THE BATTLE FOR
BALTIMORE
1814

THE BATTLE FOR
BALTIMORE
1814

by

Joseph A. Whitehorne

The Nautical & Aviation Publishing Company of America
Baltimore, Maryland

Library of Congress Catalog Card Number: 96-24506

ISBN: 1-877853-23-2

Printed in the United States of America

Picture Credits:
Illustrations appearing on openers for chapters 1-9 and 11-12 are from: William Walton, The Army and Navy of the United States From the Revolution to the Present Day, 11 vols., Boston, MA: George Barrie Publisher, 1889-96.

Illustration appearing on opener for chapter 10 is from: David D. Porter, Memoir of Commodore David D. Porter of the United States Navy, Albany, NY: J. Munsell Publisher, 1875.

Front cover painting courtesy of The Maryland Historical Society

Maps 1-4 by Steve Oltman; maps 4 and 5 by David Bennett

Library of Congress Cataloging in Publication Data

Whitehorne, Joseph W. A., 1943-
    The Battle for Baltimore: 1814 by Joseph W. A. Whitehorne

    p.   cm.

    Includes bibliographical references (p.) and index.
    1. Baltimore, Battle for, 1814.   2. Baltimore (Md.)—History—War of 1812.   3. United States—History—War of 1812—Naval operations.
4. Chesapeake Bay (Md. and Va.)—History, Naval.   I. Title
E356.B2W47   1996
973.5'2—dc203

To the memory of my father and grandfather

Tempus vita et disportati illustrati

Contents

❧

Preface

ॐ

The War of 1812 gets little attention in American History. It is cited briefly in textbooks and mentioned in college survey courses in passing with the burning of Washington cited as a sort of tragic comic opera. The impression given is that the war is of little consequence. The substantial amount of material that does deal with the conflict is often partisan, sometimes giving a false or imbalanced impression of the events under discussion while seeding considerable factual error. Historiography at the time rarely gave full names or accurate unit designations and this incomplete methodology plagues many current volumes, perpetuating inaccuracies and errors. A great deal of the material written on the war consists of local histories and memoirs. While often rich in information, these accounts suffer from what one author calls, "the law of intellectual optics." That is, one's closeness to an event makes it seem more important than it really is in relation to other events.[1]

Perhaps our distance from the War of 1812 and the magnitude of the conflicts that followed has effected the reverse. The United States showed a substantial refocusing at the close of the war, with two of our arguably greatest presidents devoting large portions of their terms to dealing with military issues and ultimately to the prosecution of a Second War of Independence. Thousands of Americans came under fire and hundreds of thousands more knew they could face the same. This two and one half year conflict was serious business, with serious consequences which have left regional memories and legends enduring to the present day.

The major actions of the war occurred along the Canadian border. These events, however chaotic, followed a pattern which allows for a logical description of their development. Themes may be deduced and objectives won and lost can be described. The Gulf, Atlantic Coast, and particularly the Chesa-

---

1. Tilghman, 145.

peake Bay portions of the conflict are less clear and are intrinsically more un-structured. Events in these areas seem less focused and consequently less capable of comprehensive treatment. While this may be due to the nature of naval and amphibious operations, it makes them no easier to understand. This is especially true in the case of operations in the Chesapeake Bay, which cov-ered a two year period of time, involved the population of all the contiguous states, and was dominated by three major events. These events, the battles for Hampton, Washington, and Baltimore, overshadow the other incidents in the bay to the point of obscuring them. This is unfortunate as these better known, larger engagements must be seen within the full context of military actions and the political and social reactions to them, in order to be under-stood.

It is interesting to note that American military success was in an inverse ratio to the scale of the federal government's involvement. The effect of Brit-ish strategy on local populations may in part explain this phenomenon, as lo-cal American defensive capabilities improved to confront it. A thorough overview of more than two years' efforts shows the British difficulties in trans-lating strategic concepts into practicalities. It reveals a substantial dedication of manpower and matériel to the Chesapeake in an effort to take pressure off the northern border while that threatened region was desperate for those very resources.

The larger battles in the bay area also reveal a great deal about the atti-tudes of the populations on both sides. This is especially the case of the City of Baltimore. Its maritime and mercantile reputation made it a major target and served as a magnet for British bay operations. Its privateers and sailors ex-acerbated British impulses to teach it and all bay residents a lesson, perhaps to the point that the British lost their strategic focus.

With that as background, my goal has been to synthesize the narratives of participants from both sides and to balance the product against later inter-pretations. Washington, Baltimore, and Hampton are now great urban areas whose development has virtually obscured any vestiges of their role in the War of 1812. And while they are the best known battles, most people assume that time has erased any outward signs of the war. This is not the case. Many of the little towns around the bay and along its tributaries retain relics and mem-ories of the conflict. One of my objectives is to acknowledge the role these towns played and show how they contributed to the better known incidents of which they were a part. I also hope to acknowledge properly the units and their members who defended their country as best as they could, whatever they thought of its policies. Central to this story is the State of Maryland and the City of Baltimore. The city supplied the ships, the men, and the money that sustained the resilience of the region and enabled it to fight its greatest battle.

One of my hopes is that the information in this book will enhance the readers' appreciation for the importance of the events described. I also hope that the book can increase one's knowledge of the region and serve as a helpful reference to make trips around the bay area more meaningful and interesting. Virtually every cove, creek, and village has a story to tell from the War of 1812.

This book was first proposed to me by my friend Jan Snouck-Hurgronje, Publisher of The Nautical and Aviation Publishing Company, as the fourth in a series devoted to chronicling battles of the War of 1812. He saw Baltimore, home of his company, as especially interesting to readers of American history because of the unique commercial, social, and political factors in the city which made its successful military defense possible in 1814. I am especially grateful to Nautical and Aviation for recognizing the importance of the War of 1812 to our national and regional history.

In addition, many other people made my work much easier; Donald Graves, author of *The Battle of Lundy's Lane,* read large parts of the typescript and made his usual incisive comments; John Frederiksen kindly advised me of many references I would have otherwise missed; Avery Hallowell helped secure some of the rare illustrations; the Reverend Parker Thompson kept me straight on the details; Robert Trotter got me on the water in his boat—my thanks to you all. I very much appreciate a grant from the Paul Wolk Fund of the Lord Fairfax Community College Foundation which offset research and travel costs. A very special thanks to Jan Brown whose interlibrary loan skills make Lord Fairfax one of the premier places to do one's research. I could not have done this without their help. The credit is theirs, the errors are mine.

Joseph W.A. Whitehorne
Cedarville, Virginia

Frigates in action, 1815.

Chapter One

❧

ORIGINS OF A FORGOTTEN WAR

In June of 1812 the United States again found itself at war with Great Britain. This time the greatest maritime power in the world was in a life and death struggle with the Emperor Napoleon and many Americans believed that Britain could not threaten them seriously in the Western Hemisphere while embroiled with the French in Europe. This complacency persisted despite the growing number of disasters and proven incompetence surrounding the first land operations. In August of 1812, a large force of militia and regulars under the elderly General William Hull surrendered at Detroit to a smaller British force under Major General Isaac Brock. Brock later lost his life shattering a second invasion attempt in October at Queenston on the Niagara frontier. The year ended with a third botched United States invasion effort at Buffalo. Because of the remoteness of these encounters the implications had little impact elsewhere in the United States. Unexpected naval successes in 1812 helped to mask the fact that the United States seemed incapable of defending itself, let alone carrying the war into British North America. Nowhere was this complacency more pronounced than in the Chesapeake Bay area,

1

which basked in the news of naval and privateering successes originating from its ports. The arrival of Royal Navy blockaders in December of 1812 plunged the region's stunned inhabitants into two years of conflict which now provide some of the best remembered incidents of the entire war.

The conflict known as the War of 1812, is today largely forgotten by both Americans and Britons. But those who fought thought it significant enough to call it "America's Second War of Independence." In reality, the War of 1812 was a by-product of the greater conflict in Europe. British and French actions challenged American sovereignty, aroused American fears, and threatened their republican form of government. Many felt that if the United States did not confront and stop European bullying, the young republic could have little practical claim to independence.[1]

In the United States, the partisan political and economic prelude to hostilities created conflicts between regions and within national political parties. The war is probably best known for the national government's disarray under pressure and for the schism between New England and the rest of the country. The disunity that existed throughout the nation was dealt with differently in the Chesapeake area which saw some of the heaviest fighting. There, the people of Maryland and Virginia, supported by their Pennsylvania neighbors, resolved their differences and focused on dealing with a common enemy. The three states' maritime economies and their coasts' vulnerability to Royal Navy actions made them privy as much as New England to the problems European developments created for the United States as it pursued its policy of neutrality. Many residents of the Chesapeake Bay region, however, shared the view of their fellow citizens in the western and southern states that war with Britain was the only solution.

The United States felt the effects of the Napoleonic Wars almost immediately. Before the turn of the century the new nation was already dealing with France and England's alternating indifference and aggression as the two powerful nations struggled for political and economic dominance. Britain's maritime policies threatened America's commerce and merchant marine and the British failure to recognize American sensibilities and their insistence on maintaining every naval prerogative pushed the United States beyond tolerance. British impressment of American sailors into Royal Navy ships showed complete disregard for United States citizenship laws and maritime sovereignty. American political leaders feared that such treatment endangered the survival of the republic itself.[2]

1. Commager, 16.
2. Egen, 73.

The pressure to go to war was increased by the growing number of younger men from frontier districts now in positions of political influence. Known as the War Hawks in Congress, they blamed Britain for hostile conduct on both land and sea. The British increase in friendly contact with the Indian nations to the west, based largely on trade to gain allies should additional military manpower be required, adversely affected American trade and coincided with the already growing Indian resistance against American expansion. Outraged at what they saw as British meddling, the War Hawks felt that eliminating the British from the area would help resolve the Indian problem.[3] Another concern was access to land. The War Hawks looked at the rapidly filling trans-Allegheny area and concluded that easy access to farmland would end within a generation, endangering their ideal of the independent landholder. Possession of the Canadas and British North America would end the problem. Southerners held the same view toward Spanish Florida, and saw the problems with Britain as an opportunity to acquire Florida from its weak ally, Spain. They saw the Spanish colony as a haven for escaped slaves and a sanctuary for hostile Indians. In the Spring of 1812, a group of Georgians occupied Amelia Island and tried unsuccessfully to provoke an uprising amongst American residents living under Spanish rule.[4]

The War Hawks saw all of this as issues of national honor and republican survival. British actions were too intolerable to be borne by any nation with pretensions at true sovereignty, and there was a growing fear that American political institutions would fragment and destroy the republican government. The followers of Jefferson's and Madison's Republican Party viewed themselves as the republic's best hope and feared the pressure created by Britain's conduct could shatter their party. And although the two presidents attempted to resolve the issue through various peaceful means of diplomacy and economic pressure, Madison saw war as the only possible option. The need for party loyalty to carry out these efforts was essential to national dignity.[5]

American politics consisted of two distinct parties by the time of Thomas Jefferson's election. The followers of George Washington and John Adams called themselves Federalists, with a philosophy formed and influenced by Alexander Hamilton, Washington's treasury secretary and a firm believer in strong central government. Hamilton doubted the average man's ability to govern and felt that the educated elite, with an economic stake in the society, had an obligation to rule. He revered law and order as an inducement to eco-

---

3. Calloway, 228.
4. Talmadge, 490; Perkins, (1961), 422-423.
5. Sapio, (1970), 195.

nomic growth and urged the development of a diverse economy. This vision embraced large capital accumulation, urbanization, and powerful government support for economic enterprise.[6] Hamilton considered close ties with Britain as essential to economic growth.

Thomas Jefferson rejected Hamilton's elitist views and by 1793 the two men were in complete opposition. Jefferson was suspicious of strong central government and felt that the average person could be politically competent. He thought the best way to assure personal liberty was to diffuse political power as broadly as possible and to control the national government by limiting its powers under the Constitution. Jefferson's vision of society was one in which wealth was broadly diffused, with an economy based largely on agriculture. He delighted at the news of the French Revolution, feeling that France had been influenced by its association with the United States and was adopting the way of the future. Despite the later excesses of the revolution which horrified Federalists, Jefferson's followers continued to sympathize with France. Those followers came to be known as Democratic-Republicans, or simply Republicans.[7]

America's first involvement in the European crisis began in 1798 during the term of President John Adams, Washington's successor, when the United States entered into an undeclared two-year naval war with France. The Republicans viewed the subsequent military build-up with great suspicion and the Federalists' heavy handed dealings with the resulting criticism led to the passage of the Alien and Sedition Acts in 1798 which discredited them throughout the country. These Acts confirmed Republican contentions of creeping dictatorship and assured Jefferson's election in 1800.[8]

Each party saw the other as a threat to its vision of the society it hoped would develop under the Constitution, and each came to represent a particular segment of the population. In general, the Federalists spoke for the established wealth of the seaboard and of those engaged in overseas commerce. The Republicans represented the interests of those in the rawer interior regions of the developing west, and received additional support from areas such as Baltimore where persons exploited the growing economy to rise to greater prosperity. Each side's view became a stereotype to the other and to potential opponents overseas. Little recognition was given to the moderate patriots of either persuasion who first and foremost wished to see their country prosper as a respected and sovereign nation.

---

6. Burns, 44-45.

7. Buel. 39, 140-141.

8. Buel, 248; Burns, 131.

War broke out in Europe in 1792 and lasted ten years before peace was agreed upon by France's new leader, Napoleon Bonaparte. The peace proved to be merely a truce, and the renewal of warfare between England and France in 1803 sharpened the divisions within the United States and tensions with both of the belligerents. The British with their larger navy emerged as the primary antagonist. The Royal Navy tried to control the flow of American goods to the French and when the British cabinet issued Orders-in-Council to establish a blockade of French controlled ports, the Royal Navy also took up station off the American coast to shut the flow of goods down at the source. The British Cabinet remained consistently contemptuous of American concerns and its underlying policy was to exploit the situation and monopolize overseas trade at the expense of the young republic.[9]

In 1806 the tension between American interests and the Royal Navy reached a critical point when the frigate HMS *Leander* pursued a merchant schooner into New York Harbor and an American sailor was killed by gunfire. There were riots in New York City during his funeral and President Jefferson banned HMS *Leander* and her sister ships from United States ports. Later, when one of them entered Hampton Roads, Virginia, in violation of the ban, the local militia was called up and strong diplomatic protests were exchanged.[10]

Both sides became increasingly embittered, and British ships experienced a constant trickle of desertions, particularly in the Chesapeake Bay area. Royal Navy manpower requirements and the cavalier British attitude towards American citizenship added to the potential for confrontation. The British tendency to take anyone they needed for their navy regardless of their birthplace, led to the impressment of many Americans. This disregard of the rights of citizenship assaulted the American's sense of national pride.[11]

Vice Admiral George C. Berkeley, RN, in command of the North Atlantic Station, became increasingly frustrated and bitter over what he viewed as American obstructionism over the recovery of British deserters. On 1 June 1807, he ordered his commanders to stop and search on sight the United States Navy frigate *Chesapeake*, rumored to be harboring British deserters amongst its crew. This order to board and search another country's warship exceeded all precedents, and when HMS *Leopard* approached the *Chesapeake* on 22 June 1807 as she left the Virginia Capes on her maiden voyage, Captain James Barron, USN, refused the British demand to board. His ship received

---

9. Dangerfield, (1956), 10.

10. Wertenbaker, 100; E.M. Gaines, 88.

11. E.M. Gaines, (1973), 89.

three broadsides from *Leopard* which killed three American sailors and wounded eighteen more. The British then boarded the shattered ship and carried off four men, three of whom were United States citizens.[12]

This attack on a neutral nation's warships shocked the entire country and united Americans against British arrogance and aggression. Great Britain ignored the fact that the United States was no longer part of its empire, and James Madison later observed that this attitude was the primary cause of the war. Contemporaries saw the *Chesapeake* incident as the first of a series of events leading directly to open conflict.[13]

Throughout the country, people joined volunteer militia organizations and clamored for war. In Virginia, large numbers of men formed such units and urged the national government to seize Canada in retaliation. In Richmond, future United States Attorney General William Wirt recalled joining an artillery company and drilling incessantly while dreaming of martial glory in the frozen north. Public meetings were held throughout Maryland as people expressed their outrage and indignation, and in both Baltimore and Annapolis, rallies urged the national government to take any measures necessary, including war, to obtain national redress. A large meeting held in Hagerstown on 14 July 1807, produced a resolution sent to Annapolis and Washington urging war.[14]

Congress reacted to this public outcry by approving increased funds for fortifications. Additionally, the Regular Army was enlarged and state governors were ordered to alert their militia for possible service. Many Maryland and Virginia volunteer units responded. In Maryland, twice the number of men needed to meet the state's quota volunteered to serve, leading to the formation of a number of new units that continued to exist after the crisis subsided. In Hagerstown, a company formed under Captain John Ragan performed a year of federal service at New Orleans. For the first time in American history, a patriotic outburst had transcended party lines and most people, particularly in the Chesapeake Bay region, put their country ahead of politics.[15]

Rather than resort to war, President Jefferson attempted a peaceful coercion. On 22 December 1807, Congress passed an Embargo Act ending all trade with Europe, and eventually overland trade with Canada. The policy did effect the English economy, but not fast enough to counter the drift towards

---

12. Wertenbaker, 100; E.M. Gaines, (1973), 83, 95; Forester, (1964), 44.
13. Rutland, 100; Dangerfield, (1956), 92; E.M. Gaines, (1973), 84.
14. Kennedy, (1834), 299; Scharf, (1882), 174.
15. Scharf, (1882), 177; Andrews, 688.

war. In the short term, the embargo severely hurt American commerce, especially in many Federalist seaboard towns. This was also the case in the more Republican Baltimore. Prior to 1807, Baltimore had profited from overseas trade despite the high risks involved but now, although faced with substantial losses, the city leadership supported the administration's goal. While some merchants traded illegally, most channeled their resources and enterprise into industrial experiments designed to produce those items no longer coming from Europe. The hardships imposed by the embargo gave the fading Maryland Federalists a new lease on life that added to political polarization throughout the state.[16]

Objections to the embargo led to its repeal on Jefferson's last day in office, 1 March 1809. In its place, the new Non-Intercourse Act allowed American trade with all countries except Great Britain and France, and prohibited British and French ships from using United States ports. Although New England seaports reacted negatively to this new Republican policy, Baltimore, suffering equally, continued to support the administration's efforts. The Madison administration attempted further economic pressures but the British remained unyielding, particularly on the issue of impressment. In 1812, Jefferson labeled the French "robbers" and the British "pirates," with the comment that, "In the hierarchy of crime, piracy stands higher than robbery." Confrontation was just a matter of time.[17]

Continued British intransigence led many Republicans to believe that the country was faced with the stark choice of war or complete submission, the latter being unthinkable in the context of both honor and national survival. Republicans saw their party and its supporters as the best hope for survival and they feared that unless the Madison administration decided on war, the rank and file of the party would abandon it in disgust, allowing the Federalists to return to power. America would then face a political crisis at home and economic disaster abroad. Republican leadership associated the survival of their party with the fate of the nation. War would ensure the survival of both, with the added benefit of the restoration of party unity.[18]

The growing dissension within the Republican Party was revealed by President Madison's attempt to select members of his cabinet after entering office in 1809. He was unable to move Albert Gallatin from Treasury to State because some Republicans felt that Gallatin's careful, cautious style would impair the conduct of foreign policy and defense measures. Thus, Gallatin had

---

16. Brugger, 175, 178; Burns, 200-201.
17. Andrews, 690; Dangerfield, (1956), 92.
18. Brown, 14; Rutland, (1990), 101; Hickey, (1976), 1.

to stay with the Treasury while Robert Smith, former Secretary of the Navy and brother of Senator Samuel Smith of Maryland, was appointed Secretary of State. Madison attempted to encourage party harmony by yielding to these pressures.[19]

Madison's moderation and his continued efforts to find a diplomatic solution to relations with Britain, led the more extreme Republicans to accuse him of being sympathetic to the Federalists. The Federalists in turn, considered him to be too pro-French! Samuel Smith of Baltimore led a group of Republicans opposed to Madison's cautious policy. A hero of the Revolution, Smith began his political career in 1792 as a Federalist, but by 1802 had become a convinced Jeffersonian and an ardent advocate for defense measures since the Quasi-War with France in 1798. He tolerated Jefferson's limited efforts, but drew the line as Madison continued the same policies. By 1809 Smith, a major general in the Maryland Militia, felt the situation called for more than "business as usual."[20]

Smith's group known as the "Invisibles," associated themselves with the War Hawks and demanded a declaration of war. The two groups grew increasingly disillusioned with peaceful coercion as a viable means of curtailing British actions. Smith felt that the Administration's caution jeopardized the country's sovereignty, and gave the appearance of knuckling under to the British. He believed that most people would endure any degree of privation, even war, if their sacrifices preserved national honor. While other Republicans could see his logic, they were ideologically or practically concerned about taking the military option.[21]

As the tensions grew between the United States and Great Britain during the period 1806-1812, Smith became increasingly critical of the Administration's actions. In 1806 he headed a Congressional committee that condemned British maritime actions and urged severe sanctions. He hoped to be appointed by Jefferson to a delegation leaving for Britain in March 1807 to discuss the issues, and was disappointed when Federalist William Pinckney, a fellow Baltimorean, got the appointment along with James Monroe. The failure of this embassy convinced Smith that Britain's real objective was to crush American commerce, not just gain wartime security. The "*Chesapeake-Leopard*" incident confirmed his suspicions and made him an ardent supporter of the embargo.[22]

19. Pancake, (1955), 27; Rutland, (1987), 206-207.
20. Dangerfield, (1956), 9; Pancake, (1955), 37.
21. Pancake, (1955), 26; Hatzenbuehler, 367-368.
22. Pancake, (1955), 18, 23.

Despite the pressure, President Madison continued to explore all options. Shortly after Madison came into office, British Ambassador David Erskine gave the new President an overly optimistic interpretation of some moderate changes to the Orders-in-Council. Madison blindly accepted Erskine's version and shocked both his party and opponents alike by announcing the end of British impositions on American trade. Clearly not the case, Erskine was recalled to London for his gaffe, leaving the embarrassed Madison with the belief that having meaningful negotiations with Britain was impossible. His belief was reinforced by Erskine's replacement, Francis J. Jackson, who had delivered the British ultimation to the Danes just before the Royal Navy bombarded Copenhagen in 1801. Relations between the two men became so icy that in April 1809 Madison requested the supercilious Jackson's recall.[23]

Secretary of State Robert Smith's obstructionism in favor of the "Invisibles" forced Madison to replace him with James Monroe in 1811, and this did not improve relations with Senator Smith. The new British ambassador, Sir Augustus J. Foster, assumed his duties at the same time. Although a more congenial man than Jackson, he continued to insist on his government's right to continue its economic policies. All efforts for a peaceful resolution had failed and President Madison's 5 November 1811 State of the Union message to Congress openly addressed the possibility of military action. He urged Congress to authorize military preparations and to appropriate the funds necessary to expand the armed forces. Congress agreed to the expansion of the Regular Army, the creation of a volunteer force, and the activation of those navy ships laid up.[24]

Although Federalists and various Republican opponents amended the bill in ways meant to embarrass the administration, most of the country supported the measures. The Virginia House of Delegates passed a series of resolutions supporting war as America's only honorable option. The debate over Madison's war message crystallized party positions in the Congress as its members wrestled with appropriations measures. Some Federalists initially supported the war measures on the belief that doing so would injure the administration, but soon shifted to complete opposition when the ploy failed.[25]

In one last effort towards a peaceful resolution, President Madison called for a ninety-day trade embargo against Britain, hoping that English reliance on the American grain needed to feed its army in Spain might have an influ-

---

23. Rutland, (1987), 209-210.
24. Rutland, (1987), 218-219.
25. Hatzenbuehler, 373; Virginia House of Delegates, Oct 1811 Sess., 73.

ence. This move inspired opposition from Federalists and Republicans representing commercial interests and they formed an *ad hoc* group to support DeWitt Clinton, a Republican, in the upcoming autumn 1812 elections. Meanwhile, with the embargo failing, Madison sent a war message to Congress on 2 June. He was out of both patience and hope and he laid out the case against England, requesting that Congress exercise its Constitutional duty and declare war. Lackluster and lawyerlike, his unemotional message put the burden of making the hard decision for war squarely on Congress. The House, divided between northern Federalists, some New York, New Jersey, and New England Republicans on one hand, and Republicans from the south and west on the other, voted for war by a margin of 79-49. The Senate, even more reluctant, finally voted 19-13 for war on 18 June. The vote for war was along party lines rather than along regional or philosophical alignment. Both sides valued party unity, although sometimes to the detriment of national interests.[26] Regardless of their motives and divisions, Congress supported a state of war with the British, who faced the climax of their struggle with France.

26. Rutland, (1987), Hatzenbuehler, 383-385.

Commodore,
United States Navy, 1813.

Chapter Two

&.

NEITHER UNITED NOR READY

M ANY Republicans, Madison included, did not consider the full implications of a declaration of war. They regarded it as a diplomatic bargain-
ing ploy rather than a prelude to open battle. Atlantic distances and Britain's
involvement with Napoleon led them to believe that war in North America
could be conducted on American terms at little cost. This helps explain the
lack of preparation and the slowness of mobilization after the declaration of
war. Once war was declared, however, unanimous support was expected and
anyone questioning national policy was viewed as little less than treasonous.[1]

There were divisions of opinion in the United States over the wisdom of
going to war with the world's greatest naval power, much of it coming from
Federalist sympathizers. The British read this as a fatal flaw in the American
capability to wage war. But most Federalists saw dissent as acceptable only
within Constitutional boundaries, and did not want to contribute to any social disarray that might stem from the war. They urged their followers to ad-

---

1. Hickey, (1976), 2; Rutland, (1990), 105.

here to the law in meeting the administration's military requirements, but stuck to their principles and made their views clear and obvious. Once again, the role and acceptance of appropriate dissent under the Constitution in a time of crisis was severely tested.[2]

The Federalists saw the increased conflict between parties as contributing to the major dangers of disunion and many predicted an all-out civil war. At the very least, they saw the war as continuing the democratization of society, to the detriment of seaboard influence. Federalists believed that if the War Hawks gained control of Canada, the presence of this vast new region would erode the Federalist influence, as the western regions tended to favor to Republican attitudes.[3]

Federalist clergymen in New England argued that since war was an unmitigated evil, no virtuous nation should resort to it. They felt that impressment was a matter between Britain and her subjects and that the declaration of war aligned the United States with the French, the embodiment of tyranny and evil. Others, less theologically inclined, deplored the lack of military preparedness but at the same time feared the growth of the bureaucracy necessary to improve it. With this came a fear of an expanding army and the threat it implied to the maintenance of civil authority and the potential it held for the growth of presidential power. [4]

But the New England Federalists failed to recognize that most of the country supported President Madison's policy, either through political loyalty or patriotism. Even in their own area large numbers of army recruits and volunteers rallied to the first calls for service. This indicated that the views of the common citizen were not in accord with their political leadership. Support for the administration was even stronger in the southern and western states, and the Federalists hoped that they could change this in the Fall 1812 elections. Instead, Madison carried every region except New England and parts of New York and New Jersey, thus indicating a wide degree of national support for his war policy. Some New England Federalists urged more extreme anti-administration measures. The British presumed this extremist rhetoric was the standard Federalist view, and excluded New England from most of their early military measures, primarily blockade.[5]

In the Chesapeake Bay area Republican sentiment was challenged more than anywhere else outside New England. Virginia's Congressional delega-

2. Cress, (1987), 139-141.
3. Callcott, 253; Cress, (1987), 136-137.
4. Cress, (1987), 131, 134.
5. Rutland, (1987), 116-118.

tion generally supported Madison's policies along party lines, and most of those members in opposition were voted out of office in the 1812 elections. Maryland representatives, were more divided, both during the events leading to war, and in the 1812 elections. But while nearly half the state's electors cast their ballots for DeWitt Clinton, Madison's opponent, the kind of schisms characteristic of New England did not occur. This was unfortunate for the British.[6]

Republicans had successfully challenged Federalist control in Maryland as far back as the elections of 1800 when they gained control of the state house and split the state's national delegation. By 1802 the Maryland Federalists seemed doomed. However, the effects of Jefferson's peaceful coercion revived Federalists' hopes and returned them briefly to a state house majority in 1808, the year of the embargo. They remained a political force throughout the course of the growing crisis with Britain, and their chances improved when Republicans split over the controversy between President Madison and Secretary of State Robert Smith, who was working with his brother Samuel's "Invisibles." In 1811 the Federalists argued that the administration was excessively anti-British while ignoring French transgressions that also threatened to destroy American commerce.[7] Maryland Republicans saw British policy as the principal threat to United States sovereignty, and accused Federalists of being elitist and dampers on free speech and economic opportunity. Jeopardizing Federalist influence in the state appealed to many voters. This rhetoric had particular effect in the city of Baltimore which remained a solid Republican enclave, marking it as distinct from the surrounding area.[8]

Baltimore started out as a small village on the Patapsco in the 1730s and 1740s. On the edge of the prosperous Maryland tobacco region, it remained on the periphery of the state's economy until after the Revolution. Then it began to tap the wheat-growing potential of the frontiers on both sides of the Pennsylvania border, and developed as a shipping and milling center. In 1796 it was chartered as a city and continued to expand until by 1812, it was the third largest city in the United States with a population of 50,000. Baltimore had tripled in size since 1790 and its rapid growth and large immigrant population made it distinct from the older planter culture. The city's commercial connections made it more anti-British than anti-French.[9]

The rapid growth of the city generated substantial change, in part ex-

6. Hatzenbuehler, 377-378; Rutland, (1987), 118-119.

7. Brant, (1961), 6: 277-6.

8. Sapio, (1969), 1, 7.

9. Hickey, (1976), 2; W.P.A., 209-210; Gilje, 61.

plaining the volatile nature of its citizens. Baltimore competed commercially with the older east coast cities and struggled for economic and political dominance of Maryland against the more established tobacco settlements in the southern part of the state. Unlike their counterparts in the traditional planter aristocracy, city leaders tended to be self-made men involved in commerce and industry. The population contained a substantial number of foreign immigrants involved in unskilled labor or basic crafts, with many aspiring to join the ranks of the entrepreneurial elite for whom they worked. This mix meant that Baltimore society was more turbulent, less deferential, and much more dynamic than that of its neighbors. Its composition and growing wealth made it a natural Republican enclave which from 1800 on, increasingly dominated the rest of the state.[10]

Despite the high risks involved, Baltimore merchants continued to prosper during the first phases of the European wars. Large profits were made both through direct trade with the belligerents, and by transshipping goods from European colonies through United States ports and on to their mother countries. This brief golden age ended with the 1807 embargo. Despite the embargo's negative economic effect, Baltimore supported the national policy and passed a resolution urging its Congressional delegation to increase national defenses. The effects of the embargo, however, generated a resurgence of Federalist activity and the confrontational attitudes of the younger Federalists contributed to the growing tensions. Differences became more pronounced in the wake of the *Chesapeake* affair when many Republicans believed that only war could resolve the problems with Britain. It was in part a growing impatience with peaceful coercion and its negative economic impact that allowed for some Federalist gains. At the same time, this sentiment led to the return of Republican Samuel Smith to the Senate in 1808, and inspired the "Invisibles'" pressure for more drastic action.[11]

Under the leadership of Governor Robert Bowie, Republicans dominated the state in the final months of crisis. The state legislature passed a resolution endorsing the Madison administration's efforts at peaceful coercion, and the majority of the delegates pledged their support for war should it prove the only solution. A special committee in Baltimore endorsed the resolution on 21 May 1812 and expressed the city's support. Governor Bowie and his fellow Republicans were pleased when the declaration of war was passed in June, since they saw it both as a means to end divisions amongst the Republicans, as well as a means for retrieval of national honor.[12]

10. Travers, 36-37; Owens, 142; Cassell, (1971), 242.
11. Brugger, 175; Pancake, (1955), 24; Cassell, (1971), 243.

There were substantial differences between certain areas of the state and Maryland's Congressional delegation. Six of nine United States Representatives voted in favor of war while in the Senate, Samuel Smith voted for war and Philip Reed, a Republican from Kent County, voted against it. Two thirds of the state lower house opposed an aggressive strategy while state senators supported such a policy. For example, the Republicans were in the majority in Talbot County on the Eastern Shore, but Federalist leaders retained considerable influence there. This was reflected by the return of the Federalists to power in the 1812 elections. The vote was not so much anti-war as it was a reflection of public disappointment over the national government's military ineptitude, and the county later supported a local man and ardent Federalist, Robert H. Goldsborough, for United States Senate. Despite this, most people were generally nationalist in their sentiments and bipartisan in their politics for the country's interest. Elsewhere on the Eastern Shore the population was solidly Republican. Voters in Queen Anne's County supported the administration by a large majority but at the same time, deplored the social divisions and mob-actions which erupted in Baltimore soon after the outbreak of war. The mood on the Eastern Shore in June 1812 was one of political moderation and unity in face of the British naval threat to the region.[13]

Public opinion in southern Maryland, the area between the Chesapeake Bay and the Potomac River, opposed hostilities with Britain. This was the oldest part of the state and its large plantations were the seats of the state's wealthiest and most established families, many of whom had been resisting the intrusion of more entrepreneurial Republican types for a decade. Despite the European war, many planters prospered through the tobacco trade with Britain and thought it folly to jeopardize such a lucrative relationship. They also knew their exposed region was vulnerable to Royal Navy attack. Nevertheless, the people of Charles, Calvert, and St. Mary's counties participated willingly in defense measures once war was declared. Later, the ferocity and nastiness of British raids galvanized them to even greater resistance.[14]

The western counties of the state also were divided politically. However, they proved to be a reliable source of manpower and support throughout the war. The Federalists in Frederick County willingly met all military requirements while remaining critical of the Madison government's mistakes. The western counties provided large numbers of troops for Western Shore defenses and several volunteer units for extended service on the Canadian border.

12. Andrews, 690-692.
13. Emory, 425; Tilghman, 144; Jones, 255; Byron, 12.
14. Stein, 147.

Many enrolled militiamen volunteered for extended periods of duty in the Annapolis defenses at great inconvenience and risk. Contemporaries argued that it was their absence in the field which enabled the Federalists to dominate politics at home.[15]

Washington and Allegheny Counties were strongly Republican in sentiment and showed it through their loyal support of state defense requirements. Voters repeatedly indicated the view that a showdown with Britain was necessary, although many were apprehensive about going to war given the level of the country's unpreparedness. However, when war came they supported the effort fully. Militia drafts were required rarely in the western counties as nearly all levies were filled by individual volunteers or whole units. The first nonlocal garrison for Annapolis was provided from Washington County in the summer of 1812.[16]

The coming of war to Baltimore created even more turbulence. The counties north of the city eagerly rallied to the war effort with enthusiasm to enlist so great in Harford County, that neither the federal government nor the state could accommodate the number of men rushing to the colors. Many of them joined a new Regular Army unit paid for in part by Baltimore and led by local lawyer Colonel William H. Winder.[17] War fever added to the social tensions in the city and led to an explosion of violence that effected local and state politics for the duration of the war, and may have influenced British perceptions as to the degree of division in the region. Social and economic differences within the population generated confrontation and the friction became more acute after the *Chesapeake* affair and the embargo. Baltimore was not unique. Once war was declared, people throughout the country resented critics of government policy, especially the extreme elements of the Federalist press. In Georgia, for example, on 12 June 1812, John S. Mitchell, an especially provocative editor, was attacked by a mob at his home. He was brutally beaten and so intimidated that he closed his paper.[18]

A Federalist newspaper was the catalyst for violence as well. The *Federalist Republican*, founded in 1808 by owner-editor Alexander C. Hanson, quickly became the foremost Federalist paper in the South. Hanson achieved this with a confrontational style and he felt the wrath of aggrieved Republicans even before the war. The paper became Maryland's undeclared Federalist headquarters and people were incensed by Hanson's caustic opposition to the

15. Williams & McKinsey, 168.
16. Scharf, (1882), 181, 184.
17. Preston, 236.
18. Hickey, (1976), 3; Gilje, 61; Talmadge, 497.

Bay area counties as of 1814.

declaration of war. On 22 June 1812 a mob destroyed the paper's Baltimore office but, still defiant, editor Hanson fled the city and continued to publish his paper from Georgetown, distributing it through the mails.[19]

The mob continued its rampage. It was composed of several hundred men, many of them recent immigrants resentful of the limitations they encountered in their quest for upward mobility. City officials did little to restrain this mob and Mayor Edward Johnson seemed completely intimidated by it. Other Republican officials sympathized with its goals while effectively trying to reason with it. The mob terrorized the city for several weeks, threatening Federalist-owned businesses and banks and intimidating people in their homes. Ships suspected of carrying grain to British markets were damaged at the same time ethnic tensions exploded. Irish Catholics attacked Orangemen and the mob assaulted blacks in city neighborhoods. Federalists' predictions that war would lead to anarchy were coming true.[20]

The *Federalist Republican*'s provocative stance was not welcomed by many of Hanson's fellow Baltimore Federalists. Nevertheless, he generated an incident by reestablishing his paper's Baltimore office at a new address on Charles Street. On 26 July he rallied a group of armed supporters, including Revolutionary War hero Light Horse Harry Lee, and issued an edition bearing the Charles Street address. He then awaited a reaction. Hanson's objectives are not clear. Perhaps he hoped to challenge and face down the turmoil in the city before it spread to other parts of the state. But none could forsee the tragedy that lay ahead.[21]

That night a violent mob descended on the Charles Street address. The Federalist defenders shot and killed one man as a group tried to enter the house which further incited the mob. City officials, from Mayor Johnson to the militia commander, Brigadier General John Stricker, Republicans all, did little to impose law and order, even though the mayhem was occurring only ten doors away from Stricker's own house. He maintained he needed a magistrate's order before he could call out the militia and this was not procured until late that night.[22]

Early on the morning of 28 July, Major William B. Barney arrived at the head of a small militia force. By this time, nearly 2,000 people were crying out for vengeance, and after hours of negotiation, Barney persuaded the besieged Federalists to surrender and move under his protection to the city jail. This

19. Owens, 162.
20. Hickey, (1976), 4; Gilje, 64.
21. Cassell, (1976), 246.
22. Hickey, (1976), 9.

they did, seeing no favorable outcome in continued defiance. Barney and General Stricker, accompanied by about fifty troops, escorted Hanson and those of his followers who did not disappear amongst the raging masses to the presumed safety of the jail.[23]

The mob was only temporarily mollified by this action. Some of its members staked out the jail while others stayed behind to destroy the emptied Charles Street house. No judge would grant bond to the Federalists and they remained in custody. With most of the crowd dispersed, General Stricker considered the crisis over and dismissed his small militia force. The jail was without external protection when the mob gathered anew later that evening. Incited by Republican journal reports of 28 July that accused the imprisoned Federalists of treason, the enraged crowd burst into the jail. Some of the Federalists escaped, but nine were brutally beaten. General James Lingan died of his wounds within hours, while others, including General Lee, suffered permanent disabilities. [24]

The injured men were tormented for over three hours before sympathetic doctors persuaded the mob to let the "bodies" be carried back into the jail under the assumption they were dead. City officials did little, although Mayor Johnson did try to reason with the mob. Congressman Alexander McKim and militia generals Stricker and Tobias E. Stansbury refused to get involved. Republicans all, they feared for their own property and did not want to antagonize potential voters in light of the upcoming fall elections. As a result, the mob continued its search for escaped Federalists and on 4 August, threatened the Post Office as it prepared to deliver copies of Hanson's paper, recently in from Georgetown. With the city teetering on the brink of anarchy, the city leadership and General Stricker finally ordered out the entire Baltimore Brigade on 5 August. Law and order was restored after five more days of curfew and patrols, but the damage had been done.[25]

People throughout Maryland were outraged at the news of the rioting, especially when a Baltimore court failed to convict anyone as responsible for the disorders. The Federalist survivors were considered heroes and Hanson was elected to Congress from his native Montgomery County in the fall elections. The riots ended Republican control of the State House and people on both sides blamed the state administration for the upheaval. Governor Bowie's inability to prosecute the perpetrators was capitalized upon by his opponents and a general fear of mob rule rippled through the state, favoring

23. Owen, 164.
24. Cassell, (1975), 252; Hickey, (1976), 11, Owen, 166.
25. Cassell, (1975), 258.

Federalist candidates. Many Maryland politicians saw in the situation a chance to curb Baltimore's growing influence. A large Federalist majority was returned to Maryland's lower house, Republican power in the senate was diluted, and Governor Bowie was ousted by Federalist candidate Levin Winder.[26]

The Maryland Federalist leadership saw it as a duty to criticize the Madison administration's policies by Constitutional means and hold it responsible for the consequences of its actions. The new Federalist Governor Winder, despite his personal views against entering the war, immediately began organizing the state for its defense. He persuaded the legislature to provide emergency funds, petitioned the federal government for help, and mobilized the militia to garrison Annapolis and Baltimore.[27]

The Baltimore riots had consequences at every level. Although Maryland kept its two parties, extremism was rejected and nearly all the members from both held similar moderate views. The local effect of the riots was to end open Federalism in Baltimore and give a veneer of unity to the city's war effort, which enabled it to develop increasingly effective defense measures and to field a growing number of efficient volunteer militia units. Nationally, the example of the riots had the effect of reducing divisive opposition to Republican national policy everywhere except in southern New England where there was massive Federalist preponderance. Authorities recognized that uncontrolled public opinion could weaken the war effort. When added to the British experience with extreme New England Federalists, the turbulence gave them a false impression of the mood in the Chesapeake region and weakened the premises of their strategic planning there.[28]

In neighboring Virginia and Pennsylvania, those with commercial interests remained apprehensive over the consequences of war with Britain. In Virginia, the majority was generally supportive of Republican policy, with only twenty-five percent of the population in opposition. Those in opposition resided in the areas of Federalist strength, the Tidewater and Shenandoah Valley which were involved in commerce and shipping. A small group of Republicans, the Quids, led by John Randolph, were personally opposed to James Madison but were voted out in the fall elections.[29]

Virginians in opposition focused on Britain's capacity to destroy American commerce and the concurrent absence of sufficient military preparedness. Like many Marylanders, they feared that war might lead to social unrest and

26. Andrews, 694; Cassell, (1976), 258.
27. Andrews, 695; Sapio, (1969), 11.
28. Sapio, (1969), 17; Hickey, (1976), 14.
29. Burns, 258.

threaten the union. They were concerned as well that the inevitable economic hardships generated by war could lead to slave revolts. The Eastern shore in particular feared national schism and slave unrest. Although largely Federalist in its views, the region strongly supported state defense measures to assure it would receive militia reinforcements from the rest of the state in the event of the slave uprising it anticipated.[30]

Once war was declared, Virginia Governor James Barbour, a personal friend of President Madison, called for unity between the parties. Newspapers in Richmond and throughout the state reported the mood as patriotic. Regardless of their politics, Virginians' sense of nationalism muted any differences and they responded to the governor's request. Militia in Federalist areas such as the Shenandoah Valley rallied as fully and loyally as did their counterparts in Republican districts. Opponents of the war experienced some harassment as people struggled to deal with wartime dissent. The elections of 1812, in which President Madison received seventy-five percent of the state vote, reflected solid Virginia support for the government's programs and a willingness to see them through.[31]

Pennsylvania was even more solidly in the Republican camp. The election of Governor Simon Snyder in 1808 and again in 1811 permanently ended significant Federalist influence in the state. By 1812, Pennsylvania was a major source of Republicanism in the northeast. When war broke out, Governor Snyder issued a stirring proclamation asking for, and receiving, the voters' backing for all necessary war measures. Pennsylvania Republicans considered prosecution of the war as essential to achieving the national respect necessary to conduct overseas business safely and to deal with the European powers on a par. Many also saw the situation as challenging the ability of the government to defend itself against foreign predators.[32]

The Pennsylvania legislature was an early supporter of the war and quickly endorsed Governor Snyder's requests for funds and manpower. Voters in the fall 1812 elections overwhelmingly supported President Madison and other Republican candidates. The state house in Harrisburg was over eighty percent Republican while twenty-two out of twenty-three Congressmen were Republicans. President Madison won all the state's electoral votes. The largest pocket of Pennsylvania Federalism was in Philadelphia and initially it was the least responsive to Governor Snyder's efforts to meet military requirements. Even here, British raids on the Delaware River and the Chesapeake

30. Wehtje, 72.
31. Bushong, (1941), 70.
32. Stevens, 170; Sapio, (1970), 166, 169.

Bay in 1813 convinced local authorities that cooperation with the Republican majority offered the only chance for security. Political support and coordination throughout the bay region was recognized as the only chance for defense, although the universal concern over military unpreparedness was well founded and soon demonstrated.[33]

President Thomas Jefferson had done nothing to build on the Adams' administration's modest efforts to strengthen the United States regular forces during the Quasi-War with France. In 1802 he approved a law which eliminated the cavalry, removed horses from the artillery, and cut the infantry in half. The United States land forces entered the peak years of the Napoleonic crisis with barely 2,700 officers and men.[34] In addition, Jefferson's administration scrapped a conventional shipbuilding program in favor of the production of small coast defense gunboats, which were to prove useless in rough water or on combat mission. The United States had only eighteen seagoing warships, plus the gunboats, when war was declared. Some investment was made in upgrading coast defense fortifications, but little thought was given to finding sources of manpower necessary for the garrisons. The small professional forces were "a kind of constabulary to police Indians but unprepared and ill-equipped for war." [35]

The tiny Regular Army was hampered by extreme partisanship. Its officer corps consisted mostly of good Republicans with little military talent. Winfield Scott, an ambitious young officer, categorized them as "swaggerers, dependents, decayed gentlemen, and others fit for nothing else."[36] Party loyalty as a criterion for leadership was added to an ideology already suspicious of standing professional military forces and filled with an uncritical acceptance of the virtues of the militia. President Madison's personal unfamiliarity with things military led to his reliance on a host of amateurs, incompetents, and elderly Revolutionary War veterans.[37]

Continued difficulties with Great Britain and France made war seem imminent. The new group of War Hawk congressmen elected in 1810 pressed legislation through to reverse earlier administration policy. As a result, in late 1811 President Madison proposed that a force be authorized that could move quickly against Upper Canada in the event of war. This proposal was opposed by his political adversaries. Senator William B. Giles of Virginia cut up the

---

33. Sapio, (1970), 175; Gibson, 163; Godcharles, 20.

34. R.C. Stuart, 109; Kreidberg and Henry, 36.

35. Kreidberg and Henry, 40.

36. W. Scott, I: 35

37. Rutland, (1990), 110; Brant, (1966), 61.

President's original bill and proposed a much larger force partly in an attempt to ridicule the administration's belated preparedness efforts. Similarly, Congress rejected many of the President's later requests for manpower increases, and what finally emerged was a classic case of too little too late.[38]

In January 1812, the Regular Army was authorized an additional ten regiments. One month later new laws allowed the president to accept 30,000 federal volunteer troops. New artillery and cavalry regiments, along with senior staffs and commanders were authorized in the following months. But creation of a paper army could not mask the harsh realities. The absence of both a trained professional force and a federal strategy to place a regular army on the Canadian border, left the rest of the country relying on its own resources for defense.[39]

The primary line of defense in Jeffersonian America was the militia. It was seen as a bulwark against central government tyranny and was recognized as such in the Constitution. Rooted in old Anglo-American tradition, the organization of the United States militia was mandated in a 1792 federal law which failed to clearly define the responsibilities expected of the states and the national government. The states were required to enroll and assign to units all able-bodied white men between the ages of eighteen and forty-five. Additionally, they were authorized to incorporate any existing volunteer military forces in their jurisdictions into their militia system. The law was otherwise very unclear as to responsibilities for maintenance of standards and training, or equipping forces thus raised.[40]

Each state and the District of Columbia adopted somewhat different approaches, none of which were very effective. In 1803 the national government tried to pump some life into the system by requiring annual strength reports from the states, but few bothered to comply. When it became apparent that many of the militiamen could not or would not provide the weapons and equipment necessary when mobilized, the national government offered to provide weapons based on accurate returns. By 1812, only Delaware, Maryland, and Georgia had availed themselves of this offer and large amounts of available funds and firearms went unclaimed by the states. A modern critic observed that "In practice Americans slighted the arts of war in order to concentrate upon the rewards of peace."[41] The states especially skirted their responsibility to maintain reasonably effective military forces and this did not

38. Brant, (1966), 60.
39. Cress, (1982), 161.
40. Kerby, 117; Cress, (1982), 151.
41. Kerby, 120.

go unnoticed by concerned Congressional elements. Several times between 1792 and 1812 the militia laws were modified to try to create a viable force. The national government received authorization in 1795 to call-up for up to ninety days all or part of each state's militia in case of emergency. Governors later were required to designate part of the militias to be ready for immediate call-up or "detachment" for immediate active service. They could be volunteers rather than drafts.[42]

The absence of a large effective standing force meant that the militia would be called upon repeatedly to meet unexpected crises and defense requirements once war broke out. The Militia Act of 10 April 1812 outlined the procedures for a call-up. The national government advised each governor of the total numbers required from the State. The governors, in turn, allocated their state's quotas amongst their various units and alerted local commanders who provided the proper number of men when required. The governors also designated rendezvous points where the mobilized militia would gather, be equipped, inspected, and mustered into federal service. Local emergencies frequently required the governors to act on their own initiative without federal instigation.[43]

The militia consisted of two different categories. Volunteer militia units were filled by men who participated as an avocation and many of these units existed before the 1792 law. Their members often clothed and equipped themselves and their units at their own expense and were usually at a higher level of training and proficiency. These volunteer units went by patriotic names such as the District's Columbian Hussars, rather than simply the name of their commander. The less effective units were part of the enrolled militia whose members were drawn from the vast pool of eighteen to forty-five year old men made available by the 1792 law. In most cases, only the officers in these units possessed uniforms. The men at best attended an annual muster day, which was more social than business, and when called up for service they often served as fillers for already active units rather than in those to which they were nominally assigned. Through little fault of their own, they were not very effective soldiers.[44]

The 1792 law required that each militia battalion have a volunteer company, designated light infantry, rifle or flank companies to distinguish them from their theoretically less accomplished colleagues. Few of the states actively responded to this weak federal initiative. Militia organizations existed large-

---

42. Cress, (1982), 172.
43. Kreidberg and Henry, 50, 53; Mil. Laws U.S., 1813, 165, 170, 239.
44. Todd, 382.

ly on paper, with little substance, although this changed after the *Chesapeake* affair of 1807. But ideological opposition to standing forces, excessive legislative parsimony, and indifference combined to produce an ineffective force. The states around the Chesapeake Bay were no different from the rest of the country.

Pennsylvania, for example, mustered more men than any other state during the war.[45] Its state militia was organized into two large divisions, each of two brigades containing six regiments for a total of twenty-four regiments, mostly associated with a particular county. The militia units usually served as pools from which state volunteer units drew to meet quotas levied on the state. Governor Simon Snyder respected Federal needs and cooperated to the fullest extent possible. He was hindered by a lack of cooperation from some Federalist leaders in the Delaware Valley. However, Pennsylvania's larger problem lay in the state's ramshackle militia laws which made supplying and paying the units difficult at best. The laws did not require any standardization of units within the state or conformance with federal organization. This made any smooth integration with other forces at mobilization virtually impossible. Despite these limitations, the state forces willingly responded to emergencies in the bay area throughout the war.[46]

The militia of Virginia was organized into four divisions with a total of twenty-one brigades and an aggregate of 124 regiments. The regiments were associated with a county or group of counties depending on regional population. Given the focus of the threat along the state coast, federal and state mobilizations usually involved calling up parts of these regional units and then amalgamating them into provisional regiments at threatened sites. Volunteer units were encouraged to muster rather than draft elements from the enrolled militia. The militias of the Tidewater and Eastern Shore had frequent short periods of active service in response to British raids. Governor James Barbour thus commanded a reasonably responsive, well led organization.[47]

The Maryland Militia was organized into three geographic divisions, each commanded by a major general. Each division had four brigades, usually containing four infantry regiments. The regiments and brigades were closely associated with their home regions, each representing all or part of a county or, in one case, Baltimore City. The latter unit had its own artillery regiment and rifle battalion. Elsewhere the artillery and special infantry were components of the basic infantry regiments although a few counties had extra battalions,

45. Sapio, (1970), 76, 82.
46. Thomson, 271.
47. Butler, 8-9.

a reflection of their large or dispersed populations. The state was further organized in January 1812 into eleven cavalry districts each producing a cavalry
regiment. They often overlapped county lines but still had strong regional af-
filiation. The Maryland Militia system, like that of Pennsylvania and Virginia,
was moribund until the *Chesapeake* affair of 1807 prompted defense preparations and a renewed sense of patriotism. A large number of men volunteered
to meet the federal levy and most of the units raised remained on the state
rolls after the crisis passed.[48]

The D.C. Militia differed from those in the surrounding states. Raised by
Congress in 1802, its officers held federal commissions. Instead of regiments,
it consisted of two legions. A legion was theoretically a self-sustaining organization containing infantry, cavalry, and artillery units. One legion was based
in Washington and Georgetown, with the other in Alexandria, then part of
the District. An 1803 law specified that the President could decide to add new
units and it required that enrolled militia regiments in each legion be augmented with four volunteer companies, one each of riflemen, light infantry,
cavalry, and artillery. In April 1813, the legionary organization was changed
to that of the two brigade Columbian Division. The First Legion north of the
Potomac became a two regiment brigade while the Second Legion in Alexandria converted into a brigade containing an infantry regiment and a cavalry
battalion. Artillery batteries remained assigned to the regiments. Throughout
the period, the volunteer units were available for immediate call-up or "detachment."[49]

Few state militia organizations exhibited a high level of proficiency, in
part because of their lack of drill and the absence of equipment. There were
officers of quality and experience such as Maryland's Lieutenant Colonel
John Ragan, and D.C.'s Major George Peter, both former regulars, who
trained and led effective units. Over time, many of these militia units became
respectable forces but it remains surprising that they performed as well as they
did. It was fortunate for the states of the bay area that hostilities first focused
on the northern border, and that Britain's mobile strike force, the Royal Navy, had problems of its own. This gave the region six months to get organized
and to iron out political differences before the enemy descended in force.

---

48. Stuart, 103; Scharf, (1882), 176; Marine, 195-197.
49. Todd, 400.

*Gun deck of a frigate
preparing for action, 1813.*

Chapter Three

⁂

BRITAIN TIGHTENS THE NOOSE

O NE of the best known ironies of the war is the British cabinet's reaction
to increasing domestic pressures over a deteriorating economy. It re-
voked the Orders-in-Council just as America declared war.[1] The cabinet did
not learn of the American declaration until 29 July 1812 and British officials
took little action other than to sequester United States ships caught in British
ports. The Royal Navy prepared to protect westward bound convoys as Britain waited for news of America's reaction to the revocation of the Orders-in-
Council. Few British leaders thought the United States would resort to war,
and few plans had been made in the event of such a declaration. With the focus on Napoleon, little had been done in America beyond improving relations
with the western Indian tribes in order to secure future allies.[2]

Once it became apparent that war was a certainty, the government of
Prime Minister Lord Liverpool decided that the primacy of the war in Europe
mandated a defensive strategy in America. The details for such a strategy were

1. Bartlett, 108.
2. Mahon, (1965), 219; Calloway, 230.

left up to military and naval commanders in North America. The most obvious American strategy would be a preliminary rush to the Canadian borders which meant that the small British and local ground forces in Britain's North American Colonies would be occupied fully in fending off American land forces. The Royal Navy represented the only possible offensive force available, but it was suffering from some severe problems that made it relatively inactive during the first months of the war.[3]

The Royal Navy's North America Station consisted of three flag level commands based respectively in Jamaica, the Leeward Islands, and Halifax, Nova Scotia. The latter was the seat of the senior admiral responsible for events on the United States coast. The Royal Navy had eighty-three vessels in American waters when war was declared, and this was judged an adequate force to deal with the smaller United States Navy. However, it proved totally insufficient to cope with the swarm of American privateers that soon ventured out to harass British shipping lanes.[4]

By 1812, the North Atlantic Station was suffering from serious Admiralty neglect. The first priority was given to the fleet operating in European waters and maintaining a blockade of French ports. Consequently, the American squadrons were plagued by crew shortages, poor ship maintenance, and mediocre leadership at the time the United States declared war. Desertions were high and the diversion of fully manned vessels to other theaters further weakened the Halifax command.[5]

Vice Admiral Herbert Sawyer, RN, appointed to command when the chances of war with America seemed remote, took little action to rectify the growing deficiencies in his command, preferring instead, to operate with the remnants of his declining force in warmer Caribbean waters. This deployment caught his small force completely unprepared to influence the situation in the first few months of the war. The Admiralty had not alerted him to the possibility of war with America until June 1812 when any effective deployment was impossible. All of his frigates were committed to convoy duty and most of his smaller warships needed repair or additional crew to become battle-ready. Neither he nor the Admiralty appear to have prepared any contingency plans in the event of a war with the United States.[6]

Admiral Sawyer compounded his weaknesses by continuing to observe his prewar orders which directed him to avoid provoking an incident with the

3. Mahon, (1965), 221.
4. Dudley, II: 167.
5. Pack, 143.
6. Lohnes, 329.

Americans. As a result, the deployment of most of his seaworthy ships was so far offshore that he could gather little intelligence, nor could his fleet prevent United States Navy warships and American privateers from heading out to sea. The Admiral further hindered his effectiveness by continuing to honor and issue trade licenses to American ships hauling supplies to British forces fighting in Spain and Portugal.[7]

The first high seas contact was initiated by the United States Navy on 27 June 1812 when part of the American squadron attacked the frigate HMS *Belvidera* several hours off New York Harbor. The British ship was damaged and forced to flee to the safety of Halifax. It was 4 July before Admiral Sawyer finally received formal notice from the Admiralty that a state of war existed. The next day he dispatched a squadron led by Captain Philip Broke, RN, in the frigate HMS *Shannon* to harass United States coastal shipping. Captain Broke's orders to find the United States fleet, which unbeknownst to him was in the Azores, allowed the escape of even more American privateers and merchantmen. The unsuccessful patrol returned to Halifax in August.[8]

This modest British effort was further nullified by the defeat of the frigate HMS *Guerriere* by USS *Constitution* on 19 August, which raised United States morale and encouraged more privateers to venture out against English merchant ships and Royal Navy egos. The suppression of these privateers became Admiral Sawyer's highest priority. An additional problem for the admiral was the loss of a number of ships to accident or weather. One frigate ran aground and sank off Cape Breton Island with the Halifax payroll on board, while in another case, a merchantman carrying military equipment for posts in New Brunswick was captured by Americans off Machias, Maine. These misfortunes combined with his lackluster leadership led Sawyer's being replaced by Admiral Sir John B. Warren in August 1812.[9]

Admiral Warren had held flag rank since 1799. He had served in American waters during the Revolution and had commanded frigate squadrons patrolling the French coast and the Mediterranean. Although not a proven strategist, his rank held the possibility that a large coordinated Royal Navy force could be organized in American waters. Warren was senior enough to discuss peace with the Americans, however, when he made overtures, President Madison insisted that impressment be abandoned as a prelude to any negotiations. Since the cabinet refused to consider that condition, Admiral Warren focused on building up the military pressure. The British goal was

7. Pack, 144.
8. Forester, (1956), 28, 59.
9. Forester, (1956), 66, 78; Lohnes, 324.

now to "chastise the Americans into submission."[10]

Warren got off to a slow start, much to the displeasure of his superiors. They ordered a blockade of the Chesapeake area in December 1812, but the logistical base for this, Bermuda, lacked the facilities and stores to sustain the fleet and little could be achieved. Not understanding the reason for the delay, Parliament and the Admiralty became increasingly critical, pressuring Warren to take the war to the Chesapeake. The bay area was not a random choice. It was the site of the United States capital and it contained two navy yards and several major ports, one of which, Baltimore, was a leader in privateering. Additionally, it was a haven for two of the increasingly respected United States frigates, *Adams* and *Constellation* and, finally, it was considered to be highly divided politically. Federalist criticism of the Madison administration's conduct of the war had persuaded the British that military pressure could crack the United States national will to continue the war, and British proximity in Canada to some of the more extreme New England Federalists led them to believe that all Federalists held similar views. Victory thus might be achieved through military operations that widened political rifts. At the very least, such a threat might divert American forces from the hard-pressed defenders of Canada around the Great Lakes and St. Lawrence River.[11]

By late 1812 Warren's command became better organized. Tactics were developed to deal with unexpectedly powerful American frigates and a more consistent strategy began to evolve, assuring a more effective blockade. The Admiral divided his command into nine stations with the first eight stations having specific geographic responsibilities. For example, station number one, the largest of them all, was assigned the blockade of the Chesapeake Bay area with six ships of the line including two 74-gun vessels. Its mission, as developed by March 1813, was to paralyze all trade within the bay, prevent the escape of merchantmen, warships, and privateers into the Atlantic, and to destroy economic resources and shipbuilding facilities throughout the region. Station number two, with three ships of the line, one of which was a 74, had a similar mission in the Delaware Bay area. Its relative size was a reflection of the differing importance of the two water systems in terms of economic activity and shipbuilding capacity. Station number nine with five ships of the line, two of them 74s, was assigned to relieve or reinforce the forces operating in the Delaware or the Chesapeake. It cruised the Atlantic area off the coast, deployed for engagement until needed in the inland waters. A 74-gun ship of the line carried a crew of about 620 men and weighed nearly 1,700 tons. It

10.   Bartlett, 111; Perkins, (1961), 19; Muller, (1963), 14.
11.   Lohnes, 324; Calderhead, 207; Byron, 23.

was the most common ship of the line, with 137 being deployed worldwide by 1814.[12]

Shortly after assuming command, Admiral Warren wrote John W. Croker, the Secretary at the Admiralty, that he had been given a bigger job than he thought their lordships envisioned. He felt his commitments far exceeded his resources and that the quality of the United States warships and their crews were much better than expected. Consequently, he was forced to double-up his frigates to protect them from their American counterparts. The huge numbers of privateers prowling in Canadian and Caribbean waters as well as along sea-lanes to Europe, posed major problems and compelled the tasking of ships for convoy duties, leaving few to conduct an effective blockade. Warren informed his superiors that early American naval successes had given them a self-assuredness which encouraged them to press any advantage, further compounding the blockader's problems. If that was not enough, Royal Navy ships close to the American shores suffered a high desertion rate as the crews were "seduced" by American propaganda.[13]

Admiral Warren's orders gave him a great deal of latitude. He translated them into putting pressure on the American coast while preparing to deal a heavier blow at some key point, possibly New Orleans, after assuring the devastation of the bay area. The immediate problem was the American navy and the privateers, and the best way to pull strength from convoys and patrols was to impose a blockade so tight that United States ships could not leave port. If they were not at sea, they would not be a problem and more Royal Navy vessels would be available to carry out other strategic objectives. The Admiralty slowly comprehended Warren's situation and gave his command a higher priority for ships and reinforcements. Orders were issued for the fleet to be reinforced with four 74-gun ships of the line and supporting vessels, and two marine battalions were withdrawn from European commitments for assignment to Warren's command.[14]

Admiral Warren still faced a daunting task. In March of 1813, the scope of the blockade was extended to include all United States coastal waters from Rhode Island to New Orleans. The objective was to completely throttle all

---

12. Roosevelt, 163; Dudley II: 80-81; O'Brian, 13, 18, The ships assigned to Station number one in March 1812 were *Marlborough* (74), *Victorious* (74), *Maidstone* (36), *Junon* (38), *Laurestinus* (26), and *Fantome* (18); to Station number two *Poictiers* (74), *Narcissus* (32), and *Paz* (10); to Station number nine *San Domingo* (74), *Ramillies* (74), *Statira* (38), *Orpheus* (32) and *Colibri* (18).

13. Dudley, I: 649.

14. Calderhead, 207; Dudley, II: 11-15, 17; Lohnes, 325.

United States coastal and overseas commerce. Warren's fleet also provided naval protection to British activities in both the Caribbean and Canadian waters. Often overlooked even by his superiors was the need to assure a continuous maintenance program to keep as many ships as possible away from extended absences necessitated by long term repairs. The build-up of United States land forces on the Canadian border necessitated mounting a credible diversion to lure U.S. troops away from that threatened area, and for this Warren selected the Chesapeake Bay. British mariners had a long-standing familiarity with the area, and its many navigable rivers and inlets made it especially vulnerable to amphibious raids. Penetration would solve the privateer problem while contributing an economic blow as well.[15]

The implementation of Warren's plan coincided with a decline in Napoleon's fortunes in early 1813. Greatly concerned by the situation in Canada, the British Secretary of State for War, Lord Bathurst, developed a strategy calling for the reinforcement of Warren's Chesapeake Station with enough ships and troops to mount a really credible diversion. He ordered Rear Admiral George Cockburn to America along with eight ships of the line and enough supporting vessels to sustain the blockade and develop information and means to raise the level of activity in the Chesapeake area. The British posture was about to become much more aggressive.[16]

The first summer of the war was not too difficult for Norfolk or the rest of the bay. Some residual trade continued and losses often were offset by profits from privateering. The merchants of Norfolk, the first city to feel the British presence, opposed the war because of the potential harm it implied for their activities and because they knew how weak the United States Navy was relative to the Royal Navy. The gunboats produced under Jefferson's naval policy were virtually useless, but their sheer numbers bred a false sense of security among many. Once war was declared, most people were determined to make the best of it, supporting the construction of defenses, performing militia duties, and financing privateers. Governor James Barbour had issued an order as far back as 19 April 1812 alerting the militia to call-up and allocating the manpower requirements to the various counties as a contingency.[17]

Except for two artillery companies, the Regular Army garrison at Norfolk was reassigned northward in July 1812. At the same time, the national government forgot to authorize militia call-ups to compensate for the Regular's departure. Governor Barbour finally received Federal authority and directed

15. Mahon, (1965), 225; Dudley, II: 78, 167.
16. Mahon, (1965), 224; Pack, 145; Dudley, II: 309; Lossing, 667.
17. Muller, (1963), 19; Wertenbaker, 109; Manarin & Dowdy, 190.

the mobilization he had anticipated the previous April. Seven regiments from the state's southern counties rendezvoused at Smithfield and proceeded to Norfolk under the command of Colonel Edmund Lucas of Greensville County. On 10 August, Captains George M. Brooke and Richard Whartenby of the Fifth United States Infantry, departed with their companies for Canada. That same day, the first contingent of Virginia Militia paraded into the city and Colonel Lucas assumed responsibility for Fort Norfolk. This post, along with Fort Nelson, dated from the Revolutionary War. Substantial local efforts following the *Chesapeake* affair had repaired them and Virginia stocked them with additional artillery. A cadre of Regular artillerymen remained to train the enthusiastic militia who took over the vacated defenses. As British privateers began to harass shipping in the fall, many lower bay residents felt it was just a matter of time before the Royal Navy made its presence known. In the meantime, the revenue cutters and local privateers had their hands full dealing with the growing menace while the militia patrolled beaches and possible landing areas with growing apprehension.[18]

In December 1812, the commander of the Ninth Virginia Militia Brigade, Brigadier General Thomas Mathews, and Colonel Edmund Lucas, the garrison commander, died within days of each other. Governor Barbour persuaded Lieutenant Colonel Robert B. Taylor of the Norfolk Cavalry to assume overall command on 9 December by promoting him to brigader general. A prominent lawyer and active Federalist, his appointment, nevertheless, was strongly supported by the state House of Delegates. The local paper commented, "Mr. Taylor is a Federalist; but he is also an American, and will no doubt prove it to the enemies of his country." The new general immediately began disciplining and organizing the militia and building fortifications. Positions were established on Lambert's Point, at the bridge over Tanner's Creek, and on the various land approaches into Norfolk. Forts Nelson and Norfolk which guarded the water approaches continued to be upgraded. Taylor also recognized the importance of Craney Island, a flat shoal-like piece of land on the west side of the Elizabeth River's mouth, and ordered the construction of earthen breastworks and battery emplacements.[19]

In early 1813 the British became more aggressive. American fishermen reported the presence of larger numbers of British ships and in early January, Princess Anne County coastwatchers verified the sightings. The news compelled Secretary of the Treasury Albert Gallatin to extinguish the navigation lights at the Capes. The British frigate HMS *Tarturus* pursued the French

18. Emmerson, 10, 12, 15, 21-22; Hallahan, 39, 41; Wertenbaker, 110.
19. Emmerson, 23; Wertenbaker, 111.

merchantman *Tamerlane* enroute from Bordeaux to Baltimore, into the Bay on 12 January. She ran aground in part because of the absence of the lights and was captured by her British pursuer. The *Tamerlane* could not be refloated and the *Tarturus* departed leaving a prize crew. Small local boats recaptured her and removed both crew and cargo. Ominously, the rescuers could see that *Tarturus* had been joined by two more men-of-war and that they were stopping all outgoing shipping. News of this increased activity led Governor Barbour to order more militia to the Norfolk area. Cavalry and riflemen from the Richmond area were sent immediately, followed by infantry and artillery units from throughout the Tidewater area. Barbour arrived with these reinforcements to discuss deployments and to give support to Taylor's organization while inspecting and encouraging the troops.[20]

The war now took on a new dimension. Captain George Burdett, RN, led a squadron of four frigates into the bay on 4 February 1813, scattering local shipping and threatening the Hampton Roads area. The force fell back to Lynnhaven Bay and established an anchorage offshore from Pleasure House. It was apparent that the British intended to blockade the bay and by 8 February nothing could get out of Norfolk while even the smallest craft were pursued and captured by barges from the British ships. Seamen released by the British identified the fleet as part of Admiral Warren's main force and reported his declaration of a total blockade. It was clear that the British were prepared to impose their will for as long as necessary.[21]

At the time Burdett's squadron entered the bay there were two United States warships in its waters. Captain Charles Morris, USN, with the frigate USS *Adams* (24) was in the Potomac and eventually evaded the blockade. USS *Constellation* (38) under Captain Charles Stewart, USN, was not so lucky. The *Constellation* had completed a refitting at Washington Navy Yard just before Christmas 1812 and had sailed to the mouth of the Potomac to avoid the ice. She conducted her gunnery tests off St. Mary's and made several short shakedown cruises. Captain Stewart assured his men attained a high level of training and discipline as he anticipated combat within days of reaching the open seas. There was a delay in the delivery of the ship's munitions, but on 1 February she finally left from Annapolis on her first voyage. As she passed Yorktown on 4 February, the ship's lookout spotted Burdett's British squadron in Lynnhaven Bay. Stewart quickly decided his only course of action

20. Muller, (1963), 17; Emmerson 24, 36.
21. Emmerson, 31, 33; Hallahan, 31; By 6 Feb. 1813 the following Royal Navy vessels were reported to be in Lynnhaven Bay: HMS *San Domingo* (74), *Dragon* (74), *Statira* (38), *Junon* (38), *Maidstone* (36), *Belvidera* (36), *Laurestinus* (24) and many smaller vessels.

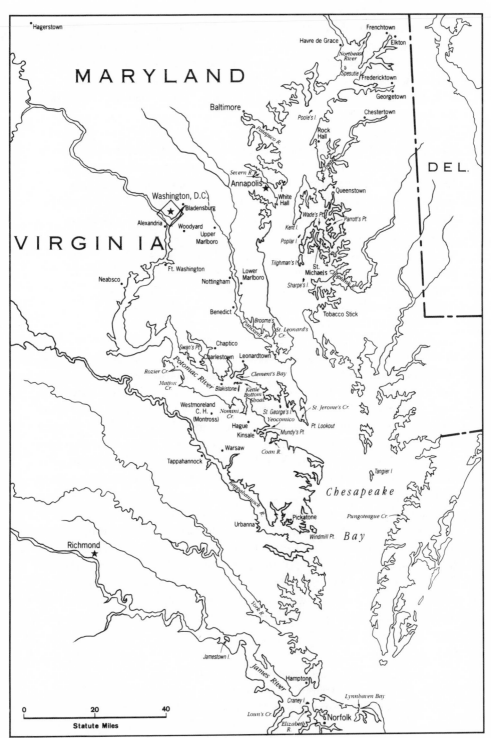

Chesapeake Bay area.

was to head up the Elizabeth River for Norfolk and get under the protection of the city defenses. He reached safety with the British in hot pursuit. In her hurry *Constellation* ran aground and hundreds of citizens in small boats turned out to get her over the bar. All the British could do was blockade the river and wait. Norfolk, however, was a prime target when the British fleet gathered strength.[22]

Some ships were not as fortunate as *Constellation*. The Baltimore privateer *Lottery* under Captain John Southcomb was spotted by Burdett's lookouts early on 4 February. The American was trying to evade through shoals to the open sea. Lieutenant Kelly Nazer, RN, led nine British barges after *Lottery*. They caught up with her after nearly four hours of rowing, boarded her under a brisk fire, and subdued the American crew after a fierce hand-to-hand brawl. Captain Southcomb was killed and eighteen out of a crew of twenty-five were wounded. The British suffered two casualties. *Lottery* was taken into British service and renamed HMS *Canso*. Southcomb's body, sent home with honors to Norfolk, was received by Captain Stewart with ceremony. The war had been brought home to Norfolk in a way it never had before.[23]

The war got rougher with the arrival of Admiral George Cockburn in response to Lord Bathhurst's orders of late November. Promoted to Rear Admiral the previous August, Cockburn had considerable experience commanding men-of-war in the long struggle against France and her allies and had performed a wide variety of combat and administrative duties. He was in command of a small force cruising off Cadiz when he was ordered to move his flag to HMS *Marlborough* (74) and proceed to North America where he had last served as a lieutenant in 1804. The new admiral left for Bermuda on 23 September 1812, but did not reach there until mid-January of 1813 after a very rough passage. He waited in Bermuda for nearly a month until Warren arrived from Halifax. The two officers discussed their mission and decided to focus on blockading the Chesapeake with a secondary effort in the Delaware. Warren ordered Cockburn to make particular efforts to capture or destroy all commercial and military shipping in the Chesapeake and its tributaries, and to collect all possible prizes and send them to Bermuda. Additionally, he charged Cockburn with gathering information about the disposition of American forces and about the navigation of the bay. Finally, he was to select a safe anchorage for the fleet while it was in the bay, and Burdett chose Lynnhaven Bay.[24]

22. Muller, (1963), 17; Roosevelt, 163; Wertenbaker, 110; Hallahan, 32.
23. James, 83; Dudley, II: 318-319; J. Scott, III: 63.
24. Pack, 141-140, 145; Dudley, II: 309, 318; Lossing, 667; Ralfe, 283-285.

The two admirals' combined force headed for the Chesapeake on 5 February only to encounter weather which further delayed their arrival. Enroute, the frigate HMS *Dragon* encountered and captured two United States Navy schooners which were patrolling the Virginia Capes in order to warn American ships of any British presence. These two beautiful little ships were added to the British fleet with appreciation. Cockburn finally arrived on 3 March, relieved Burdett and increased intelligence gathering activities about the Norfolk defenses. The Americans noticed the arrival of Cockburn's force including HMS *Marlborough*, *Ramillies*, and *Poictiers*, all 74s, hours after they anchored in Lynnhaven Bay. Within days the whole fleet shifted to the Hampton Roads area to gauge American reaction and defenses. The move isolated Norfolk and Hampton from the water and diminished the James River waterborne traffic. Cockburn was pleased to discover that no batteries had been established at Point Comfort or Sewall's Point to interdict the approaches to Norfolk. The vulnerability of the entire region was apparent to Cockburn. In his first report to Admiral Warren on 22 March, Cockburn observed it would be possible to revictual at least in part through shore raids. He also noted Washington, D.C.'s susceptibility to a raid. After assessing the situation, the officers concluded that their small forces limited their activities to commerce raids and harassment until they could be reinforced with land troops. After that, they regarded USS *Constellation* and its base at Norfolk as being the first priority for an attack.[25]

Cockburn's presence in the Chesapeake injected British activities with a new aggressiveness. Each night while the fleet lay at anchor in Lynnhaven Bay, its small craft eased into the area of Point Comfort in the hopes of interdicting local water traffic. They also had their eye on a coup against *Constellation*. Captain Charles Stewart, USN, was the senior American naval officer in Norfolk and he worked with the Gosport Naval Base commander, Captain John Cassin, USN, to improve the area's defenses and possibly help his ship escape. *Constellation* had been kedged up the Elizabeth River as far as Fort Norfolk in the first excitement of early February but Stewart later brought his ship down to Craney Island where he hoped to make a break for it. This was noted by the British and their night patrols rowed so close to the ship that Lieutenant George A. Westphal, RN, of HMS *Marlborough* was inspired to organize a raid. He planned to maneuver a rocket boat close to the American ship and destroy it with point blank fire. The 10 March raid was hampered by high winds and took too long to develop. The Americans took alarm and moved *Constellation* back up the river.[26]

25. J. Scott, III: 61; Emmerson, 50; Pack, 146-147; Dudley, II: 320, 322.

It was obvious *Constellation* was stuck for the duration of the British blockade. Consequently, Stewart prepared his ship to function as part of Norfolk's overall defense system and concentrated on improving local defenses on both land and water. One of the first things he did was reorganize the gunboat fleet. Crews were consolidated and equipment was redistributed, reducing the number of boats to seven. Block ships were sunk off Lamberts Point and everything useful for the land defenses was removed from *Constellation*. These actions frustrated Cockburn who began a risky series of probes up the James. British barges carrying out this task were sometimes cut off by American gunboats and captured. Several times enemy craft ran aground and were taken by militia rowing patrols in the James. By the end of March three or four British sailors were deserting to the more attractive comforts of America each night. The resulting manpower problem led the cabinet to approve more troops in the hopes they would increase Cockburn and Warren's success which, in turn would divert American resources from Canada to the Chesapeake Bay.[27]

The British had enough men to conduct forays similar to those begun up the James River. These went up as far as Hog Island and were intended to disperse American defenders and allow the British to probe Norfolk. A few prizes were taken and Cockburn got the impression that the Virginians in the area did not support the war. Unable to get at *Constellation*, and presuming that more raiding might influence local opinion in British favor, Cockburn and Warren turned their attention northward. Almost immediately, contact was made with some American naval defenders. United States Master Commandant Arthur Sinclair had moved his small force of a schooner and three gunboats to the mouth of the Potomac on 10 March. There he learned that the British were at Lynnhaven Bay and that their small craft were launching raids throughout the region. He immediately shifted Lieutenant Edmund P. Kennedy, USN, with the schooner and a gunboat to an anchorage off Gwins Island to be in a better position to intercept the raiders. This move placed Kennedy just above Mobjack Bay where part of the British fleet was anchored. Within hours of his move, he was challenged by a schooner later identified as HMS *Canso*, the former Baltimore privateer *Lottery*. The two ships exchanged fire for several hours with *Canso* getting the worst of it. She staggered away but sank before reaching New Point Comfort. On 17 March, two armed Baltimore privateers were chased by British patrols up Piankatank Creek but militia firing from the creek banks chased the British away. All of

26. J. Scott, III: 74; Dudley, II: 327; Pack, 147-148.
27. Dudley II, 315, 318; Wertenbaker, 110; Pack, 148; Anderson, 7.

these incidents signaled to the residents the arrival of the Royal Navy, and that no place was immune from its attention.[28]

The northward movement of the fleet generated near panic in many of the towns bordering the Chesapeake. Alarm was especially severe in Annapolis, presumably a British target. Throughout March, as British scouts cruised the area more and more citizens evacuated inland. The state archives were removed to Frederick as the city prepared to defend itself. Annapolis was home to many Federalists who had deplored the descent into war. Nevertheless, despite a feeling of near helplessness in the face of British naval power, the city responded to the threat as best as it could. A small force of Regulars with a rotating garrison of militia occupied Forts Severn and Madison at the mouth of the Severn River, while other troops built earthworks. Meanwhile, Governor Winder sought assistance from the Federal government.[29]

Winder wrote a letter to Secretary of War Armstrong pointing out the weakness of the defenses of the Eastern shore and Annapolis. He asked for Federal troops to assist the state in its efforts. After a long silence, the Secretary authorized Federal funding for a militia battalion at both Baltimore and Annapolis. He pointed out that most Federal forces were committed along the Canadian border and that local defense must be provided by the states. Despite their indignation at this indifference, most Marylanders continued to support the war effort and recognized that their defense was up to them. Governor Winder mobilized state militia and coordinated their flow to threatened areas. These forces, mostly from the western counties, were intended to augment forces in Baltimore and Annapolis which were on a permanent state of alert.[30]

General Samuel Smith, the senator, commanded the Baltimore defenses and energetically began to improve the city fortifications and militia while coordinating with Regular Army and Navy units in the city. Once Baltimore became aware of the British arrival in the bay, maritime insurance groups queried the Department of the Navy over the possibility of commissioning privateers to guard merchant vessels and to distract the British. They hoped their offer would serve to augment the more conventional naval resources. Secretary of the Navy William Jones admitted that the forces at his disposal were inadequate to guard everything, but proposed to deploy the forces he did have to the southern bay. Captain Charles Gordon, USN, in command of naval forces in Baltimore, was ordered to send nine of his ten gunboats to the

---

28. Dudley, II: 327, 332, 333; Emmerson, 50; Hallahan, 34.
29. Calderhead, 208; Riley, 233.
30. Andrews, 697, 702; Riley, 234.

Annapolis area in support of Sinclair's and Kennedy's forces located further south. They later went up the Potomac, and on to Norfolk where their dubious services were lost for the duration, leaving one lightly manned gunboat in Baltimore harbor. Thus, when General Smith solicited Gordon's support in readying Baltimore's defenses he had little to give but advice. He pointed out that the Patapsco's shallow draft meant that men-of-war could not reach the city without running the great risk of lightening themselves. Thus, the principal danger to the city was from shallower draft vessels such as bomb ships. These could be countered with properly equipped privateers, shore batteries, and a mobile force to deal with landing parties. While Smith set about his preparations, Gordon requested authority to procure and equip some privateers to defend the city's water approaches and local commerce.[31]

31. Dudley, II: 329, 331-32.

Infantry outposts,
1810-13 uniform.

Chapter Four

ða

THE FIRST RAID: 1813

L EAVING only HMS *Victorious* (74) and a frigate in Lynnhaven Bay, Cockburn's fleet sailed north on 31 March. Within a few days it was apparent that Norfolk might have a brief respite. Captain Charles Stewart took the opportunity to improve the Craney Island fortifications despite Secretary Jones' admonition that it was the army's job. Action continued in the area despite the absence of the fleet. On 11 April the blockade runner *Flight* enroute from Bordeaux to Baltimore was pursued by four barges from *Victorious* and ran aground off Willoughby Point. The barges foundered in a squall and were forced ashore, some at Hampton and some at Lamberts Point. The ships and their crews, fifty-nine men in all, were captured by the revenue cutter *Jefferson* and boats from *Constellation*. It was one of the few times the Americans had the upper hand.[1]

Cockburn's fleet reached Point Lookout, Maryland late on 1 April where it waited while elements explored the Potomac. The shipboard marines land-

1. Emmerson, 58; Anderson, 8.

41

ed on Point Lookout and extended their control of the peninsula for several miles as far as the village of Ridge. Others occupied St. George and Blackistone Islands and dug wells for drinking water. In both cases the men helped themselves to whatever the local farms could offer and encouraged the slaves to join them. Other parts of the fleet probed the Virginia side of the river in search of shipping.[2]

As the fleet moved northward on 2 April, five American privateer schooners were sighted off New Point Comfort and chased into the Rappahannock River. The large ships could not pursue further and held at the mouth of the river at Wind Mill Point. Lieutenant James Polkinghorne, RN, took 105 men in four boats from HMS *San Domingo* and began a grueling fifteen mile chase. The British rowed all night and at daylight came up on the Americans who had deployed for battle at a wide point in the river. They were advancing in the cool morning air discussing what tactics to adopt when the Americans opened fire. All the British boats immediately pulled for the *Arab*, the largest American ship, to neutralize it first. The American captain tried to alter position in order to deliver a broadside, moving away from the protection of his sister ships as he did so. The British boarded his ship and capture it after a sharp fight. *Lynx* and *Racer* were overcome quickly and their guns turned on the fourth schooner, *Dolphin*, commanded by Captain Stafford. After a severe fight on board, her resistance was crushed. Two British were killed and eleven, including Lieutenant Polkinghorne, were wounded. The privateers lost six killed and eleven wounded.[3]

The captured ships were taken downriver to the fleet but at low tide the *Arab* could not cross over the bar at the river's mouth. While she awaited high tide, Major John Chewning's detachment of Lancaster County militia gathered on an island just offshore, beyond range of the ship's guns. The British were launched an amphibious assault toward the bridge linking the island to the mainland at Chewning's Point, and compelled the Americans to withdraw after an hour's fighting. One marine was killed while no other Americans were reported injured although the British estimated they had inflicted twenty casualties. By the morning of 5 April, all five captured ships were incorporated into the fleet and assisted in the capture of nine more unsuspecting American craft cruising the area. *Arab* and *Dolphin* kept their names but *Racer* was christened HMS *Shelburne* and *Lynx* became HMS *Musquedobit*.[4]

Major Chewning's command had been mobilized on the orders of the re-

2. Hecht, 142; Norris, 353.
3. James, 83; Dudley, II: 339; Muller, (1963), 23.
4. J. Scott, III: 78, 91; James, 83; Pack, 150; Hoge, 1267.

gional militia commander, Colonel Richard E. Parker of Westmoreland County. News of the British probe up the Potomac led Parker to prepare for the worse. On his own authority, he ordered his units along that river and along the Rappahannock on alert. His foresight enabled the troops, led by future militia general Captain John R. Hungerford, to fend off British probes at Nomini Cliffs and Mattox Creek. The British withdrew, but not before burning Nomini Plantation and looting the chapel. On 6 April raiders landed near Urbanna and sacked Rosegill Plantation before being confronted by the militia. A running fight lasting several hours followed the British as they descended the river under fire from militia groups along the shores. Colonel Parker wrote Governor Barbour requesting greater munitions and supplies for his region and relating the need for outside militia support for his hard-pressed men. One of the only reactions to his request was the shift of Captain William L. Rogers's Company of the Thirty-Sixth United States Infantry from Leonardtown, Maryland to Sandy Point in Westmoreland County.[5]

The British juggernaut continued northward to Annapolis, attacking Sharp's, Tilghman's, and Poplar Islands enroute. The British occupied Sharp's Island on 12 April and briefly held its owner, Jacob Gibson, captive. They took most of his livestock, but paid and released him and a slave a few days later. The two men headed up the Choptank River to St. Michaels, and conceived a practical joke on the way. Gibson tacked a red cloth to the mast and had his companion beat a drum roll on a barrel. This caused a full alarm in the village and the entire militia mustered to repel an attack. Gibson was lucky not to be shot as few of the inhabitants of St. Michaels were amused. But the militia had undergone an effective drill and the chastened joker paid for two cannon to soothe any hard feelings. The improved defenses would be tested later that year.[6]

The first British ships appeared off Annapolis on 9 April. Two privateers were chased into the harbor but the enemy ships did not complete their pursuit, choosing instead to hover menacingly at the mouth of the Severn. It was at this time that the last of the state archives were transferred inland. Major Charles S. Ridgely commanded local militia forces and supervised the militia rushed in by Governor Winder to complete the manning of the city's defenses. Tension was high and there was an atmosphere of confusion and panic as anyone who could, departed the city with what possessions they could cart away. Surprisingly, the fleet made no landward move. Instead, Admiral Warren remained at anchor with most of his force while Admiral Cockburn ven-

---

5. Norris, 353; Hoge, 1267; Muller, (1963), 24; Hecht, 143; Meade, II: 148, 154.
6. Preston, 164; Byron, 22.

tured northward with a smaller force. The junior admiral had his flag on *Marlborough* (74) and had with him the frigate *Maidstone*, brigs *Fantome* and *Mohawk*, and the tenders *Hornet, Dolphin, Racer,* and *Highflyer.* He had on board a special force of 180 sailors and 200 Royal Marines and Royal Marine Artillery borrowed from the ships remaining off the Severn.[7]

Baltimore's reaction to Cockburn's appearance on 16 April was more controlled than that of Annapolis. Although some residents evacuated the city, their departure was offset by an influx of militia from throughout the region in accordance with plans begun by General Smith as soon as he took command of the city's defenses. Smith was the right man for the job. He had served nearly four years in the Continental line during the Revolution distinguishing himself in the tenacious defense of Fort Mifflin in 1777. He later supervised defensive preparations for Baltimore. After the war he rose to command of the local militia division and gained great political and commercial influence in his adopted city. He was the best connected man in Baltimore, ideal for the persuading and cajoling role his new military responsibilities required.[8]

General Smith already had discussed a plan of defense with the amiable United States Navy Captain Charles Gordon. It was a bigger challenge to turn his plans into action. He had to train and organize his polyglot militia force, continue the pressure to get help from state and federal officials, and begin the construction of effective defenses around the city. His job was made difficult by the fact that he had no authority over federal facilities in the town such as Fort McHenry. Its commander, Major Lloyd Beall, was loathe to permit militia to stay on his post overnight. Smith overlooked this pettiness and persuaded the major to include his men in guard mounts and to allow them to perform other fort duties. This provided his men the opportunity to train without being mobilized and gave them a sense of purpose. He created cavalry posts around both shores of the Patapsco for the same reasons and to familiarize his troopers and officers with the terrain.[9]

Despite Major Beall's reservations, Smith pushed for improvements around Fort McHenry on the assumption that an attack was possible from both land and water approaches. The fort was strengthened and earlier engineering plans were revived to develop two large water batteries to better protect it. Guns were procured for the emplacements from government sources, but many more came from local ships immobilized by the blockade. Especial-

7. Riley, 234; Pack, 151; Muller, (1963), 24.
8. Cassell, (1971), 181; Sellers, 19, 23.
9. Cassell, (1971), 184.

ly impressive were twelve 42-pounders taken from a wrecked French man-of-war.[10]

As news of the northward British movement became known, the garrison was put on full alert. Neither Secretary of War John Armstrong nor Governor Winder shared Smith's belief that Baltimore would be a British target. Their views were seconded by the senior Regular Army officer in the city, Colonel Decius Wadsworth, who did not think the British had enough ground troops to deal with the city but just in case, Armstrong authorized Smith to mobilize the full city brigade. The orders Armstrong sent were so vaguely worded that it was unclear who was in overall command and the general took advantage of this by assuming full charge of all military components in the city. A few days after learning of the federal government's slow response to the British threat, the Baltimore City government created a Committee of Public Supply to support Smith's efforts. The Committee was filled by many of the General's civilian business associates. As its name implies, it sought to assume the logistical burden for Smith by providing the funds and procuring the supplies his soldiers and defense construction required. The Committee also raised and funded a corps of Sea Fencibles from amongst the unemployed sailors in the city who proved especially useful in harbor patrolling and gunnery training.[11]

Thus Baltimore was reasonably ready when Admiral Cockburn sailed his squadron to the mouth of the Patapsco where he discovered that nearly all American shipping had gained the protection of Fort McHenry. Only Captain Gordon's single gunboat was visible and it, too, hovered close to the fort. Cockburn dispatched some barges and the shallow draft HMS *Hornet* up the river in pursuit of stragglers and captured some while exchanging fire with Gordon's gunboat. The main fleet remained further out while its small boats procured water from nearby North Point. Baltimore was in a state of alarm over the threat of British attack and hulks near Fort McHenry were prepared to be sunk to block the harbor entrance. The hours of drill and rehearsals paid off as the militia moved to their positions with a minimum of confusion. The British sent a flag of truce boat ostensibly to discuss prisoner exchange, but really to assess the situation. What they saw before they were ordered away must have been unnerving. The land and naval defenses were a beehive of organized activity and the big French 42-pounder guns were very noticeable.[12]

Although the fleet seemed deterred by the defenses, it continued to hov-

---

10. Pancake, (1972), 108.
11. Cassell, (1971), 188; Scharf, (1881), 88.
12. Calderhead, 212; Dudley, II: 340, 350; Niles, IV: 134, 24 April 1813.

er off the river's mouth. Each night Captain Gordon deployed six guard boats three or more miles below the city on a rowing patrol to guard against a surprise attack. Militia cavalry increased their forays as well, patrolling the riverbanks in earnest and reporting all British activities to Smith's headquarters. One cavalryman, Baltimore businessman Leverett Saltonstall Jr., later wrote his father that one look at Cockburn's 74 (HMS *Marlborough*) almost made a pacifist of him. He felt that if the War Hawks had had the same experience, peace would soon follow. There was little panic. Work increased on Fort McHenry and the surrounding defenses as General Smith took advantage of the larger numbers of men available and most people were confident that the city could be defended successfully. The men were kept under arms on a weekly rotation. Very few exemptions to duty were allowed and heavy fines were imposed if a man failed to report. Militia from outlying regions periodically relieved the city brigade from two large camps on Hampstead Hill and Bear Creek on North Point. The city was more than Cockburn could handle and within a few days, he shifted his force northward in search of easier targets. HMS *Maidstone* and its tender remained to observe and blockade Baltimore.[13]

As early as 20 April the residents of the extreme northern part of the Chesapeake Bay were aware that trouble was coming their way. There were rumors of farms being raided and small boats destroyed north of Baltimore. Newspapers reported that the British had occupied Poole's Island and the one hundred or so fishing families residing there had fled to Harford County. The British fleet hovered briefly off Worton Point in Kent County where local militia fended off a foraging party trying to land at Still Pond. Finally, on 27 April, a brig and three schooners anchored in the waters off Havre de Grace. Old men recalled they were in exactly the same place used by the British in 1777 as they readied themselves for the Philadelphia campaign. Once these vessels were joined by another brig and schooner, they disappeared around Turkey Point and headed up the Elk River. These were Cockburn's raiders. His force had departed the Patapsco and reached and occupied Spesutie Island then continued northward, leaving the deeper draft HMS *Marlborough* there.[14]

Interrogation of locals led Admiral Cockburn to conclude that Frenchtown on the Elk River was a major logistical site. It was located on the Baltimore-Philadelphia stage road and had become a depot for military goods and agricultural produce. On 28 April, Cockburn led the force seen disappearing

---

13. Moody, II: 530-531; Dudley, II: 350; Hanna, 341-342.
14. Sparks, 157; Usilton, 97; Lossing, 670; J. Scott, III: 99.

from Havre de Grace, consisting of the brigs *Fantome* and *Mohawk*, and the tenders *Dolphin*, *Racer*, and *Highflyer*, up the river. Once the larger ships had reached bottom, the foray continued with 150 marines in small boats under the command of Lieutenant George A. Westphal, RN. The expedition detoured erroneously up the Bohemia River, giving the militia time to establish some defensive positions at Frenchtown. It was early morning of 29 April when the British encountered a six-gun battery that opened fire on them. This was engaged by guns on the barges while a marine force landed and flanked the American position, routing the defenders. One American was allegedly killed by rocket fire, no marine was hurt. The guns were spiked and the troops advanced into the village where large quantities of flour and military goods were destroyed along with five small ships. The exhilarated British then withdrew.[15]

This devastation marks the beginning of a policy which became Cockburn's trademark. He let it be known that his forces would do no harm to anyone or any place that did not resist, but, if fired upon, he promised the persons or place would be devastated and any property destroyed. This policy aimed to convince opponents of the Madison government of British reasonableness, while laying the war's horrors at the feet of its supporters. What it created was a license to pillage and some glaring anomalies. For example, Cockburn's forces often made token payments for livestock and produce taken from local farms but, prize law treated the same items found in a boat as subject to confiscation. Cockburn's policies displeased some British officers. Many of the naval officers were American-born and several had family members in the beseiged areas and they did not relish the idea of destroying property in which they might have an interest. The exception was Cockburn, whose uncle, Martin Cockburn, and his family lived on an estate south of Mount Vernon on the banks of the Potomac. One British officer likened the situation to an "almost civil war" and these depredations ultimately increased popular support for the national government. As harsh as they were, United States newspaper rhetoric made them appear even worse, and many Americans came to believe that resistance was the only answer to barbarism.[16]

One of the most notorious alleged atrocities occured during the British withdrawal from Frenchtown. The British ships, of necessity, passed through their old anchorage opposite Havre de Grace, a town of forty to fifty houses on the Philadelphia post road and although at extreme range, they were fired upon by a battery outside the town which ran up its colors in unusual defi-

15. James, 85; J. Scott, III: 96; Pack, 151; Muller, (1963), 25; Lossing, 670.
16. James, 85; Hoge, 1266; Pellew, 3:121; Napier, 225; Fortescue, X: 322.

ance. Admiral Cockburn decided to deposit his plunder with the main fleet at Spesutie Island and return to discover why Havre de Grace should act so aggressively.[17]

Havre de Grace officials had been hard at work since 20 April getting their town, the home of naval hero, Commodore John Rogers, ready to defend itself. Local militia were called up and artillery sent by the state was emplaced. One 9-pounder and two 6-pounder guns were mounted at Potato Hill just south of town. Two 9-pounder guns were dug in at Concord Point where the Susquehanna flows into the bay, and the battery was manned by volunteers usually exempt from military service. Preparations hit a fever pitch when British ships first appeared on 28 April. The militia conducted nightly patrols along the river and bay shores, but when the British ignored Havre de Grace by sailing away, the defenders lost their sense of urgency. Many drifted home, leaving a weakened, unorganized force. British plans were foiled briefly on 1 May when a deserter alerted the Americans to the imminent attack. The town went into an uproar, the militia returned, and families departed. When nothing happened that night, guard was again dropped and numbers of militia dispersed.[18]

Cockburn had merely held his punch. Shallow waters precluded approaching Havre de Grace in the larger ships. At midnight on 2 May Lieutenant Westphal led a group of small boats with a detachment of marines and artillery against the town defenses. Overall coordination and command of the operation fell to Captain John Lawrence of HMS *Fantome*, while *Dolphin* and *Highflyer* came close enough to provide additional fire support. The British reached their attack positions at dawn and began firing on the American batteries with artillery and rockets. The alarm sounded as soon as the barges were detected leaving the fleet's anchorage, but there was little semblance of order amongst the defenders. The men manning the battery at Point Concord began firing, only to get a Congreve rocket barrage in reply that killed one of the militia infantry, a man named Webster, and so panicked most of his comrades that they fled.[19]

The boats carrying the marines passed under the American gunfire and landed their men while British gunboats continued to pound the battery. The marines captured the American guns and turned them on the remaining defenders, forcing them to flee and severely damaging houses in the town. The marines entered Havre de Grace and cleared it of militia after a brief fight.

17. James, 86; J. Scott, III: 104.
18. Sparks, 159; Lossing, 670.
19. Sparks, 160; J. Scott, III: 100; James, 86; Muller, (1963), 27.

One of the few militiamen to hold his position during the British attack was a fifteen-year resident originally from Ireland named John O'Neil. He single-handedly manned one of the artillery pieces until the attackers were virtually upon him, then retreated into the village. There, he and a fellow militiaman fired on the British until they ran out of ammunition. O'Neil ran to the village common and signaled his comrades to return but was captured by Lieutenant Westphal. He was taken on board Cockburn's ship where the first reaction was to treat him as a traitor, but Cockburn soon released him.[20]

The British force broke into small groups and scattered throughout the town. A company of marines pursued the militia for about one mile while their comrades ransacked the town. About forty of the sixty structures were burned, although Admiral Cockburn personally saw to it that Commodore Rogers's home was preserved. A British patrol rowed five miles up the Susquehanna to the head of navigation and burned a warehouse, but was unable to harm several small vessels scuttled nearby. They returned to discover that unaware of the situation, the Philadelphia stage had innocently rolled into town. Admiral Cockburn, again, personally intervened to prevent the looting of passengers. Having done considerable damage, the British reembarked and rowed three or four miles to Principio Foundry, or Cecil Furnace, near Cress-well Ferry on the Susquehanna. They destroyed the foundry and forty-five gun barrels found on the premises were rendered useless. After twenty-two hours of action, Cockburn led his men back to the fleet. The region was shocked by the destruction of property and it galvanized people everywhere to greater resistance, especially in Baltimore where one of the local papers said the choice was now simple, "For or against the English is the only Touchstone." [21]

After a day's rest the British turned their attention to the Sassafras River. This was one of the few places they had not examined and Cockburn had heard from informants that the small towns of Georgetown and Frederick-town, each of about twenty houses, were havens for ships and important commercial centers. He used the same force that had hit Havre de Grace, led this time by Captain H. D. Byng of HMS *Mohawk*. The raiders rowed through the night of 5 May, reaching a point within two miles of the twin villages at dawn on 6 May. There they encountered two Americans and Cockburn sent them ahead to advise the townsmen not to resist. If they did, he promised them the same fate as Havre de Grace. This threat did not have the desired

20. Sparks, 161; J. Scott, III: 106.
21. Sparks, 160-162; Dudley, II: 341; J. Scott, III: 102, 108; Muller, (1963), 27-28; Niles, IV: 165.

effect. The British proceeded about one mile closer when they encountered heavy fire from an estimated 400 riflemen and an artillery piece under the command of Colonel Thomas W. Veazey of the Forty-Ninth Maryland Militia. The Americans had deployed on both sides of the river where it narrowed at Pearce's Point. Cockburn's force immediately responded with rocket fire and landed marines to flank the gun position and flush out the militia. Five marines were wounded and the raiders proceeded on to the villages where they sacked first Fredericktown then Georgetown.[22]

Both villages were defenseless. All of the able-bodied men had been mustered into the militia companies, leaving the town full of women, children, and the elderly. Many fled with their valuables and hid in the countryside. The British set about destroying warehouses and four ships lying at anchor in the river. Things soon got out of hand and houses also went up in smoke. One resident of Georgetown, Catherine "Kitty" Knight, had not fled as she was determined to prevent the destruction of her house and that of an invalid neighbor in her care. She refused to leave when a fire party approached, brazening it out first with the young officer in charge and finally with Cockburn himself. With the strange gallantry he often displayed, the admiral acknowledged her courage and ordered her house and that of her neighbor to be spared.[23]

The amphibious force rejoined the fleet on 7 May. Upon their return they encountered a delegation from Charlestown offering to surrender to avoid harm, and later landed at a riverside village where the inhabitants appeared cowed and cooperative. The British took this as evidence of their success in dividing American support for the war. Tactically, they had proven the vulnerability of the Chesapeake shores, and their experience raised the possibility for even more intensive land operations in the minds of both Cockburn and Warren. However, despite the short term negative effect on local morale, the cumulative effect of the raids caused a shift in public opinion duly reflected in the Baltimore newspaper observation quoted above. There was a growing dislike for the British and many previously neutral or indifferent Americans now openly opposed them. The raids had a further effect on Pennsylvania. On his own initiative, Governor Snyder mobilized the militia in southeastern Pennsylvania and large numbers of them rushed to Elkton to help Maryland meet the British threat. This was not only a rehearsal for later cooperation, but a challenge to the attitudes of Delaware Valley Federalists who had previously been unresponsive to Pennsylvania support for the war.[24]

22. James, 88-89; J. Scott, III: 110; Dudley, II: 334.
23. Usilton, 47, 50; Pack, 153; Muller, (1963), 28.

Cockburn's flotilla headed southward on 7 May to rejoin Warren's main force off Annapolis. Enroute, they continued to harass targets of opportunity. HMS *Maidstone* landed a group of foragers at Plum Point in Kent County and plundered George Medford's farm, removing all of his livestock. Militia arrived and chased away the foragers before they could do further damage. In retaliation, *Maidstone* fired fifteen rounds at the next farm house, Stephen Wilmer's, hitting it six times. This sort of activity emphasized how defenseless parts of the shore could be and the combined fleet returned to the St. Mary's River area for further foraging. Southern Maryland was especially exposed and both federal and state officials felt that its vulnerability to waterborne attack from both the Potomac and the bay sides, made it an unwise choice for the stationing of troops. Thus, whenever a large British force appeared it became routine to order Colonel Henry Carberry's Thirty-Sixth United States Infantry, stationed at nearby Leonardtown, to move closer to Annapolis or Washington. The same policy prevailed for most of the region's militia. Its commander, Brigadier General Philip Steuart, was ordered to keep his forces concentrated in northern Calvert County, or in Anne Arundel County, to support Annapolis whenever danger threatened. This did little to inspire the largely Federalist population and compelled many of them to appear sympathetic to the British. Their conduct added to the continued British misconception about American attitudes.[25]

For nearly a week the British fleet trickled into Lynnhaven Bay. In Norfolk, Captain Stewart anticipated an attack and pressed completion of the Craney Island defenses and the establishment of a 500-man garrison. He got a brief reprieve, however, as the two British admirals knew that their activities in the bay had no perceptible effect on American activities in Canada. Admiral Warren felt that a larger gesture using the troops ordered to the area by Lord Bathhurst was necessary. Consequently, he left for Halifax with forty prizes and ordered HMS *Dragon* to escort thirty more to Bermuda. After attending to business in Halifax, Warren planned to join *Dragon* to escort the ground reinforcements heading for Bermuda.[26]

Admiral Cockburn on HMS *Marlborough* remained in the Chesapeake, taking station near Point Comfort while HMS *Victorious* (74) anchored at Lynnhaven Bay. *Marlborough*'s crew frequently visited Smith's Island, both to converse with the pretty daughter of the only family in residence and to

24. Lossing, 674; *Naval Chronicle* XXX: 167-8; J. Scott, III: 110; Thomson, 271; Ellis & Evans, 75.
25. Hecht, 143; Usilton, 97.
26. Hallahan, 36; Dudley, II: 347, 357.

hunt wild sheep. Wherever they went, they tried to increase their knowledge of the navigable routes in the bay. Their primary mission remained keeping *Constellation* bottled up in the Elizabeth River and throttling bay commerce.[27]

This first raid up the bay generated changes throughout the area. In Baltimore, Captain Charles Gordon, USN, received authorization from the Navy Department on 15 April to lease and man four privateers to compensate for his depleted fleet. During the crisis, he had negotiated successfully to lease *Revenge* and *Patapsco*, both with fourteen 12-pounder guns and the smaller *Comet* and *Wasp*. Once the British left the area, he would cruise the northern bay to protect local shipping. As it turned out, most ships stayed in harbor, although his activity did compel the British to hold their roving small boats closer to the fleet for safety. Although Gordon was responsible only to the Navy Department, Secretary Jones told him to work closely with General Smith whenever Baltimore was threatened. The little privateer fleet was not ready until mid-May because of the difficulties Gordon had luring sailors away from better paying privateer billets.[28]

The first British forays prompted Governor Winder to call a special session of the Maryland legislature on 17 May. It was apparent that the national government would not or could not devote more resources to Maryland's defenses and the delegates wrestled with methods of financing the myriad military commitments they faced. They also passed a resolution urging the federal government to allocate its resources as equitably as possible. It was their impression that the national government's focus on the fate of *Constellation* meant that Virginia was getting the bulk of any federal resources available. The lawmakers sensed that any concrete measures would be up to them and, they developed their own means to defend the state as best they could. One choice was to authorize the governor to rotate militia from less threatened western areas into the bay defenses to give their eastern counterparts some relief. By mid-May a steady flow of Frederick and Washington County troops streamed in and out of Baltimore and Annapolis.[29]

The slow federal response in the first crisis persuaded Samuel Smith and the Baltimore City fathers that they must continue to look to their own resources to maintain the safety of the city. Consequently, even after the British moved south following their foray in May, Baltimore maintained a high level of activity. Supported by the Committee of Public Supply, Smith emphasized

27. J. Scott, III: 116; Brenton, 498; Pack, 156.
28. Dudley, II: 348, 351; Calderhead, 211.
29. Andrews, 207; N.H. Williams, 165, 167.

the need for more work on the harbor defenses and the system of earthworks growing on Hampstead Hill. In his capacity as federal senator, Smith pressed the national government for more resources and enlisted the Committee to lobby the Secretary of War. The city proved its sincerity by raising $500,000 towards defense costs. Although little came from the federal level lobbying, Smith did get the obnoxious Major Beall replaced by the more amiable and competent Major George Armistead, who had both the funds and authority to complete the improvements to Fort McHenry. Smith refused to diffuse his forces in futile efforts to protect indefensible sites, opting instead to concentrate his force around the city and make it as impregnable as possible.[30]

He also developed a system to gather intelligence on British movements in the region. As early as March 1813, Post-Master General Gideon Granger ordered a courier system be developed linking St. Mary's County and Washington. It would report both friendly and enemy ship movements and serve as an early warning system for Washington. News of any ship's movement into the Potomac would reach the capital within twenty-two hours and by July postal employees operated a system that reported routinely on all British movements visible from Point Lookout.[31]

British intelligence gathering improved over the spring of 1813 largely due to the numbers of slaves seeking protection. Many of them proved excellent sources of information and others served as guides, allowing the British to select targets where the greatest possible damage could be inflicted. The former slaves' knowledge of the countryside now made British night patrols feasible, and any area within ten miles of a waterway became vulnerable to British raids. Prior to this assistance, British raids had been random and ineffective.[32]

British commanders were not to incite any kind of slave revolt. They were directed to be as receptive as possible to any black fugitives, but this became difficult given the large number wanting protection. As early as May 1813, the Norfolk newspapers were commenting on the number of slaves that had fled from Princess Anne County farms to Royal Navy ships at Lynnhaven Bay. There they were kindly received and completely unresponsive to their master's pleas to return. In fact, many returned to their old homes only to persuade others to run away.[33]

Admiral Cockburn saw other uses for this unexpected reinforcement.

---

30. Cassell, (1971), 193, 195; Pancake, (1972), 108.
31. Pancake, (1972), 110; Hecht, 150-151.
32. J. Scott, III: 115, 119.
33. Cassell, (1972), 145; J. Scott, III: 118; Pack, 156.

The escapees were a welcome source of additional manpower and he thought of training them as soldiers to augment his land forces. Long before he received permission to do so, other ramifications of slave discontent became apparent. Citizens of the Virginia and Maryland countryside feared that a slave revolt might be part of British strategy. As a result, some militia were retained during major alerts to assure a force was available in case of an uprising. Additionally, a great deal of militia energy was diverted to catch runaways escaping to the British. All these factors worked to the British advantage. The situation compelled many people in the region opposed to the national government's policy to cooperate fully as it was the lesser of two evils.[34]

The withdrawal of the Royal Navy to Lynnhaven Bay changed the mission of Gordon's privateer fleet in the Patuxent. This little flotilla's job shifted to observing the enemy forces and keeping the defenders informed as to their capabilities and deployment. Once satisfied with its equipment, Gordon led his command as far south as New Point Comfort, often coming in sight of the British. They did not respond to his presence and he did not dare close with real warships, but he harassed any enemy detached ships and foraging parties he could in an effort to reduce the extent of their mischief. His presence compelled the British to keep their small craft well in hand and to maintain night patrols whenever the big ships were at anchor.[35]

The privateer fleet also supported more novel forms of harassment. Whenever possible it destroyed buoys and other navigational aids deployed by the British and experimented with devices such as fire ships and torpedoes. The latter, also known as "Fulton Machines," were gunpowder rafts intended to be towed close to enemy craft and detonated by manual or timed fuse. Sailing Master Elijah Mix worked with Gordon's fleet to use these devices as early as May. The first plan called for using them in the defense of Baltimore Harbor, but when the British shifted south, Mix relocated along with Gordon. He made several efforts in June to use the torpedoes but was foiled by both bad weather and technological problems. Finally on 24 July, after several tries he and his crew exploded a torpedo next to HMS *Plantagenet* as it lay at anchor near Cape Henry lighthouse. The massive detonation hurled a huge fountain of water skyward. Other than that, all it did was soak the British ship and frighten its crew. The torpedo's time had not yet come although Captain Gordon would use them as barriers in Norfolk Harbor after assuming command there in 1814. The Americans brushed off British protests over torpedo use by citing the British use of rockets as an equal violation of fairness.[36]

34. Cassell, (1972), 146.
35. Dudley, II: 352; Calderhead, 213-214.

Concurrent with these experiments, a new phase of operations forced Gordon and his men northwards. On 13 June Admiral Cockburn began concentrating his command in Lynnhaven Bay in anticipation of Admiral Warren's return with the land force requested earlier in the year. Channels were marked and *Marlborough*, *Barossa*, and *Junon* anchored in Hampton Roads to observe Craney Island and the approach into Norfolk. The British build-up presaged a new crisis for the American defenders.[37]

36. Calderhead, 217; Niles, VII: 55, 6 October 1814.
37. J. Scott, III: 136; Brenton, 498.

Infantry skirmishing at bridge,
Maryland Eastern Shore, 1813.

Chapter Five

ह⠀

AGGRESSION REPELLED: 1813

T HE successes against Napoleon allowed the shift of British army and
navy resources to America. Warren was provided additional warships,
raising the total for his Chesapeake Bay station to eight ships of the line and
twelve frigates with numerous smaller craft, a large force by any standards. It
was made even more formidable by the addition in May of marine and army
forces under the command of Colonel Sir Sydney Beckwith. Beckwith was a
veteran light infantry officer who had fought against the French in Iberia. He
had been appointed to North America as assistant quartermaster-general in
Canada but, enroute, was given command of the expedition requested by
Cockburn, while he waited for the St. Lawrence to clear of ice. Well liked by
the soldiers, his senior subordinate, Lieutenant Colonel Charles Napier, characterized him as "a clever fellow - but a very odd fish."[1]

The Admiralty informed Warren that he should focus primarily on the
destruction of United States Navy capabilities and, secondarily, stage a series

---

1. Lee IV: 91; Fortescue III: 375; Lossing, 675.

of raids at a level of destruction which might lure United States forces from Canada. Beckwith arrived with orders of his own. His overall mission was to work with his naval counterparts in creating a diversion spectacular enough to effect the Canadian front. His actions should be no more than raids and he should not permanently occupy any site. His orders stated that he should not stir up the slaves, but to protect them if they came to him as fugitives. Beckwith understood his orders to give him veto power over the Admiral's decisions if the latter conflicted with his own instructions. The command relationship that evolved from each officer's understanding of his orders, although cordial, was often difficult and disjointed.[2]

Beckwith's force sailed from England on 30 March and reached Bermuda on 23 May. His command consisted of two battalions of Royal Marines, two companies of Royal Marine Artillery, each with a Congreve rocket section, a 300-man strong detachment from the 103rd Regiment, and two companies of Independent Foreigners. Upon arrival in Bermuda the 103rd Regiment element was reassigned to a force bound for Canada. It was replaced by the 102nd Regiment from the Bermuda garrison.[3]

The units of the command were a uneven, mixed bunch, reflecting the manpower priorities and deficiencies of the British Army in the last full year of war against Napoleon. The two marine battalions had been formed in 1810 from shipboard and depot units in Britain and had served in garrison and raiding duties in Spain until returning to England in December 1812. Both battalions were composed of eight infantry companies and a Royal Marine Artillery company. Although the marine detachments were made up of handpicked men, they had little experience in battalion and larger formations, a deficiency which led to confusion and casualties in the forthcoming operations.[4]

The regular regiment, the 102nd, had an unusual background. It was raised in 1789 as the "New South Wales Corps" and sent to garrison the British penal colony at Botany Bay, Australia. The unit became a dumping ground for men from units throughout the British Colonies. In 1808 the regiment's officers mutinied against Captain Edmund Bligh, the governor of the colony, who had been the object of an earlier, more famous, mutiny. The regiment returned to Europe and while stationed on Guernsey it was redesignated as the 102nd. It had a very poor reputation but this changed when Lieutenant Colonel Charles Napier, a superb officer and disciplinarian, be-

2. Dudley II: 325; Mahon, (1965), 224; Muller, (1963), 32.
3. Fortescue IX: 321; Field I: 291.
4. Field I: 262-265, 289-291; Napier I: 212; Nicolas II: 241.

came its commander. Napier took the 102nd to Bermuda in July 1812 and embarked upon an extended program of garrison duties and training which brought his regiment to a very high level of proficiency. By the time the 102nd was assigned to Beckwith's force, it was an excellent unit.[5]

Colonel Beckwith immediately sized up the Independent Companies of Foreigners as marginal troops. The insubordination and rowdiness of the men both on board ship and upon arrival in Bermuda, confirmed his first impressions. These two companies were among Britain's least successful military experiments of the Napoleonic period. They were recruited in 1812 from French Army deserters in Spain and French prisoners of war in England, with the intention of sending off to the disease-ridden West Indies as garrison forces. The two 152-man companies assigned to Beckwith's force were officered by French emigrés with one exception, Captain Sylvester Smith, and there was little respect or loyalty between officers and men. Considerable confusion surrounds the correct designation of these units. They have been called the "Chasseurs Britanniques" or "Canadian Chasseurs" which were, respectively, another unit of French troops in British service and a Canadian militia unit. The origins of the Canadian association was a request from Beckwith who thought such a designation might calm the men's fears of being sent to the Caribbean. Whatever their name, the Independent Foreigners, properly identified, proved to be an unsavory collection of thugs.[6]

In Bermuda, Beckwith organized his force into two brigades with Napier commanding one, Lieutenant Colonel Richard Williams of the Royal Marines the other. He assigned a company of foreigners to each brigade in order to dilute their potential for trouble. He formed a staff by taking officers from the Bermuda garrison. Lieutenant Frederick Robertson, RA, was an especially welcome addition as he had commanded the artillery detachment during the spring foray into the Chesapeake and could serve as a guide.[7]

In late May, Admiral Warren arrived in Bermuda and he and Beckwith began planning an attack on Norfolk. They exchanged information with Admiral Cockburn by courier. Already in the Chesapeake, Cockburn stressed the vulnerability of the Norfolk area and slighted the quality of the defenders in his reports. He had acquired some information about troop movements, perhaps the earlier deployment of Brigadier General Joel Leftwich's Virginia Militia regiment to Fort Meigs, Ohio, and concluded that Brigadier General Robert B. Taylor's defenders were dangerously weakened. It was obvious

5. Butler, 55; Napier I: 185-186; Hill, 135-136.
6. Hitsman & Sorby, 11-17.
7. PAC, Beckwith Letters 1813; Elting, (1991), 125.

from the questions coming from Bermuda that a landing to the west of Craney Island was under consideration. A survey of the island's shoal-ridden approaches by Lieutenant George A. Westphal, RN, showed that reaching it would be very difficult. Cockburn advised against the approach because the Americans could reinforce the proposed landing area from the opposite river-bank. It also cut off a line of retreat which would compel the defenders to stand instead of run.[8]

Admiral Warren's force slipped Bermuda on 8 June and began assembling in Lynnhaven Bay ten days later. British movements indicated that Norfolk was the likely target, but their appearance frightened the entire bay region. The sheer scale of the British effort had all coastal towns preparing for the worst. Defensive preparations increased everywhere, especially in Baltimore. General Samuel Smith believed the city was on the British target list and convinced the governor and the legislature of this likelihood. Larger numbers of militia from surrounding counties were added to the rotations just begun, with 2,000 additional troops under the command of Colonel William Miller of Cecil County joining Smith's Division for the remainder of the summer.[9]

The District of Columbia forces became more active. On his own initiative, Major General John P. Van Ness, their commander, put his cavalry on full alert in May during the crisis of the first British raid. He used them periodically thereafter to patrol the Maryland bank of the Potomac and to maintain contact with the Maryland militia and Thirty-Sixth United States Infantry troops which were observing the British at the Potomac's mouth. A civilian Committee of Vigilance was formed by concerned citizens to prod the War Department into accepting a militia battalion led by Major Adam King, for purposes of augmenting the elements of the Thirty-Sixth Infantry stationed at Fort Washington and Indian Head. The militia cavalry was kept on active duty briefly in June, but was sent home when the War Department objected to the cost of their maintenance. The strange complacency of the national government was not justified or explainable in light of the increased British activity.[10]

Even before Admiral Warren returned to the bay with Beckwith's force, it was obvious that the British intended to renew their raiding activities. On 12 June, Lieutenant John Crerie, RN, took the boats of HMS *Narcissus* and forty Marines under Lieutenant Patrick Savage, RN, up the York River to at-

8. Hallahan, 54; Pack, 156-157.
9. Scharf, (1881), 87.
10. Todd, 426-427.

tack the United States revenue cutter, *Surveyor*. The sixteen-man crew led by Captain Samuel Travis learned of the British search and prepared for an attack. Travis's picket boats spread the alarm as the British approached. The Americans, each armed with two loaded muskets, delivered a vicious fire on the British boats, killing three and wounding six. Despite this small arms fire, Lieutenant Crerie persisted, selecting an angle of approach which prevented the American's bigger guns from coming to bear. The marines boarded and captured *Surveyor* after a short brawl in which another marine and six Americans were wounded. Lieutenant Crerie returned to the fleet with his prize and the prisoners were transferred to HMS *Junon*. The next day Crerie returned Travis's sword to him as a token of respect. A few days later, several British vessels probed up the James River, harassing small craft and farms alike. This was a reconnaissance preliminary to the full fleet shifting from Lynnhaven Bay to Hampton Roads. The movement began on 18 June and the American defenders knew that the long awaited crisis was finally at hand.[11]

On 19 June HMS *Junon* (38) with HMS *Laurestinus* (24) and *Barossa* (36) anchored off Newport News to blockade the Elizabeth River. The currents caused *Junon* to drift some distance from her sister ships, with all three ships becoming becalmed in the stillness of the night. Captain John Cassin, USN, Norfolk port commander, noticed *Junon*'s vulnerability and immediately ordered Master Commandant Joseph Tarbell to lead a gunboat attack to cut her out. Tarbell used men from *Constellation* and fifty militia volunteers from the Craney Island defenses to create a fifteen-boat force divided into two divisions, commanded respectively by United States Navy Lieutenants Robert D. Henley and John M. Gardner. Although the gunboats pulled out at 11 P.M. on the 19th, adverse winds prevented them from getting in range of *Junon* until about 4 A.M. the following morning. *Junon* spotted them and opened fire at a distance of three quarters of a mile. The increasing swells prevented the gunboats from holding position or shooting accurately. After forty-five minutes of firing, *Junon* made headway in a fresh breeze and pulled away. At the same time, *Barossa* and *Laurestinus* arrived and forced the American gunboats to withdraw. The entire action had lasted about ninety minutes. One American, Mr. Allenson on gunboat 139, was killed and two were wounded while three gunboats were damaged.[12]

Master Commandant Tarbell was convinced that he had severely damaged *Junon*. Captain Samuel Travis from *Surveyor*, and still a prisoner on *Junon* at the time of the action, reported that the British ship was hit only four

11. Hallahan, 54, 58; James, 90; Muller, 33.
12. Lossing, 675; James, 90; Roosevelt, 194.

times. A marine was killed and three sailors were wounded in the attack while another tar died in an accident. The performance of the gunboats validated the fear of their unsuitability both in rough weather and after they had fired their gun because of pitching from the recoil. Additionally, a single hit from enemy fire rendered them virtually inoperable. Of more immediate concern to the Americans was the effect the raid had on the British. The entire enemy fleet began shifting closer to Hampton Roads. A major assault appeared imminent.[13]

On 21 June, the American defenders on Craney Island reported the appearance of eight 74-gun men-of-war, twenty frigates, and numerous small vessels. They considered the gunboat raid a success if for nothing else, that it compelled the British to keep a healthy distance from the mouth of the Elizabeth River. Undeterred by the *Junon* affair, Cockburn completed his plans for an attack on the Norfolk defenses, with Craney Island as the first objective. A boat from HMS *Marlborough* twice scouted the island and noted the wide shoal surrounding it which threatened to ground landing craft well short of the beach. When Warren arrived on 20 June, Cockburn offered to lead the attack because of his local knowledge, but was turned down. Royal Navy Captains Pechell and Hanchett would command the naval parts of the assault. A bit non-plussed, Cockburn shifted his flag to the frigate HMS *Barossa* so he could direct some fire support when the time came.[14]

Admiral Warren's goal in attacking Craney Island was to gain control of the Elizabeth River entrance so he could get upriver to attack *Constellation* and destroy the growing complex of fortifications in the Norfolk-Portsmouth area. Craney Island was the key to the region's defenses. This flat fifty-acre expanse was situated on the west side of the river's mouth opposite Lamberts Point. It was separated from the mainland by a narrow channel known as the Thoroughfare. The shoals around it extended outwards for as much as two miles, denying close approach by large ships. Ever since assuming command, General Robert Taylor had pressed for the improvement of its defense. Captain Walker K. Armistead, a Regular Army Engineer, had supervised the start of construction of a blockhouse on the southeast, or main channel, side of the island along with earthworks and trenches at other possible approaches. By June 1813, three heavy guns were emplaced in the unfinished fort and units from the Norfolk garrison were rotated to the island's defenses for short stays.[15]

---

13. Brannan, 171; Dudley II: 357; Roosevelt, 194; Hallahan, 59.
14. Rowland, 229; J. Scott, III: 139-141.
15. *Naval Chronicle*, 243; Muller, (1963), 35; Hallahan, 42-43.

In late May, American commanders on the island noticed the increased British interest in their position and correctly assumed it presaged some kind of attack. Since *Constellation* was an obvious target, it was equally evident that Craney Island would be an intermediate objective. They remained confident that they could keep the British out of Norfolk. One officer wrote that he felt his men's inexperience was more than offset by their determination and courage. While more British ships entered Hampton Roads after the *Junon* incident on 21 June, a second enemy force threatened areas in Princess Anne County near Pleasure House. General Taylor correctly viewed this as a diversionary ploy and continued reinforcing the Craney Island garrison.[16]

Captain Richard Pollard's Company of the Twentieth United States Infantry was dispatched from Fort Norfolk along with thirty militia volunteers from Culpeper and Isle of Wight Counties. They joined the defenders commanded by Lieutenant Colonel Henry Beatty of Frederick County. Beatty had a well trained battery of artillery from the Norfolk militia led by Captain Arthur Emmerson, and Captain John P. Richardson's militia battery from Charlotte County. All the artillery was under the supervision of Virginia Major James Faulkner. Colonel Beatty's infantry force was commanded by Major Andrew Waggoner of Berkeley County and included Waggoner's own battalion from the Fourth Virginia Regiment and Captain Thomas Roberts's Frederick County Riflemen. General Taylor asked Cassin for additional men to help with the big guns on the island and the Navy sent three officers and one hundred sailors from *Constellation*, as well as a large part of its marine detachment. Cassin stationed a line of gunboats across the main channel of the river. By 21 June the defenders were as prepared as they could be. They continued to work on their positions on the island and around Norfolk, all the while keeping a wary eye on the British.[17]

Unconcerned by the American activity, Admiral Warren continued planning and preparations for the attack. He stuck with his earlier decision to place Captain Samuel G. Pechell of *San Domingo* in command of the naval aspects of the attack despite Cockburn's greater familiarity with the area. The main attack would land 800 of Colonel Beckwith's men west of Craney Island. While they advanced toward the American position, they would be supported by an amphibious diversionary attack against the island led by Captain John M. Hanchett, RN, of *Diadem*. Hanchett's objective was to land and neutralize the American artillery. His force consisted of about 500 shipboard marines from *Marlborough*, *San Domingo*, and *Plantagenet*, a company of In-

16. Hallahan, 61.
17. Rowland, 228; Flournoy, 427; W.H. Gaines, 34; Lossing, 667-8; James, 91.

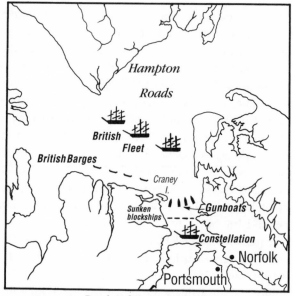

Battle of Craney Island.

dependent Foreigners, and part of the 102nd Regiment in fifteen barges. None of the troops had any time to rehearse, and there was no attempt at reconnaissance.[18]

The British activity was plain to see from Craney Island and the defenders were in hourly anticipation of being attacked. At midnight on 21 June, the edgy garrison experienced a false alarm when sentinel William Shutte fired on an object in the Thoroughfare which he thought was a boat but which turned out to be an uprooted bush. Colonel Beatty chose to maintain an alert throughout the night and the men stood to until dawn when they were dismissed for breakfast. Just as they returned to the camps, a cavalry vedette from the mainland splashed across the Thoroughfare and announced that a large British force was landing two and one half miles away at Hoffleur's Creek near the mouth of the Nansemond River. The men rushed to their positions again and, as daylight increased and the morning haze burned off, they could see the redcoats organizing, and marching out of sight into the woods. Beatty and his senior officers decided to realign their main strength along the Thoroughfare to confront this threat. All the while, they feared the British might head right for Portsmouth and cut them off.[19]

It was fortunate for Beckwith that his men encountered nothing more

18. Pack, 158; Fraser & Carr-Laughton I: 236; Lossing, 675.
19. Lossing, 678; W.H. Gaines, 34; Hallahan, 65; Emmerson, 182.

than a few vedettes at their landing place. The British troops had been on board ship since leaving Bermuda almost two weeks before, and were not in the best physical condition, nor had they ever worked together before. The force consisted of about 200 sailors, three companies of marines, four companies of the 102nd led by Colonel Napier, and a company of the Independent Foreigners. The landings in the early morning darkness were confused due to the absence of any rehearsal and the barge crews' desire to get back to the fleet to carry Hanchett's diversionary force. As soon as the troops were organized, Beckwith moved them off the beach into the woods to avoid the occasional fire coming from Craney Island. The forest was virtually impenetrable, however, and he had to move the men back onto the beach to enable them to advance with sufficient speed to support the waterborne attack.[20]

The landing force availed itself of a local guide captured near the landing point and pressed along the wooded shore. As they did, they began to hear fire being directed toward the diversionary attack. However, they were delayed in reaching their destination by the brush and high water in the tidal streams that intersected their line of approach. While they were held up, the Royal Marine Artillery rocket section tried to contribute by firing a barrage at the island from a position near George Wise's farm. The Americans were startled but unshaken by what proved to be a harmless display of pyrotechnics. However, the British fire gave away their positions and Major Faulkner ordered some of his guns to return the fire, killing a man in the 102nd, and wounding one of his comrades and eight marines. It also forced Beckwith to withdraw his force out of range and essentially out of the fight just as the diversionary force needed all the help it could get.[21]

The diversionary attack began at about 8 A.M. when Hanchett regained control of the barges which had dropped off Beckwith's men. Brandishing an umbrella, Hanchett, allegedly a natural son of the Prince Regent, led his flotilla sixty yards ahead of the rest of the boats in Admiral Warren's barge, *Centipede*. Captain Samuel Romilly of the Royal Engineers was also in *Centipede*, taking soundings as they approached the island. The movement of the flotilla was not well managed and Lieutenant James Scott, RN, in command of *Marlborough*'s barge, later recalled there being too many people in charge, all giving conflicting orders.[22]

The Americans reacted effectively to the British threat. Captain Thomas Rourke, an unemployed sea captain who was serving with Emmerson's Bat-

20. Nicolas II: 243; Napier, 217.
21. Napier, 213, 217; Robinson, (1942), 1; Jarvis, 138, 140.
22. W.H. Gaines, 34; Napier, 212; Scott, 141.

tery to which he had once belonged, volunteered to move the heavy guns
when Colonel Beatty decided they had to be shifted. With Major Faulkner's
help, all the pieces in the unfinished fort on the southeast side of the island
were manhandled to the threatened northwest side. Faulkner ordered Emmerson's lighter 6-pounders to be shifted so they could fire either toward the
Thoroughfare or into Hampton Roads. The heavier guns were set up on the
west side to fire in Beckwith's direction. Faulkner relied on the line of gunboats in the river mouth to provide artillery support on the eastern side of the
island. The infantry took position in breastworks parallel to the beach while
the guns were about forty feet to their rear on higher ground. Once the men
were settled in, they found a long pole, nailed a United States flag to it, and
raised it overhead—a symbolic gesture especially meaningful to the sailors and
marines amongst them.[23]

Hanchett led his division in the direction of the Thoroughfare while the
following division showed its right flank as it made for a point further east.
Major Faulkner ordered his gunners to hold their fire until it was impossible
to miss, as the brief Congreve bombardment from Beckwith's force fell harm-
lessly in the sandy soil. Lieutenant Godwin's big 24-pounder gun was diverted to deal with Beckwith's force. Finally, the Major nodded to Captain
Emmerson who shouted to his men, "Now boys, are you ready?—Ready!
Fire!!" and a hail of grape and canister blasted the British. The British plight
was made even more acute as their barges ran aground on mudflats some 300
yards from shore.[24]

When the attacking boats shoaled, they tried to push off while under the
heavy fire. This caused confusion amongst those following behind and prevented them from closing. No thought was given to wading to the beach, in
part because of the American fire and in part because of the assumption that
the muddy bottom would not allow dismounting and charging. Seeing the
growing chaos, Lieutenant George A. Westphal, RN, who had scouted the
site, rowed from near Beckwith's landing site to try to correct the problem.
In the meantime, Hanchett pushed off and shifted in the direction the follow-
on column was heading but in so doing, he presented his barge's side to the
American artillery and was seriously wounded by canister when *Centipede* was
hit and foundered. Two other boats were severely damaged and Hanchett
was transferred to another boat for evacuation. When others saw his new boat
pulling out, confusion mounted over whether to stay or withdraw. Despite
Westphal's efforts, Captain Pechell saw no point in continuing the slaughter

23. Emmerson, 180; Dudley II: 359; Jarvis, 137; Muller, (1963), 34.
24. Jarvis, 140; W.H. Gaines, 34.

and signalled the surviving barges to return to the fleet. Once the British withdrew, United States Midshipman Josiah Tatnall proved the solidity of the mudflats by leading some sailors across them to capture what was left of *Centipede* and to help the British wounded.[25]

The battered British attackers were rowed to Beckwith's landing beach to recover from their shock. One man had been killed and seven wounded in the ordeal and they joined Beckwith's men in taking out their frustrations on local livestock and property. The men began to circulate rumors that the Americans had shot at the wounded in the water, thus explaining the large number of missing, but later investigation proved the rumors unfounded. In fact, most of the missing were deserters from the Independent Foreigners. Nevertheless, what they heard led many to think of vengeance. Late that afternoon, Beckwith and Pechell got Warren's approval to call off any further attempts and the men returned to their ships.[26]

While Beckwith was withdrawing, the small British force hovering in Lynnhaven Bay to the east, landed at Pleasure House in an attempt to create a distraction. Captain Richard Lawson's Company, stationed in the area for just such a contingency, repulsed the attack. Taylor correctly assumed that this action was of little significance and concentrated on reinforcing Craney Island and calming the citizens of Norfolk. When the attack began, many had rushed to Town Point to see what was going on, but the action was too short and too far away. However, everyone feared the worst when the Craney Island ammunition bunker erupted in a gigantic explosion at about noon—a prearranged signal to be used if the British were overrunning the position. But it was an accident, possibly caused by the bunker's sentry and it left the defenders with little ammunition and increased fears that the British would return. Captain Blackwell Foster from Colonel William Sharp's Second Virginia Regiment rushed 120 men, mostly from Norfolk, to the island that afternoon. Taylor also placed Lieutenant Colonel Armistead Mason's Fifth Virginia Regiment in a position where it could attack a force around Wise's farm, the area used by Colonel Beckwith that morning. But the threat was over. The American soldiers spent most of their time evacuating British wounded and receiving the nearly forty deserters, almost all Frenchmen, who began to trickle in.[27]

The Americans were both pleased and amazed at their success. They had engaged a formidable foe and suffered no combat casualties. Both Beatty and

25. Scott, 145; Brannan, 172; Napier, 212; *Naval Chronicle*, 182.

26. Jarvis, 141; *Naval Chronicle*, 182, 243.

27. Lossing, 685; Flournoy, 428; W.H. Gaines, 35; Emmerson, 185.

Mason reported a surge in confidence amongst their men. Apparently, many had held an unrealistic, but understandable, fear of rockets but found them not as intimidating as expected. The same could be said for the British themselves; defenders throughout the bay area took heart at the victory at Craney. For the British part, Napier believed that the failure was due to overconfidence—"we despise the Yankee too much." In other words, they had greatly underestimated their opponent. Unfortunately, events at Hampton a few days later would undermine the achievement at Craney Island.[28]

After the fiasco at Craney Warren concluded that any successes against Norfolk would exact a considerable price. He was impressed by American defense of the island and felt that taking it would result in too many casualties. Besides, an attack could also be construed as contrary to Beckwith's orders to raid but not occupy places for any length of time. The three senior British officers looked for an easier target now that it was obvious that the Craney fiasco would have little influence on the situation in Canada. The feisty garrison at Hampton, across from Norfolk, was a possibility. It had been a minor irritant by impeding small boat forays. If Hampton were strengthened with heavy artillery, it might combine with that at Norfolk and make the Roads and the James inaccessible to British ships. Warren hoped that a blow at Hampton would isolate Norfolk by severing its communications with the Peninsula.[29]

Hampton was defended since February by a battalion of Peninsula militia commanded by Major Gawin L. Corbin. It was reinforced in April by a battalion of Virginia militia infantry from Fauquier, Albemarle, and Orange Counties commanded by Major Stapleton Crutchfield. As senior officer, Crutchfield assumed command of the defenses and by June his force consisted of a seven-gun artillery company, a small cavalry company, and miscellaneous rifle and infantry companies for a total of 440 troops. Crutchfield kept his headquarters and the cavalry in Hampton proper while the rest of the command encamped at Little England Plantation about one mile away. Located on Sunset Creek south of the village, the plantation was accessible via a small footbridge.[30]

Before the attack, a water patrol led by Captain Samuel Romilly, RE, scouted Hampton Harbor. It drew American fire, revealing the defenses, and Romilly took soundings. Warren and Cockburn decided on the same tactics used at Craney Island. A water diversion led by Cockburn would harass the

28. Rowland, 230; Hallahan, 85, 88; Napier, 217.
29. PAC, Beckwith to Bathurst 23 July 1813; *Naval Chronicles*, 244.
30. Butler, 228; Anderson, 351-352; V.C. Jones, 39; Rouse, (1968), 321.

harbor while Napier conducted a landing on the American flank. Once the landing force was engaged, Cockburn would support it with gunfire, squeezing the defenders between the two forces.[31]

The landing force left the fleet late on 24 June and rowed for a point two miles from Hampton near Celey's Plantation. They reached the shore at about 2 A.M. and amidst some confusion got themselves organized. Napier's 650 men advanced through the trees and brush, dragging two 6-pounder guns along with them. Because of a lack of communication, the two follow-on Royal Marine battalions under Lieutenant Colonel Richard Williams did not land for several hours. While waiting for them, Napier's men skirmished with American pickets patrolling Celey's road, which paralleled the shore. The information was sent back to Major Crutchfield at the same time an outpost at Mill Creek reported spotting a large number of British barges approaching the mouth of Hampton Creek from the south.[32]

When the pickets sounded the alarm, the American camp at Little England quickly fell in and the troops advanced in the direction of the fire. Crutchfield was still in Hampton, about one mile away, but he arrived in camp in time to order that the men remain in place, fearing the British boats that had appeared at about 5 A.M. at the harbor's mouth off Blackbeard's Point posed the main threat. This caused a critical delay. The Royal Marine Artillery unleashed a spectacular rocket and artillery demonstration offshore and then were silent. Meanwhile, the increased pressure on the pickets near Celey's indicated that the main attack was coming from there and Crutchfield ordered the infantry to resume its march while he deployed his artillery to deal with the gunboats.[33]

Napier's force pressed the American skirmishers toward Hampton until encountering the American infantry. The Virginians tried to deploy from column into line in a cornfield on the British flank and prepare for a bayonet charge, but Napier's men fired from inside a woods line and his artillery went into action. United States volunteer Adjutant Robert Anderson reformed the men into column and marched them off the field into the shelter of some woods where they tried to form a line for a second time and advance on the British. Under a heavy return fire they lost much of their cohesion. Major Corbin retained control of two of his companies and tried to link with a battalion led by Captain John B. Goodall. The combined force moved rearward briefly, but, when Major Corbin was grievously wounded near Pembroke

31. Napier, 214; Rouse, (1969), 83; Emmerson, 81.
32. James, 93; Nicolas II: 244.
33. Anderson, 352; J. Scott, III: 151.

farmyard, the men scattered.[34]

Napier then redirected his advance toward Hampton under heavy fire from the American artillery in the camp. Captain Brazure W. Pryor's gunners continued firing at the gunboats and advancing British infantry long after the infantry had run away. Napier ordered his men to hold behind a hedge line and while his artillery fired on the Americans, he sent Williams with his two Royal Marine battalions on a flanking move. When the marines approached to within sixty or seventy yards, Pryor ordered his men to spike their guns and then led them to safety across the creek through the scattered British forces. Napier's force advanced into the virtually empty town while the marines captured the abandoned guns and occupied the American camp by 10 A.M. The British had suffered seven killed and thirty-three wounded to seven Americans killed and twelve wounded despite a British claim of 300.[35]

The ordeal had just begun for the American civilians in the conquered village. The British troops swept through the town to the Point Comfort lighthouse, where many of them turned to plunder the town and worse. The undisciplined Independent Foreigners went berserk. The rumor that some of them had been shot at Craney Island seemed to have incensed them. Many pledged revenge and their conduct during the attack presaged their later actions. Napier saw a Frenchman deliberately shoot a prisoner. A naval officer saw a similar incident in the town. After the fighting there were several rapes and a bedridden civilian was shot and killed. Houses were looted and other helpless civilians robbed and beaten. The Royal Marines and 102nd Regiment stood back from the mayhem and were used eventually to restore order.[36]

For two days the British remained in the area foraging and shipping goods to the fleet. The Episcopal Church was used as a cookhouse, its cemetery a place to slaughter stolen livestock. Americans returning after the British evacuation reported it was damaged by numerous fires and carcasses littered the surrounding area. Cockburn and Beckwith established their headquarters at the Savage House. The Admiral was particularly taken by Captain Hancock Lee, one of the captured Americans, a veteran of the Revolution from Fauquier County who was in the United States camp visiting his son at the time of the British attack. The old man had fought with his son's company until he was captured and sent aboard HMS *Marlborough*. His firm demeanor,

34. Rouse, (1968), 322; Guy, (1929), 2-3.

35. Fraser & Carr-Laughton II: 237; Nicolas, 244; Rouse, (1968), 323; Lossing, 683; *Naval Chronicle*, 244-246.

36. J. Scott, III: 151; Napier I: 213; Lossing, 683; Rouse, (1969), 83.

courage, and courtesy intrigued the British who released him after three days, treating him more like a guest than a prisoner.[37]

These courtesies could not mask the terrible harm the British had done to their reputation. They left Hampton on 27 June and when American authorities reentered the town on the 29th, the terrible excesses quickly became known and the American press capitalized on every atrocity, especially the treatment of women. The news persuaded even greater numbers of people that resistance to British incursions was the only option. Many families evacuated coastal towns while others sent livestock and valuables inland out of reach. "Remember Hampton" became a militia rallying cry and eventually even the British came to understand the raid's counterproductive effect. Napier thought that the operation showed more enthusiasm than sense. He felt it was characteristic of British bay operations where admirals tried to be generals and the army and marine officers accommodated them. He predicted that sooner or later this would prove disastrous because "Cockburn's confidence in his luck is the very thing to be feared; it is worse than 1,000 yankees."[38]

As soon as he learned of the atrocities, Taylor sent a letter of protest to Warren. Beckwith replied saying that as regrettable as the incidents were, they originated in the need for revenge inspired by the alleged American actions at Craney Island. Taylor denied Beckwith's accusations and directed a board be formed to investigate them. The board found no wrongdoing on the part of the Craney Island defenders and was able to explain and justify each alleged incident. The responsibility for the sack of Hampton rested squarely on the British. General Taylor in a 7 July letter to Secretary of War Armstrong pointed out that British conduct at Hampton did more to unite his area than anything he had done since taking command.[39]

The incident gave Beckwith ample reason to get rid of the troublesome Independent Foreigners. Warren fully supported his recommendation as several ship's captains had expressed concern over having mutinous armed foreigners on their ships. By the end of the month the companies left and reached Halifax on 12 July. Here they became a mobile crime wave, causing severe discipline problems until they could be returned to Britain in September. Their departure had no effect on Warren's plans in the bay.[40]

37. Emmerson, 94; Meade I: 236.
38. PAC, Beckwith to Bathurst 23 July 1813; Rouse, (1969), 85-86; Rowland, 230; Napier, 218, 229.
39. ASP MA I: 378-381.
40. Hitsman & Sorby, 16; Napier I: 224; Elting, (1988), 125.

United States Marine, 1813.

Chapter Six

ช.

THE SECOND RAID: 1813

A DMIRAL Cockburn kept up the pressure on the Americans even as he argued Hampton's finer points with General Taylor. Five frigates and several smaller craft headed up the James River on 27 June to acquire supplies and pin the local militia in place. This probe, which threatened Smithfield and reached up the James to Sandy Point in Charles City County, led to a wave of activity as far inland as Richmond, which many presumed to be the actual target. With news of Hampton fresh in their minds, the people of the region were afraid. Richmond had always maintained a high level of alertness to every crisis in the southern bay area. However, until now, in the words of William Wirt, "it survived many attacks which were threatened without being made; and was favored with the most satisfactory opportunities, short of bloodshed, to evince her patriotism and public spirit." This time, the threat seemed more real.[1]

An alarm bell rang in Richmond on the morning of 28 June and all mem-

1. Kennedy I: 300; Fraser & Carr-Laughton II: 238.

bers of the volunteer and enrolled companies reported to predesignated sites. Everyone was aware of the British behavior at Hampton and the mood was one of concerned determination. Lieutenant Colonel John Ambler's Nineteenth Virginia Regiment speedily rallied and within hours marched to Fort Powhatan at Hoods Point on the river in Prince George County. Another 4,000 troops marched to Malvern Hill in Henrico County while others rushed to Sandy Point in Charles City County itself. The latter arrived in time to see the enemy ships turn about for Hampton.[2]

The call-up revealed several problems in organization and planning, so despite the British withdrawal, a new level of military fervor was sustained by public and private groups alike. A citizens' Vigilance Committee was formed to aid city and state authorities in fortifying Richmond and to assist in raising defense funds. Governor Barbour prevailed upon several veterans to form and train a battery of horse artillery to augment the large numbers of infantry. This unit ultimately was manned by one hundred of the most distinguished young men from Richmond society. The men devoted all of their spare time and some personal funds, and by the end of the summer the battery was highly efficient. Their unit exemplified the ultimate effect of this phase of British operations. Although bruised, the whole region was more determined to resist and its militia was evolving into a reckonable force. The vital points throughout the state had become so formidable that the British could not threaten them. As a result, Warren was compelled to look for other vulnerable points.[3]

That part of the fleet left in Hampton Roads during the James River probe was pulled back to an anchorage off the Back River north of Hampton to take on water. Hampton Roads was strangely quiet for several days, when the James River expedition began returning between 4 and 7 July. The ships took on water and supplies and by 11 July, the entire force left the area, only *Plantagenet* (74) and a few small craft remained to blockade the bay. Local water travel quickly resumed in Hampton Roads and up the James while Sailing Master Mix prepared his last torpedo to frighten *Plantagenet*. Admiral Warren had divided his force, taking one element north. Admiral Cockburn sailed with the other to the Outer Banks of North Carolina to seal the back door to Norfolk.[4]

Cockburn transferred his flag to HMS *Sceptre* (74) and on 3 July left with six other warships carrying one of the Royal Marine Artillery companies along

2. Anon., Vigilance Committee, 225, 227; Kennedy I: 318.

3. Kennedy II: 319; Anon., War's Wild Alarm, 217; Anon., Vigilance Committee, 227.

4. Emmerson, 87; For Elijah Mix, see previous Chapter.

with Napier and 500 men from the 102nd Regiment. Winds delayed the force, but it finally reached the bar at Ocracoke Island leading into Pamlico Sound on 12 July. Several boats probed for the channel throughout the night, finally allowing boats carrying troops into the Sound near dawn on the 13th. These headed for the village of Ocracoke, but bad weather delayed their approach and allowed the surprised Americans to evacuate valuables and to prepare defenses. The British were fired on by the privateers *Atlas* and *Anaconda*. They rushed toward *Anaconda* which fired a broadside before being boarded and forced to surrender after a brief fight. Seeing this, *Atlas*'s captain surrendered without further opposition. The British then futilely chased a number of river craft before occupying the villages of Ocracoke and Portsmouth on opposite shores of the channel entrance. Cockburn thought an attack on New Bern was unfeasible and after two days ashore, the fleet departed for the Chesapeake on 16 July with *Anaconda* and *Atlas* (renamed HMS *St. Lawrence*) in tow. By the evening of the 19th, Admiral Cockburn was back with Warren's force off Point Lookout where the Potomac flows into the bay.[5]

This incident caused the rapid deployment of North Carolina militia to New Bern and was led by Governor William Hawkins himself. The British had carried off great numbers of livestock after token payment and vandalized private property. One civilian had been shot but lived to tell Cockburn who tried to make amends. This incident horrified residents of the Carolina coast and led to increased defense construction and militia activity. The latter were deployed to guard transportation routes to Norfolk and other points on the James as well as to reinforce the city itself.[6]

His recent foray to Ocracoke convinced Cockburn that the blockade should extend to the North Carolina coast because of the Americans' ability to divert goods from Virginia. The British had been unaware of the relative ease of access of southeastern Virginia to the Outer Banks and of how much trade had shifted there once the Chesapeake blockade began. Goods came down the James to the Norfolk area where they were transferred to small boats and carried to Kempsville. From there they moved about ten miles by road to North Landing where they went back on small craft that carried them to Beaufort or Ocracoke where they were loaded on oceangoing vessels. By June 1814, another route from the hinterlands had developed when a vessel successfully carried goods from Scotland on the Roanoke River to Albemarle Sound. These efforts combined with the shifting winds and shoals made an

---

5. James, 95; J. Scott, III: 156-158; Lossing, 689; Park, 159; Nicolas II: 246.
6. Lemmon, 133-137.

effective blockade very difficult. One insurance company reported that thirty of the thirty-seven ships it was covering on the run to the Caribbean completed safe trips, while six of eleven ships on the European run were successful.[7]

A spectacular move by the British fleet in Chesapeake Bay was still Britain's best chance for a strategic victory. The Admiralty pressured Warren to be more aggressive, frequently giving him suggestions on ship deployments and urging him to use his forces with greater efficiency. While the Ocracoke raid was underway, Warren moved the remainder of his force from Hampton Roads up the Chesapeake in search of targets. The fleet entered the Potomac a few days later, hoping to capture the United States frigate *Adams* reportedly cruising the mouth of the river. The main fleet anchored off St. George and St. Clement's Islands, which the marines occupied, while the advanced naval elements pressed on, searching for the American ship. *Adams* reacted quickly and headed up the river beyond Kettle Bottom shoals and eventually to Washington Navy Yard. British ships sailed no further than Cedar and Maryland Points where, without pilots, they did not want to risk the shoals and shallow water.[8]

The departure of *Adams* left the small Potomac Flotilla under the command of Lieutenant George C. Read, USN. He was under orders to patrol the river's mouth and defend the lower reaches of the Potomac. On one of his sweeps of the area his sloop, *Scorpion*, and Lieutenant James B. Sigourney's *Asp* encountered two British brigs, *Contest* and *Mohawk*, at 10 A.M. on 11 July. The fast sailing *Scorpion* outran the British, but Sigourney's slower *Asp* was forced to sail up Yeocomico Creek and tie up under the protection of the 200 militia stationed on the bank. The British brigs anchored in the Potomac and Lieutenant Roger C. Curry, RN, of *Mohawk* led small boats up the creek. *Asp* opened a tremendous fire but, after several tries, the British boarded her. Following a hard struggle in which Lieutenant Sigourney and nine other Americans were killed, the remaining Americans abandoned the ship. Two British were killed and six, including Lieutenant Curry, were wounded. They hastily torched the ship and withdrew under fire from the militia. *Asp*'s survivors immediately returned, doused the flames, and, under Midshipman H. McClintock, restored the ship to fighting order.[9]

On 17 July, the British raided the Mattox and Rozier Creek areas. The Virginia militia under Colonel Richard E. Parker's command fell out in force, this time reinforced by a company of the Thirty-Sixth United States Infantry

7. Wertenbaker, 113-114; Dudley II: 365.

8. Nicolas II: 247; Fraser & Carr-Laughton II: 239; Dudley II: 139, 369.

9. Roosevelt, 195; Dudley II: 366; James, 96.

stationed in Westmoreland County. The enemy first probed Rozier's Creek but encountered a large number of militia. Undeterred, they returned on 19 July to Mattox Creek. Colonel Parker thought the British objective was a large house across from his force on Mattox Creek, and he commandeered a schooner to ferry his men over. The first unit to cross was Captain John Hungerford's Company which rushed into the attack despite artillery fire from the British boats and evicted the British before the rest of Parker's force joined him.[10]

The promise of extensive action in the area prompted Governor Barbour to order Lieutenant Colonel James McDowell and his regiment of Shenandoah, Frederick, and Stafford Counties militia to the threatened area. On 20 July, while enroute to his new base at Montross, McDowell learned of a battalion of British marines with artillery landing at Hollis's Marsh on the west side of Nomini Bay. Diverting his troops there on 21 July, he arrived in time to see the enemy force withdraw after burning a sloop. Evaluating the British hit and run tactics, he ordered his cavalry to join him from Fredericksburg, and stationed it at Stratford Hall to serve as a quick reaction force. He advised Governor Barbour that Colonel Parker's men could not be effective unless he was allowed to keep some of them on extended tours of duty. Otherwise, by the time they could muster, the British damage was already done.[11]

The probe up the Potomac and the unprogrammed return of *Adams* caused the mustering of the complete Columbian Division. The men gathered on 15 July and deployed to Fort Washington. From there, detachments of infantry took up positions to block the roads leading from points on the Potomac between Piscataway and Port Tobacco. They conducted around the clock patrols in an effort to detect and repulse any British landings. The Columbian cavalry ranged even farther afield, assisted at one time by Secretary of State James Monroe who rode with them as an "observer," and who came under fire on 20 July when a British landing at Swan Point was repulsed. The area had been visited earlier by the Secretaries of War and Navy driving a sulky. All three cabinet members declared the Potomac defenses sufficient to repel invasion.[12]

This sort of hit and run went on for one week until on 21 July, observers on both sides of the Potomac noted that the British were returning to the Potomac's mouth, surveying and sounding as they went. Warren had hoped that his thrust toward Washington and Alexandria might lure troops destined for

10. Hoge, 1268-69.
11. Norris, 355; Nicolas II: 245.
12. Nicolas II: 247; Rutland, (1990), 130; Todd, 427-28.

Canada to the defenses of the capital. The opposite happened, as regulars and volunteer militia continued northward even at the height of British activity. American fixation with Canada was inexorable. Warren noted the inconvenience caused by the large militia turn out on both sides of the Potomac, and reported rumors of panic in Washington. The fleet gathered off Blackistone and St. Catherine's Islands where Cockburn's force rejoined it and the sailors landed to dig wells. The Marines and 102nd Regiment landed at Point Lookout, providing security for foraging parties which swept accessible parts of St. Mary's County. Finally, on 29 July, the great force headed into the Chesapeake and nosed its way northward for a second time.[13]

The first objective was to secure a base from which to operate while also providing the soldiers and marines a place to recuperate from cramped and increasingly unhealthy shipboard conditions. Cockburn's force surveyed Watts, Tangier, and Smith's Islands as possible sites where prizes could be held and escaped slaves housed and possibly trained for military duties.[14] Undefended Kent Island, scouted as early as 26 July, seemed an ideal temporary solution, with Tangier a possibility for a more permanent base. Cockburn, still on board *Sceptre*, along with *Barossa* reached the area on 4 August and set about occupying the island before the arrival of the delayed main body. While his ships blocked the ferry to the mainland, Royal Marines with artillery landed on the island, trapping the local militia. The 102nd Regiment led by Colonel Napier followed and soon captured the cut off militia whose captain proved to be a native of England. He and his officers were paroled after interrogation. The Royal Marine Artillery detachment reported that the biggest enemy at the ferry site were the clouds of mosquitos which made life absolutely miserable.[15]

On 6 August the remainder of Beckwith's force landed on the south side of the island and marched northward, deterred only by the fierce heat. By 8 August, the entire command was united in wooded camps around "Belleview," the home of Jonathan Harrison. Located on the Annapolis side of the island, "Belleview" became Beckwith's headquarters. Relations between the inhabitants and the occupiers were cordial and the British officers were open with their views and objectives. One British officer declaring that the reason they were there was to "ship the Democrats for being enemies to the British government, and drub the Federalists for being enemies to their own." The statement reveals not only the contempt most British officers had for their op-

13. Anon., War's Wild Alarm, 219; Dudley II: 369; Hoge, 1269; Beitzell, 245.
14. Pack, 158-159.
15. J. Scott, III: 160; Brenton, 449.

ponent ("Jonathan") but also their stereotyping of American attitudes.[16]

The British presence in the middle bay caused great concern in Annapolis and Baltimore. British scouts appeared at the mouth of the Severn on 3 August and the state capital immediately went on full alert. It was Warren's goal to paralyze ship movements in the area, damage Gordon's small flotilla if possible, and create a distraction which might somehow help Canada. He certainly created an alarm but achieved little else. In Annapolis, Colonel Henry Carberry of the Thirty-Sixth United States Infantry assumed command of militia and regulars alike and supervised the evacuation of large numbers of civilians. Captain Charles Morris, USN, bottled up at Washington with his crew from *Adams*, rushed to reinforce the city and assumed command of Fort Severn on 12 August. By then, militia from the western counties secured the city but it remained in a high state of nervous alert throughout the British foray.[17]

In Baltimore, Smith took matters in hand once he learned of the British approach. He did not wait for mobilization authority from Governor Winder on the assumption that the situation in Annapolis had his full attention. Smith called in the militia from the surrounding counties in case of an attack. He was confident his well trained city Third Brigade could muster very quickly, but outside forces were needed to back them up. They also needed extra training which Smith did not think their commander, Maryland Brigadier General Tobias E. Stansbury, took seriously enough. His measures were approved by the governor and the War Department on 8 August, coinciding with the appearance of the British.[18]

That day three British ships of the line, five frigates, three brigs, two schooners, and numerous tenders appeared at the mouth of the Patapsco. All of the city's defenses were manned and Major William Jamison's Seventh Maryland Regiment from Baltimore County's Eleventh Brigade took up positions at Bear Creek, along the road to North Point. Few people expected an attack from this small fleet, however, the mobilization was taken seriously. No militia substitutions were allowed and fines were levied against laggards and shirkers. The militia cavalry worked out of their homes rather than from one of the camps, to make caring for their horses easier. They rendezvoused daily at Hampstead Hill and patrolled out to North Point. Under the command of Lieutenant Colonels James Biays of the Fifth Regiment and Nicholas Moore of the Sixth Regiment, they became familiar with the terrain throughout the peninsula.[19]

16. Tilghman, 161; Nicolas II: 248.
17. Riley, 234; Dudley II, 383.
18. Cassell, (1971), 195.

The federal government's eyes were fixed firmly on the northern border. Consider the story of Captain Richard Booker's Virginia Company. This Richmond unit had been enlisted and organized in June and began to march northward at the height of the panic following the attack on Hampton. It was in Annapolis when the British threatened that city in early August. Ordered northward, the men reached Baltimore at the peak of that city's mobilization. The city fathers took care of their supply needs, believing they were federal reinforcements for Baltimore's defense. The company stayed for three days, but then received orders to continue its march. It reached Sacketts Harbor, New York, just in time to play a minor role in the ill-fated campaign along the St. Lawrence River in the autumn of 1813, before being discharged to walk back home. The War Department thus continued to disappoint the bay area with its demonstrated and puzzling indifference.[20]

Despite the absence of help, this second crisis gave Smith the opportunity to perfect his plans. He had originally considered it best to hit the enemy at its landing places, most likely North Point, but once he observed British mobility on the water, he reconsidered and chose Bear Creek, much closer to the city, as a better defensive position. Forces stationed there would be less vulnerable to being cut off by an amphibious landing. Smith directed Generals Stricker and Stansbury and the officers from the Baltimore City and County brigades to familiarize themselves with the site, and Jamison's Regiment was placed there when the British appeared on 8 August. Smith also assured completion of the Hampstead Hill position and arranged for a fifty-gun artillery park to support it. Because of earlier British threats, Smith understood the need for water barriers, such as sunken hulks, to reduce Fort McHenry's vulnerability to a flank attack. He built additional supporting batteries for his main positions to offset British waterborne mobility even more. The menacing British posture gave him the opportunity to develop and perfect his defensive plans while providing just enough threat to keep his forces highly motivated. By the time the last British ships left the Patapsco on 24 August, Smith, his men, and the city were as ready as they could be.[21]

The action was more direct on the Eastern Shore. The senior militia officer in Talbot County, Maryland Brigadier General Perry Benson, a veteran of the Revolution, was especially concerned that Easton might be a British objective. It was the largest town in the area, the site of the regional arsenal, and a prosperous port full of ships trying to avoid the British. Benson ordered

19. Moody, II: 538; Scharf, (1874), 87.

20. Anon., War's Wild Alarm, 224.

21. Cassell, (1971), 196; Cassell, (1971), Crisis, 360; Scharf, (1874), 87; Niles, V: 286.

companies from the Fourth and Twenty-Sixth Maryland Regiments to concentrate in the St. Michaels area under the command of Lieutenant Colonel Hugh Auld of the Twenty-sixth. The little port on the Miles River was the most direct approach from Kent Island to Easton. The militia were quartered in the village and patrolled the shoreline to provide early warning of any enemy activity. Captain William Dodson and his local artillery consisting of four guns were in the breastwork at Parrott's Point. Built in the spring, Parrott's Point was a system of earthworks established on the high ground overlooking the spot where Corsica Creek flows into the Miles River near Spencer's Wharf. The river was so narrow at this point that artillery could control its entire width.[22]

Artillery fire from Parrott's Point could also cover a log and chain boom that was drawn across the St. Michaels harbor entrance. Captain Clement Vickers took two guns from the Talbot County Volunteer Artillery Company and stationed them at the junction of Broad Creek and Bayside roads to block any land or westward approach to the town. The two 6-pounder guns donated by prankster Jacob Gibson, were positioned within the town at a site called Dawson's Wharf and commanded by Lieutenant John Graham from Captain Joseph Kemp's St. Michaels Patriotic Blues. Captain Vickers later moved his guns to earthworks at Mill Point when the direction of the British attack became apparent.[23]

British leaders on Kent Island looked for opportunities to keep their idle troops engaged. When news came of the concentration at St. Michaels, Admiral Cockburn approved a request by Lieutenant James Polkinghorne of the brig HMS *Conflict* to carry out a raid. British actions betrayed their intentions as *Conflict* anchored in the Miles River near Deep Water Point and her small boats began surveying and sounding approaches. The actual assault began early on the morning of 10 August when eleven barges containing an estimated 300 men left the brig under cover of darkness and fog, and rowed along the shore opposite St. Michaels to avoid detection from the outposts around the town.[24]

The British began their final approach at about 4 A.M. and landed without opposition. Dodson's men at Parrott's Point heard their leaders giving commands and many Americans panicked and fled. The British fired at them, to do nothing more than speeding them on their way. Dodson, Lieutenant Richard Kennemont, and John Stevens, a slave, stayed behind, manhandling

22. Emory, 429.
23. Tilghman, 162.
24. Scott, 161-162.

a gun into position and firing a barrage of canister and scrap metal. The gun was dismounted, but its blast into the unsuspecting British caused enormous carnage. Believing the position abandoned, the British approached it casually in a tight cluster. Nineteen of them were killed including Admiral Cockburn's nephew, a lieutenant in the Royal Marines. The disciplined British rushed the battery just as Dodson and his companions made their escape. Once on the position, they spiked the captured guns.[25]

While the British landing party was busy dealing with the Parrott's Point Battery, some of their barges rushed the harbor only to run into the blocking boom. They pulled off and started bombarding the town. Lieutenant Graham's guns responded and soon were joined by those of Vickers. The fog made aiming difficult, but a few of the barges were hit. The British, misled by the American placement of lanterns on high ground behind the village, succeeded only in hitting the upper stories of several houses. General Benson drew up his infantry and cavalry in the center of the town to repel any further landings. The British broke contact after only an hour, and rowed to the opposite shore, from where they returned to *Conflict* and Kent Island around 10 A.M. The Americans had suffered no losses. When Cockburn learned of the raid and its casualties he mourned his nephew, commenting that he "had lost an officer worth more than the whole damned town."[26]

The whole Kent Island operation seemed pointless to many army officers in Sir Sydney Beckwith's force. He devised a plan, primarily to keep the troops busy, to attack the nearby village of Queenstown and disperse a militia force known to be there. The scheme began when the marines guarding the ferry crossing were relieved on 12 August by their shipboard comrades. They could now support an advance by the 102nd against the village by landing their artillery at Hall's Farm on Love Point north of Queenstown. They would attack the Americans in the rear while Napier's troops engaged it from the ferry side of the town. The 102nd watched the marines depart at 5 P.M., and then departed, accompanied by Beckwith at about 11 P.M.[27]

The Kent County militia guarding the town consisted of 244 men from the Thirty-Eighth Maryland Regiment commanded by Major William H. Nicholson. He also commanded one hundred cavalrymen from the Ninth Maryland led by Major Thomas Emory, and Captain Gustavus Wright's two 6-pounder guns. Cavalry vedettes became aware of Beckwith's advance at about 3 A.M. and gave the alert. The militia garrison was fully deployed within

25. Dudley II: 381; Miller, (1963), 40.
26. Tilghman, 171; Lossing, 944.
27. Nicolas II: 249; Napier, 215.

thirty minutes, about the time the vedettes began firing. Signal rockets fired by the waterborne force gave away the British plan and Major Nicholson ordered a withdrawal to high ground about one mile further inland. Both British columns were in trouble. The marines at Love Point landed on the wrong side of the creek and made no contribution to the engagement. Beckwith's advance guard had not silenced the American cavalry vedettes as planned and they panicked when the Americans opened fire. The British main body assumed it was under attack and some of its members started shooting at each other. Beckwith restored order and led the advance into the deserted village. One look at Nicholson's strong position outside Queenstown persuaded Beckwith to halt the operation. The British did little damage other than carrying off a large part of the militia's stockpile of bread and bacon, although the column at Love Point did vandalize Hall's farmhouse before withdrawing. The force was back in its Kent Island camps by the night of 13 August.[28]

After such a performance, it was time for the British to depart. The soldiers began boarding the ships on 22 August. When Benson discovered this, he alerted his troops to the possibility that the enemy might make a second push up the Miles River to avenge its failure at St. Michaels. The fleet hovered off Kent Island for several days when Cockburn decided to attack. Cockburn's plan called for Napier's 102nd to attack the rumored militia camp and drive its occupants toward a second force led by Beckwith. On the morning of 26 August, Napier's column of sixty barges landed at Wade's Point, not too far from Lieutenant Colonel Hugh Auld's house. It advanced inland about two miles with its artillery against what turned out to be only Captain John Caulk's small company of startled local militia, who beat a hasty retreat across Harris Creek to avoid capture. This ended any further attack. The British burned a few small ships, plundered a few farm houses, and were back aboard ship by 5 P.M. The high point of the fiasco was Admiral Cockburn's jovial crashing of a young ladies' tea party at Colonel Auld's house. A few days later the fleet disappeared to the south.[29]

On 1 September, coast watchers in Princess Anne County, Virginia noted the appearance of large numbers of enemy ships sailing straight out to sea. An especially large group gathered on the 4th and sailed on the 8th. By 11 September, only one 74, *Dragon*, two frigates, and a schooner remained in Lynnhaven Bay. Warren had decided to terminate operations for the season. Many of his men suffered from malaria and he feared the warm autumn weather would increase the danger of fever. Additionally, the force continued

28. Nicolas II: 249; Napier, 216; Emory, 431.
29. Tilghman, 172; Napier, 220; J. Scott, 164.

to lose a steady stream of deserters. He advised the Admiralty that the onset of hurricane season made it dangerous for a large fleet to operate in such confined waters. Along with Beckwith's force, he left the bay for Halifax on 6 September. They reached Halifax on 13 September and Admiral Cockburn left for Bermuda a few days later.[30]

Captain Robert Barrie with HMS *Dragon* and its small force, stayed behind to blockade over the winter. Barrie considered his command too small to carry out the mission, but continued a program of aggressive patrolling to keep *Constellation* bottled up. As the winter weather worsened, a steady trickle of large Baltimore clippers outsailed his squadron and escaped into the Atlantic, as did Captain Charles Morris with USS *Adams* in January 1814. The British withdrawal reduced the need for Captain Charles Gordon's makeshift privateer fleet and the ship's owners began to press for their return to pursue more lucrative raiding ventures. By the end of September, the little fleet was dissolved and accounts settled. The command had been very effective and had contributed to Baltimore's defense. Its success demonstrated the need for a more permanent force and it inspired Commodore Joshua Barney to suggest that such a force be established. Secretary of the Navy William Jones authorized Barney's venture in late August but it took until early 1814 to ready the new fleet. Unfortunately, built up around *Scorpion* and Gunboat 138, its twenty-one armed barges represented a much weaker force than its predecessor.[31]

Captain Barrie remained aggressive, despite the small size of his force. On 22 September, a landing party surprised a militia force in Princess Anne County, captured several men, and burned Pleasure House. Thereafter, the militia defenders made it a special point to harass British watering parties. A severe clash occurred on 27 December when Captain Griffin Lampkin's Botetourt County Riflemen attacked a group which was reinforced from its mother ship. A day long fire fight developed until ammunition was exhausted and darkness had fallen. Earlier, crews from *Lacedemonian* and *Mohawk* tried to capture two schooners moored up Kings Creek near Cheriton in Northampton County. They attached tow lines to their prizes but had to abandon their task when two artillery pieces appeared and swarms of militia fired upon them. One of Barrie's last forays of note was again in St. Mary's County, Maryland, where his men raided up St. Mary's Creek, burned some ships and buildings, and made off with 170 slaves who were sent to Bermuda. They landed briefly on St. George's Island for water and returned to Lynnhaven Bay where Barrie

30. Dudley II: 383; Brenton, 499; Emmerson, 103.
31. Dudley II: 307, 310, 384, 395; Calderhead, 219, 221.

made futile attempts to enforce the total blockade of the American coast, per Admiral Warren's orders of 13 November.[32]

The 1813 bay operations should have been a learning experience for both the British and the Madison government. The federal government failed to contribute much to the bay's defense and left the state governments struggling to fill the void. The British increased their knowledge of the bay and its tributaries and became aware of the vulnerability of Washington. The weakness of the entire region, its susceptibility to raids of any size, and the chance for plunder and prizes made it an obvious target for the next campaign season. From a strategic standpoint, Warren's and Cockburn's forces were not well used. Their raid and harassment tactics achieved little considering the investment in ships and manpower. The regional economies did suffer from depredations, the loss of labor represented in militia musters, escaping slaves, and the disruption caused by refugees fleeing westward. Many bay residents had been terrified. But the net effect was a stiffening of public resolve. People opposed to the Madison government's policies were determined to resist British incursions against their homes and reluctantly came to support the war effort. The British performance in the Chesapeake was strategically insignificant because it had little impact on the northern frontier as intended. This is attributable mostly to poor leadership. In the words of John Fortescue, "Cockburn an excellent sailor, tried to be a general and Beckwith, an admirable soldier, attempted to play the admiral."[33]

For British forces in Canada, 1813 was an uneven year and they certainly had not benefited from the Chesapeake actions. In most cases, the outnumbered Crown forces held their own, but some setbacks had long term repercussions for the Chesapeake region. In April 1813 an amphibious force led by Generals Henry Dearborn and Zebulon Pike captured Fort York and its adjacent village (now Toronto) on the west shores of Lake Ontario. The Americans pillaged and burned the public buildings before departing to capture Fort George at the mouth of the Niagara in May. Activity shifted to the Thames area in western Ontario where Major General William H. Harrison defeated a British-Indian force in October. The major American offensive of 1813 was a two-pronged attack on Montreal which was repulsed handily by the British. The New York militia commander at Fort George panicked and abandoned his post to move to Fort Niagara on the American side of the river. In the process, his men burned down the villages of St. Davids and Newark (now Niagara-on-the-Lake). The British retaliated for this last atrocity by

---

32. Emmerson, 107, 113; Dudley II: 260, 385, 395; Byron, 32.
33. Dudley II: 311; Calderhead, 208; Rowland, 231; Muller, (1963), 40-41; Fortescue, X: 321.

capturing Fort Niagara and burning the entire length of the American side of the Niagara River as far south as Buffalo. Disgusted by the destruction on both sides of the border, the British commander-in-chief, Sir George Prevost, issued a proclamation in January 1814 that he would abandon these tactics in the future if the United States would do the same. The stakes for both sides had grown and the next campaign would be fought with even greater determination to reach a decision.

Master Commandant,
United States Navy, 1813.

Chapter Seven

❧

BRITISH RETURN: 1814

T HE hard-pressed Captain Barrie in HMS *Dragon* (74) was unaware of a massive shift in policy as he tried to sustain the blockade amidst Chesapeake gales. The strategic situation began to shift decisively in the latter part of 1813 with the blockading of United States Navy Captain Stephen Decatur's squadron in Long Island Sound, and frigate HMS *Shannon*'s victory over the USS *Chesapeake* off Boston. These victories ended the American naval threat and enabled the Royal Navy to direct its resources to enforcing the blockade and harassing American targets. The demise of Napoleon meant the release of land forces that could support the fleet's activities and reinforce the hard-pressed Crown forces defending the Canadas. American successes on Lake Erie made it even more essential that action be taken in the Atlantic and Gulf areas during the 1814 campaign season to take the pressure off the northern border. Once again, the Chesapeake region seemed the best suited for a diversionary operation.[1]

---

1. Lohnes, 325-6; Mahon, (1965), 227.

Early 1814 saw a peak in British public opinion demanding that the United States be taught a lesson for attacking Great Britain while it struggled against Napoleon. Rising pressure from domestic commercial interests caused the British government to focus on ending the American war as quickly as possible so trade could return to normal and government spending could be curtailed. Sir George Prevost, the governor general in the Canadas, urged that his forces receive greater reinforcements to allow for a favorable outcome in his area. The decline of the French threat allowed this gradual shift of talent and support to British forces in America.[2]

The Admiralty decided in November 1813 to replace Admiral Warren with the more aggressive Vice Admiral Alexander F. I. Cochrane. He was appointed on 25 January 1814 with orders to prosecute the war along the Atlantic coast more vigorously. Some Royal Navy officers felt that the relieved Admiral Warren had not been supported by the Admiralty. The necessities of war had precluded his being given the numbers of ships necessary to perform his mission and the nature of the Chesapeake Bay shallows often rendered the vessels assigned ineffective. Uses for the deep draft ships of the line were limited and a larger number of shallower draft vessels should have been provided. The growing reinforcement of the British fleet and the availability of more frigates, enabled the new admiral to tighten the blockade and pursue more aggressive tactics.[3]

Admiral Cochrane was up to the task. The fifty-six year old officer had extensive operational experience, including actions against France and her colonies and in amphibious operations both in Egypt in 1801, and Martinique in 1809. His brother had been killed at Yorktown in 1781 and he harbored a deep hatred for Americans, telling Lord Melville that the war could not end before they had been "drubbed into good manners," like spaniels. But, he had few specific campaign ideas beyond urging his second in command, Admiral Cockburn, to sustain a retaliatory approach in the Chesapeake area to draw United States attention away from Canada while more comprehensive plans were being developed.[4]

On 1 April 1814, the new admiral assumed command and ordered the blockade extended from New England to Louisiana. He ordered his captains to "destroy and lay waste such towns and districts upon the coast as you may find available." This new policy was soon evidenced by raids up the Connecticut River and by attacks on Massachusetts ports and ships, which climaxed

2. Mahon (1965), 229; Mullaly, 229; Lohnes, 327.
3. Mullaly, 75; Bourchier, I: 311; Pack, 197-198.
4. Lehmann, 58; Pack, 166-167; Muller, (1963), 45.

with an advance into northern Maine and the occupation of Machiasport and Castine. At the same time, Cochrane looked for the most effective point for a diversion in support of Canada. Cockburn's successes in the Chesapeake Bay made the region seem the most favorable place to use the new forces coming from Europe.[5]

As early as March 1814, Lord Bathurst, the Secretary of State for War, began making arrangements for reassignment of British troops to America. Most of those identified were headed for the Canadas to seize positions within the northern United States in order to assure the security of British possessions along the St. Lawrence River and the Great Lakes. Other units were to reinforce Cochrane's fleet enabling him to make diversions helpful to the troops on the northern frontier. On 6 May 1814, Admiralty orders reduced the size of Royal Navy crews in the Mediterranean to free the manpower needed to augment the forces already in America. On 20 May a land force was identified to come mostly from Wellington's Peninsula veterans. Bathurst ordered on 6 June that it be used to bring pressure wherever possible so that the United States felt the war everywhere—a form of total war.[6]

The strategy being developed consisted of a three-point attack using the newly available forces. Cochrane's orders included a full blockade coupled with raids developed at his own discretion. The intent was to lure United States forces away from the northern frontier where the major land attack up the Lake Champlain Valley was expected. His raids would then be followed by an attack on New Orleans and other points in the Gulf of Mexico. The combination of these assaults would presumably result in control of land in New York and Maine, and along the Mississippi. population centers and on the Mississippi. This would provide a buffer around Canadian population centers and effectively limit America's southwestern expansion, while at the same time creating a haven for Britain's Indian allies in the west. Chesapeake diversionary operations were critical to these larger plans.[7]

Sparring between Captain Robert Barrie's small force, centered around HMS *Dragon* (74) in Lynnhaven Bay, and American forces in Norfolk continued throughout the winter. Barrie's ships tried unsuccessfully to sustain the blockade due to both bad weather and the need to keep a close watch on Norfolk where the USS *Constellation* waited for a chance to escape. The American port experienced a change of command in January 1814 when Brigadier General Thomas Parker, a veteran of the Revolution, replaced Brig-

5. Byron, 46; Rutland, (1990), 157; Mahon, (1965), 229.

6. Mahon, (1965), 229, 234; Lohnes, 327-328.

7. Cassell, (1971), 198; Muller, (1963), 44-45.

adier General Robert Taylor who requested release from active duty to command the city militia. On 9 April, Brigadier General Moses Porter took command of the city garrison as well as the 5th Military District. Meanwhile, sloops from Richmond arrived with Captain William Morris's Winchester Artillery Company and Captain Isaac van Horne's Frederick County Rifle Company. They had been sent by Governor Barbour in reaction to the renewed British activity.[8]

Norfolk's economic situation grew worse in February when the federal government imposed an embargo on blockade running in an attempt to keep goods out of British hands. Customs agents from as far up as Richmond held goods destined for the port area or diverted them to Albemarle Sound. This measure was resented by Norfolk merchants who felt that local trade was virtually risk free and should be allowed to continue until the British fleet could reassert itself in the new campaign season.[9]

The situation began to change on 23 February when Admiral Cockburn returned with his flag on Captain Charles B. H. Ross's *Albion* (74). He had spent a few weeks in Long Island Sound coordinating the blockade, then sailed to Norfolk to ensure the continued pressure on *Constellation*. The frigates HMS *Armide* (38), *Lacedemonian* (38), and some additional tenders shifted to Mobjack Bay thirty miles to the north while *Albion* and *Dragon* hovered in the Hampton Roads area. The British also spent a great deal of time marking channels with buoys. Some thought this indicated another attempt on Norfolk, while others felt that the British were considering targets further north. Barrie's force patrolled the middle part of the bay, sounding and scouting, but primarily foraging as they felt the pinch of both bad weather and the American embargo.[10]

Barrie's ships anchored off New Point Comfort and used two prize schooners as watering vessels. Wells were dug near a lighthouse on a sandy spit of land that linked the point to the mainland. Virginia militia artillery sniped at the water parties when they drifted into range and a British boat that menaced the entrenched battery sustained some damage, mostly to the ego of the midshipman in command. Severe winter weather continued into March. Temperatures were so low that the men in the watering parties, inevitably soaked during their task, had to be relieved every fifteen minutes. At

---

8. Emmerson, 120, 127, 135; Br. Gen. Thomas Parker assumed command on 31 Jan., he was replaced by Col. Constant Freeman on 19 Feb. who was supplanted by Br. Gen. William B. Chamberlayne, Va. Militia, on 15 March and, finally Gen. Porter.

9. Emmerson, 118-119.

10. J. Scott, III: 179; Pack, 165; James, 168; Emmerson, 132.

least once, livestock foragers on Smith's Island were prevented from carrying off their prizes and were compelled to impose on the local farmer's hospitality. The British crews were on duty night and day, either manning guard boats to prevent an attack on the main ships, or pursuing clippers trying to sneak south. Their knowledge of the region became so good that many Americans suspected that treasonous pilots were helping them.[11]

Admiral Cockburn arrived with orders from Cochrane to secure an island somewhere in the bay to serve as a land base and rendezvous point for prizes. In early April Barrie shifted his anchorage to a point between Watts and Tangier Islands and began developing facilities on Tangier Island. The location allowed quick coverage of the tributaries of the middle bay between the York and Patuxent Rivers, and allowed interdiction of traffic from the north.[12]

Lieutenant J. H. Fenwick, RE, began supervising work to fortify the site and erect the necessary buildings. By July a very elaborate base had been created. Centered around an earthen fort named for *Albion*, its four walls each were 250 yards long and bristled with twenty-six 18-pounder guns. A one hundred-bed hospital, twenty small officers huts, a chapel, and troop barracks completed the base. Vegetable gardens also were laid out to provide eventual ration supplements. Building materials for the project came from Tangier and nearby Watts Islands. The British also built barges at improvised docks. They received cooperation from the locals by agreeing not to raid adjacent farms if the residents kept them apprised of militia activities.[13]

Admiral Cochrane envisioned Tangier as a gathering place for escaped slaves, at least some of whom could be formed into a corps of Colonial Marines. On 2 April he issued a proclamation encouraging slaves to "emigrate" to British control. In it he offered the chance to enlist or to be sent as free persons elsewhere in British America, Halifax if they volunteered, the Bermuda Navy Yard if they chose to work. This policy added to the worries of the region's defenders. With their large Tidewater slave population, Virginians were concerned about a slave revolt and considerable resources were devoted to projects more for social control than defense against the British. By May, as the first naval raids began in earnest, Cockburn reported progress in the development of the Colonial Marines. Sergeant William Hammond, RM, received local commissioned status and began molding the ex-slaves into a reliable force. They began deployment with the fleet in late May.[14]

11. J. Scott, III: 181-3, 187.
12. J. Scott, III: 187; Fortescue, X: 140.
13. J. Scott, III: 188-189; Emmerson, 139; Pack, 166.
14. Shomette, (1995), 63; Cassell, (1972), 150, 152; Pack, 167; Brenton, 520.

While the base developed, Cockburn's force continued to grow, first easing into Lynnhaven Bay, then dispersing to harass American shipping. In early April Norfolk newspapers reported that over the preceding two weeks sixteen coastal craft had been seized and burned, including two sloops off Sharpe's Island well to the north. HMS *Jaseur* (18) chased a Baltimore sloop, *Grecian*, into the York River on 15 April and pursued it with its small boats under the command of Lieutenant Henry West. The British rowed all night, reaching *Grecian* at dawn. The American ship had been on alert all night and its crew had stood down just before West's arrival. The Lieutenant held up to wait for his other boats, but *Grecian*'s watch spotted him and gave the alarm. West and his five men dashed for the ship, cut down the watch, and secured the hatchways before the rest of the crew could get back on deck. The ship was captured without further loss. From 18-22 April, raiders probed up the Rappahannock River as far as Carter's Creek where they captured several flour-laden schooners and carried off some livestock. They landed below the creek to allow sixty-eight slaves to board and had one sailor wounded by the militia arriving in belated response to news of the raid. Other raiders probed the Virginia side of the Potomac. Brig HMS *Highflyer* (16) encountered the privateer *Roger Quarles* and was badly shot up and her captain killed before she escaped. Cockburn was so impressed by the gallantry of Midshipman Edward Gordon, the ship's only other officer, that he ordered he remain in command of the brig.[15]

Cockburn maintained his policy of attacking any place that resisted his forces. When a passing schooner was fired on by artillery at Rumley's Gut near Chesconessex on the Virginia Eastern Shore, he directed Captain Ross of *Albion* to launch an attack powerful enough to squelch any further resistance. It took several days to get organized as raiders came in from various points of the bay, and the captain was finally ready to go on 30 May. Early the next morning a sloop and seven barges noisily attacked a militia position at the mouth of Onancock Creek as a diversion, while eleven barges headed up nearby Pungoteague Creek. This second force was supported by fire from several schooners and brigs while *Albion* displaying Cockburn's pennant hovered in deeper water offshore.[16]

Lieutenant Colonel Thomas M. Bayley, commander of Accomack County's Second Virginia Regiment, mustered two companies and an artillery section local to the area and advanced toward the suspected point of the British landing on Pungoteague Creek. At about 7 A.M. an estimated 400 British sail-

15. Hoge, 1273; J. Scott, III: 117, 197; Emmerson, 136; Tilghman, 177.
16. Whitelaw, I: 43; J. Scott, III: 199.

ors and marines, including thirty Colonial Marines, landed under the cover of rocket and ship's artillery fire and established a beach head at John Smith's farm, where they captured a militia observation post. The British had expected to find an emplaced battery near their landing point, and it took them a few minutes to realize that Captain Thomas Underhill's guns were mobile field pieces. It took a few minutes more to pinpoint their location.[17]

Colonel Bayley presumed the British were holding a temporary position in the hopes of enticing local slaves to "desert" to them. He proposed to break this "stand-off" by luring the British further inland and cutting off their line of retreat. Major John Finney and Captain Isaac Smith each led a small force against one of the British flanks. The British counterattacked Finney's detachment, forcing it back and capturing one 6-pounder gun. Both sides were fully engaged at this point and British rocket and artillery fire reached a crescendo. The Colonial Marines pressed Finney's force to a second position in some woods about one mile from the creek, where a second American gun was captured and spiked before bugles recalled the attackers. Screened by a company of Royal Marines, the remaining British force withdrew by 9 A.M. One American had been wounded, one Colonial Marine was killed, and five others were wounded. The otherwise pointless exercise had proved the value of Cochrane's and Cockburn's hopeful experiment and Captain Ross praised the discipline and initiative of the ex-slaves. Ultimately, two full companies (400 men) would see service in the Chesapeake while others trained on Tangier Island served in the Gulf of Mexico operations.[18]

Admiral Cockburn was pleased with the relative ease with which his forces operated in the bay and the vulnerability of virtually every target in the region except for Norfolk. He discarded that well-defended city as unsuitable for the kind of diversion he and Cochrane were considering. His plans took on a new urgency when some of Barrie's foragers, the schooner *St. Lawrence* (13) with *Albion*'s and *Dragon*'s boats, encountered an American flotilla led by Commodore Joshua Barney near the mouth of the Patuxent River.[19]

The origins of this new American force lay in the improvised privateer flotilla of Navy Captain Charles Gordon. Raised in Baltimore in response to Cockburn's 1813 raids, Secretary of the Navy William Jones saw it as only temporary and that a more permanent solution was required for the naval defenses of the upper and middle bay areas. This was provided for in Barney's 4

---

17. J. Scott, III: 199; Cassell, (1972), 151.

18. Whitelaw, II: 816; Pack, 168; Cpt. Smith's Company at Chesconessex was attacked again in June.

19. Niles, III: Supplement.

July 1813 recommendation to develop a defensive flotilla. Barney was a veteran of the Revolution who had distinguished himself in 1812 as commander of the Baltimore privateer *Rossie* when he captured fifteen vessels worth more than one million dollars over a three month period. Any suggestion from a naval officer of his reputation was treated with respect. In his July proposal, Barney estimated British naval strength and predicted that, in addition to Norfolk, both Washington and Baltimore had to be under consideration as British targets. He envisaged a large flotilla of well-armed, shallow draft vessels manned by Baltimore sailors unemployed because of the British blockade. They would harass and attack the British fleet in a form of waterborne guerrilla warfare. Barney submitted designs for the craft he had in mind along with estimated costs. His proposal was approved by the Navy Department and scheduled to begin on 20 August. The flotilla would be distinct from the rest of the Navy with Barney reporting directly to Secretary Jones. The cutter *Scorpion* and the schooner *Asp* soon joined Barney's force.[20]

Contracts to build the flotilla barges were given to Spencer's shipyard in St. Michaels and Thomas Kemp at Fell's Point near Baltimore. The flotilla construction continued throughout the winter in the absence of large-scale British activity. In the meantime, Barney recruited crews and clarified his discreet operational links with Secretary Jones. His special status and the competition for manpower between the United States Sea Fencibles and General Samuel Smith's defense plans created some tensions with the city's leadership, but most crews were filled out by March. The tempo of British activities in the southern part of the bay picked up, and Baltimore learned of a threat to Annapolis on 15 March, while growing numbers of its coastal craft were captured and burned within days of their departure.[21]

By 17 April 1814, the flotilla consisted of twenty-six different vessels and 900 men mostly from Baltimore, and was sufficiently ready for a shakedown cruise. *Scorpion* and ten of the barges headed into the bay to test the new vessels and crews and to serve as a deterrent to any raiders in the area. Barney pressed as far south as Annapolis to find that HMS *Dragon* and her tenders had shifted anchorage further south to the Piankatank River. The flotilla returned to Baltimore to work on some design changes which continued through May.[22]

Information about the growing British presence at Tangier Island was received and Barney set out on 24 May with *Scorpion*, two gunboats, thirteen

20. Dudley, II: 373, 376; Pack, 172.
21. Shomette, (1995), 60; Pack, 172; Muller, (1963), 48.
22. Andrews, I: 707; Byron, 38; Barney, 255.

barges, and a lookout boat to harass enemy traffic. The little force sailed southward to anchor at the mouth of the Patuxent. On 1 June the lookout boat spotted two small enemy vessels and Barney immediately ordered a pursuit. These turned out to be HMS *St. Lawrence* along with seven barges from *Albion* and *Dragon*, all under the command of Captain Barrie who wisely headed his force toward the protection of *Dragon* anchored off Smith's Point. The American flotilla gained on the fleeing vessels which were firing rockets and making signals. At St. Jereme's Point, *Dragon* came into view and blocked access to the Potomac. Barney had no recourse but to order a turn-about and a quick dash to the safety of the Patuxent, just ahead of the hotly pursuing British.[23]

Scorpion's fire drove off *St. Lawrence* and *Dragon*'s cutter as they chased the flotilla into the Patuxent, while rocket fire prevented the Americans from turning on their pursuers. Barrie sent some boats to cut out and burn an American schooner that had happened onto the scene in hopes that Barney would reemerge to protect it. *Dragon* and *St. Lawrence* along with their smaller craft blocked the Patuxent until reinforcements arrived to break the stand-off.[24]

On 6 June, the frigate *Loire* (38) commanded by Captain Thomas Brown, RN, and the brig *Jaseur* (18) commanded by Captain George E. Watts, RN, joined Barrie's force. The next day he transferred from *Dragon* to the shallower draft *Loire* and moved his force into the river towards the flotilla, forcing Barney early on 8 June to withdraw into St. Leonard's Creek. The British tried to stop this move by blocking the creek's mouth, but *St. Lawrence* ran aground and *Jaseur* diverted to assist her, leaving the smaller boats on their own. They probed forward gingerly but were repulsed by fire from the flotilla which had successfully gained the safety of the creek. The small British boats continued to fire on the Americans in the hopes of luring them into range of their larger ships which could not get up the creek. Instead, Barney formed the flotilla in a line across the high-banked creek and waited for the British to approach. Barrie tried again early on 7 June when his scouts located Barney's position. He landed marines and sailors on each side of the creek's mouth where they chased away a large militia force and burned some warehouses and barracks in an unsuccessful effort to flush Barney out of his position.[25]

Barges from *Loire*, *St. Lawrence*, and *Dragon* probed Barney's position

---

23. Andrews, I: 707; Byron, 39; Roosevelt, II: 290; Barney, 255; J. Scott, III: 208.
24. James, 168; Shomette, (1995), 65; Footner, 267.
25. Andrews, I: 708; James, 169; Log of *Dragon* 7 June.

again at 8 A.M. on 8 June, peppering it with rockets. At noon they withdrew to the cover of the larger ships hovering at the creek's mouth when the flotilla advanced toward them, but made a second foray in the afternoon. A rocket from this thrust went right through one of Barney's men, killing him, and igniting some ammunition and injuring several others. The barges withdrew again as the flotillamen prepared to counterattack. On 9 June, Barrie shifted his major ships close to the creek's mouth and tried to lure Barney within range by sending small boats up the creek to exchange a few shots. Barney refused to react to this "broken wing" trick and the firing died down at about 8:30 P.M.[26]

This activity was the prelude to a stronger effort. 10 June began with the boats from *Loire* and *Jaseur* deploying near Sotterly Plantation on the Calvert County side of the Patuxent. They were to interdict boats carrying militia and Thirty-Sixth United States Infantry reinforcements going to aid the flotilla. The main British attack began when twenty-one barges with at least 800 men advanced into St. Leonard's Creek. Barney rushed the attack head on. He unstepped his barge's masts so their movement would be harder to detect through the trees, culled out slower, less maneuverable vessels, and organized the flotilla into three divisions—his own red, Lieutenant Solomon Frazier's blue, and Lieutenant Solomon Rutter's white. The flotilla deployed in a line opposite Johns Creek, a small tributary of the main creek, and awaited the unsuspecting British. They came into sight at about 2 P.M. with a band playing and flags flying. The two forces simultaneously opened fire when they were about 300 yards apart, engaging in a wild melee. One of Barney's barges sank during the exchange and another caught fire. The blazing ship was saved through the heroism of Major William B. Barney, USMC, the commodore's son, who jumped on board and doused the flames before they could ignite the ammunition and cause even wider destruction. The British barges slowly yielded, then broke and rowed pell-mell for the protection of the bigger ships at the mouth of the creek.[27]

Barney's boats immediately pursued them and by 3:30 P.M. the wild fight engulfed *St. Lawrence*, anchored closest to the creek entrance, and shattered the sloop with numerous hits to her masts and hull. She grounded trying to get away and was abandoned by her dazed crew. The Americans were forced back when *Loire* and *Jaseur* came to the rescue, their heavy guns blazing. *St. Lawrence* was taken under tow, but she was so badly damaged that she was

---

26. Barney, 257; Shomette, (1995), 69; Muller, (1963), 48; Log of *Loire*, 7-8 June; Log of *Jaseur*, 8 June; Log of *St. Lawrence*, 8 June.
27. Shomette, (1995), 69, 71; Fortner, 269.

later beached at Peterson's Point to be repaired. In the meantime, Captain Barrie landed some of *Jaseur*'s marines on the creek-side bluffs above the Americans, and drove them back to their base with a combination of rifle and naval gunfire. *Loire*'s boats rowed back into the creek a short distance and waited until about midnight with no further incident. This so-called "First Battle of St. Leonard's Creek" ended with an American tactical success but no change in the strategic situation.[28]

The British changed their tactics after this engagement, leaving Barney alone while they conducted a series of savage raids along the Patuxent Shores in the hopes that he would emerge from his sanctuary for a showdown. On 11 June, *Jaseur* and her tenders began a systematic devastation as far up the river as Lower Marlboro. One British officer recalled that "...the inhabitants within ten miles of the shore, with the assistance of the negroes, were completely in our power." Frigate HMS *Narcissus* (32), commanded by Captain John R. Lumley, RN, joined Barrie's blockaders on 15 June, giving him sufficient force to detach twelve small boats and over 200 black and white marines to harass the entire region. Barrie led this force to Benedict, where it drove away a small militia force, burned some warehouses, and carried off large quantities of tobacco. He repeated these forays at Lower Marlboro on 16 June where the village was pillaged, and a patrol rowed as far as Hall's Creek, frightening the residents of Upper Marlboro. On 17 June the raiders headed downstream again, hitting Magruder's Landing, Cole's, Kent's, Ballard's, and Graham's Plantations. The raiders took livestock, slaves, and tobacco as prizes, and the tobacco that could not be carried off was burned. At Benedict, more tobacco and other provisions were loaded on a captured schooner and sent to the base at Tangier Island. The force then returned to the mouth of the Patuxent, having been threatened only once by a Thirty-Sixth United States Infantry battalion which appeared briefly near Holland Cliffs and was dispersed without loss by the marines.[29]

On 19 June, *Dragon* escorted the remaining prizes to Tangier Island while Captain Thomas Brown led *Narcissus* and *St. Lawrence* crewmen on a second expedition up the Patuxent to Benedict to gather more tobacco. They landed at 2 P.M. and while the ships were being loaded, two naval officers led a small party of marines on a local reconnaissance. The officers and Sergeant

28. Logs of *St. Lawrence, Loire,* and *Jaseur,* 10 June 1814; Logs of *St. Lawrence, Loire,* and *Narcissus,* 19-20 June 1814; Shomette, (1995), 73; James, 169; Byron, 40; J. Scott, III: 235; Klapthor, 102.

29. *St. Lawrence, Loire, Narcissus,* Logs 19-21 June 1814; Shomette, (1995), 73; James, 169; Byron, 40; J. Scott, III: 235; Klapthor, 102.

Mayo, RM, got separated from the patrol and encountered D.C. militia cavalry under Maryland Brigadier General Philip Steuart. Steuart saw his chance and led his horsemen in a direction intended to cut off the men from the ships. The British recognized the danger and ran toward Benedict while the charging Americans captured some members of the main patrol. The British officers jumped a hedge and got away, but the more heavily encumbered marine sergeant was brought to bay. Trooper Francis Wise of the Columbian Dragoons made a pass at Sergeant Mayo, but overrode him and was shot and killed by his intended victim who presented bayonet to the other startled Americans. Trooper Alexander Hunter fired his pistol at the determined marine, wounding him slightly, but lost control of his startled horse. Mayo then turned on General Steuart with his bayonet until Hunter, now dismounted, rejoined the fight. The sergeant dropped his musket and ran under fire to the shelter of a nearby swampy area. Hunter borrowed General Steuart's sword and went in pursuit with two other cavalrymen. The British sergeant was mortally wounded in the ensuing struggle and died within minutes of being carried out of the swamp. Eventually, more than 400 D.C. and St. Mary's County militia, including three guns from Major George Peter's Georgetown Artillery, ringed the village and the British hurried back to their ships, covered by fire from *St. Lawrence* and unaware of Sergeant Mayo's amazing struggle.[30]

The small fight at Benedict was the first contribution made by United States ground forces due to the greater British mobility on the water. As in Virginia, the militia lost too much time in mobilizing and rallying, giving the raiders time to depart before any confrontation could take place. The United States Regulars had the same problem; when the Thirty-Sixth United States Infantry did react, it was criticized for uncovering the land approaches to the flotilla's St. Leonard's Creek sanctuary. On 5 June when Washington received news of the British presence in the Patuxent, city officials persuaded Secretary Armstrong to call up some of the Columbia Division's volunteer companies for service. He did little else until the British struck deeper up the river on 18 June. Armstrong then ordered Major Peter to reinforce the struggling Patuxent area ground forces with his artillery company, a rifle company and three companies of horse. On 19 July, Captain John Davidson led out another D.C. militia force, consisting of his own company, the Union Light Infantry, Burch's Washington Artillery, and Doughty's Rifles to Wood Yard, Maryland to screen for British raiders. After only ten days in the field, it was discharged from federal service for reasons of economy, but remained on active duty on

---

30. J. Scott, III: 112; Quebec Gazette 25 Aug 1814; *St. Lawrence,* Log 21 June 1814; the sergeant's name also appears as Mayeaux and Mahiou in various reports.

the District payroll at Major General Van Ness's insistence. It was Peter's command that assisted General Steuart and the militia in the brief fighting around Benedict.[31]

The growing British presence in the Patuxent alarmed both Washington and Annapolis. Some thought was given to destroying Barney's flotilla, thus ending the focus of British interest and the cause for their proximity to the two capitals. Secretary of the Navy Jones twice suggested Barney move his vessels overland to the Chesapeake, a concept which the commodore rejected as impractical. More sensibly, Barney ordered a log boom be deployed across the creek to secure the flotilla and directed Major Stephen Johns's battalion of the Thirty-First Maryland Regiment, Calvert County to patrol the area and snipe at British forays. Meanwhile, cooler heads in Washington prevailed and Colonel Decius Wadsworth, now the Army Commissary General of Ordinance, proposed that a larger ground force with heavier artillery be deployed to assist Barney to break out. Soon, Captain Samuel Miller, USMC, with one hundred marines arrived with a gun section of three 12-pounders and elements of the Thirty-Sixth United States Infantry from Leonard town which patrolled the area along with the local militia.[32]

On 24 June, Wadsworth arrived from Washington accompanied by two long 18-pounder guns and their crews and he and Barney began planning for a break-out set for 26 June. The big guns and Miller's field pieces were emplaced on high ground at the north side of the St. Leonard's Creek mouth where they could fire down on the unsuspecting larger British ships riding at anchor. The Thirty-Sixth United States Infantry set up along the Patuxent shore to the rear of the guns and were joined by Major George Keyser's Second Battalion, Thirty-Eighth Infantry which set up slightly more inland, also behind the artillery. This unit had sailed to Annapolis from Baltimore, then marched the thirty miles from there in a day to be in position the night of 25 June.[33]

On 26 June at 4 A.M., the battle began when Wadsworth ordered the 18-pounders to open fire on the British ships. *Loire* and *Narcissus* were caught by surprise and their guns had difficulty achieving sufficient elevation to return the fire. They recovered quickly and sent a launch and rocket boat onto the American battery's river flank while they tried to pull out of range. They

31. Todd, 429-430; Shomette, (1995), 74; Peter's D.C. battalion consisted of the Georgetown Artillery, the Washington Light Horse, Columbian Dragoons, Columbian Hussars, and Stull's Rifle Corps.

32. Pack, 173; Muller, (1995), 49; James, 170; Fortner, 271; Stein, 152.

33. Shomette, (1995), 75; Anon., Calvert Historian, 11; Byron, 41.

soon had greater concerns as Barney's barges raced down the creek and by 5:30 A.M. got within 400 yards of the British ships and began blasting them with their guns. Struggling to get underway, both ships sustained damage, particularly *Loire*, before they could return the fire. They concentrated on the flotilla because Wadsworth and Barney were not in communication and were unable to synchronize their efforts, allowing the fire from the land based guns to become ineffective.[34]

Wadsworth had emplaced the big guns on the reverse slope, well behind a position selected earlier by Sailing Master John Geoghegan, one of Barney's officers. As a result, the guns fired blind, their recoil shoving them even further down the slope and requiring time and great effort for the crews to muscle them back into firing position. There was additional confusion among the supporting infantry and marine field artillery. When they shifted to deal with the Royal Marine movement against their river flank, their officers lost control and the troops began to withdraw. This action, combined with a reduction in the artillery ammunition supply, ended any land side support and exposed the flotilla to the undistracted fire of the British ships. Just as Barney was considering calling it off, the British blinked first and the damaged *Loire* and *Narcissus* pulled away southward to Point Patience, lifting the blockade of the creek. Barney saw his chance and moved the flotilla up the Patuxent to Benedict that night. The damaged British ships could see him going from where they were making repairs, but were unable to interfere.[35]

The next day, Wadsworth regained control of the wandering infantry and a small detachment led by Captain Thomas Carberry returned to recover the abandoned artillery. Lieutenant Solomon Rutter, Barney's second in command, remained behind to salvage material from the flotilla's old anchorage and to strip the damaged craft left behind when it escaped. On 30 June, he sent usable equipment by water to Benedict, then left with the remainder overland when the British renewed their blockade and began sending marine patrols along the creek shore. On the morning of 2 July, *Loire*'s boats supported by those from newly arrived HMS *Severn* (40), Captain Joseph Nourse, RN, advanced up the creek with 150 marines to destroy two dismantled gunboats, several small craft, and a storehouse abandoned by Rutter. In the meantime, Secretary of the Navy Jones decided that Barney should keep his flotilla intact around Nottingham in the upper Patuxent, while Rutter was to go to Baltimore to assume command of the fourteen barges and 500 sailors

34. Fortner, 275; Logs of *Loire* and *Narcissus*, 26 June 1814; James, 170.
35. James, 170; Muller, (1963), 49; Shomette, (1995), 78; Byron, 41; Log of *Loire*, 26 June 1814.

left there when the adventure began in May. Barney's continued presence in the Patuxent provided the basis for the next phase of British strategy.[36]

After inspecting developments at Tangier Island on 2 July, Cockburn headed north on board *Albion*, raiding several farms enroute to the Patuxent which he reached on 6 July. The delays were explained by some *Albion* deserters who told their Accomack County Militia captors that many of their comrades suffered from the "flux" and complained about living on short rations. The ship's marines and crew immediately went ashore to dig water wells and to scour local farms for livestock and produce while Cockburn assessed the situation with Nourse and the other ships' captains. The admiral dismissed Barney and the flotilla as of no concern and left just *Severn* and *Narcissus* to watch the Patuxent while the rest of his growing force probed other parts of the bay. The Thirty-Sixth United States Infantry moved into the vicinity of Nottingham to support Barney, but when *Albion* and *Jaseur* threatened Annapolis on 9 July, it shifted there along with much of the Anne Arundel County Militia, leaving Barney to his own devices and whatever dubious support Steuart's local forces could provide. The western counties of Maryland sent reinforcements to the bay shore, with Captain Jacob Alexander's Frederick County Company, for example, volunteering for service at Annapolis in July, well before its scheduled August rotation. While this was going on, *Loire* cruised as far north as the Elk River where on 11 July her sailors landed at Frenchtown, spiked a gun and made off with some supplies in a captured schooner. By the night of 15 July, Cockburn and his force had returned to the Patuxent and a strategic plan began to form.[37]

These early operations that showed American inability to effectively counter the British thrusts, confirmed Cockburn's observations from the previous year that an attack on a major target such as Washington or Baltimore could be achieved with little risk. Thus, when Admiral Cochrane, still in Bermuda, solicited his views on the best use of the ground reinforcements reported to be on the way, Cockburn recommended a landing at Benedict on the Patuxent. In a 17 July response to the Admirals' inquiry, he said the site was relatively secure from adverse weather, assuring a safe landing, but more importantly, its location offered a number of strategic options to keep the American defenders confused. Barney's flotilla might be the objective, but Annapolis and Baltimore were still vulnerable to a landward approach, partic-

36. Log of *Loire*, 30 June, 2 July 1814; Fortner, 276; Shomette, (1995), 82; Byron, 42; James, 170; Andrews, I: 708.

37. Emmerson, 139; Riley, 234; Fortner, 277; J. Scott, III: 216; Log of *Loire*, 11 July 1814; Williams & McKinsey, 167.

ularly since their water defenses and the shallowness of their rivers made them more difficult to approach from the bay. Washington was exposed from the east and it was possible to bypass its only major defenses on the Potomac at Fort Washington. These could be distracted by a naval feint on the river concurrent with the land attack.[38]

Cockburn's response tied in with Cochrane's thoughts. The senior admiral had received a letter from Sir George Prevost in Canada describing a devastating raid on Dover, Long Point, Ontario made by Colonel John B. Campbell's Eleventh United States Infantry from Presqu'Ile, Pennsylvania. A great deal of private property was destroyed in the raid in actions later disavowed by the Madison government. Nevertheless, Sir George suggested to Cochrane that some sort of retaliation was appropriate as a deterrent, if nothing else. The admiral understood his mission to include any actions that could pin down United States troops in the bay area and keep them from reinforcing the northern frontier. On 14 July, he had written Lord Bathurst and identified Washington and Baltimore as the most sensitive spots in the region, adding that such attacks also would influence recruiting from the slave population while adding to American fears. He added, "I have it at heart to give them a complete drubbing before peace is made." On 18 July, after receiving Prevost's letter, he authorized his captains to raise the level of violence, sparing lives but never property, in retaliation for Long Point. He sent a copy of his order to Secretary of State Monroe, at the same time directing Cockburn to develop a plan against Washington and Baltimore to cause the greatest possible diversion in favor of the Canadas.[39]

Since the Patuxent was to play such an important role in the growing British plans, Cockburn transferred the bulk of his force to the Potomac. He left Captain Nourse with his own *Severn* and *Narcissus* in the Patuxent as a credible threat to the flotilla, a force not so large as to alarm Washington authorities. He instructed Nourse to continue the riverside raids while encouraging runaways, leaving the countryside sufficiently preserved for foraging ground forces. On 16 July, Nourse's raiders landed at Battle Creek, sacked nearby Calverton, and moved up the river the next day to Dr. John Gray's plantation at Sheridan's Point. Here they raided George Mackall's house, "Godsgrace," which served as a militia headquarters, burning several houses enroute. On the night of 18 July, 300 marines and sailors occupied Huntingtown and torched its tobacco warehouses. The fires got out of control and

---

38. Andrews, I: 708; Cockburn, 16.
39. Linthicum, 573; Muller, (1963), 59; PAC Cochrane Letters, D1-8; Robinson, (1942), 273, 279; Mullaly, 80; Pack, 175; Brant, (1961), VII: 285.

the village was destroyed. It was never restored, rather, its inhabitants rebuilt about three miles away after the war. Returning to their boats, the British destroyed Colonel Benjamin Mackall's plantation at Hallowing Point and hauled off thirteen hogsheads of tobacco. The next day a fifteen-man patrol attacked Prince Frederick, but as it prepared to burn the Calvert County Court House, a large force of militia suprised it, forcing it to withdraw. By the 23rd Nourse brought his sated force back to the mouth of the river just ahead of any attempted thrusts by Barney.[40]

In the meantime, Cockburn embarked on a series of raids on both sides of the Potomac intended to convince the defenders of Washington that that was the intended avenue of British approach. This focus coincided with the arrival of the first reinforcements from Europe, sent from Bermuda by Cochrane who hoped to increase the tempo and scale of Cockburn's raids in accord with their developing strategy. The troops consisted of a Royal Marine Artillery company and the 3rd Battalion, Royal Marines commanded by Major George Lewis, RM. During the winter of 1813-14 the battalion was formed by the consolidation at Portsmouth of several Royal Marine companies serving in England and the Netherlands. On 7 April the force sailed on the frigates *Regulus*, *Melpomene*, and *Brune* and reached Bermuda on 9 June where it spent several weeks training and acclimating under Cochrane's critical eye. It left for the Chesapeake on 30 June escorted by *Asia* (74), bombship *Aetna*, and the sloops-of-war *Thistle* (18) and *Manly* (14), passed through Lynnhaven Bay on 11 July, and joined Cockburn in St. Clement's Bay at the mouth of the Potomac on 15 July.[41]

On the night of 18 July, Cockburn led the marines and some sailors from the fleet who he was training to be part of a naval landing force on a raid against Leondardstown in St. Mary's County. Their objective was the Thirty-Sixth United States Infantry camp located in the village. The force made a combined land and water approach, reaching the target early on the morning of 19 July. The few United States regulars not at Annapolis withdrew when they learned of the British presence, abandoning most of their camp equipment and supplies. The raiders sacked a few shops, took the material they wanted, including two schooners full of tobacco, and destroyed the rest before departing at 2 P.M. Steuart's cavalry arrived just in time to see them depart, as Cockburn shifted his raids to the Virginia shore.[42]

40. Shomette, (1995), 85; Stein, 152; Anon., Calvert Historian, 12; Klapthor, 102.

41. Log of *Jaseur*, 14 July; Brenton, 421; J. Scott, III: 238; Lovell, 150; Fraser and Carr-Laughton, I: 259.

42. Hammett, 107; James, 171; J. Scott, III: 240; Andrews, I: 708; Byron, 89.

The fleet anchored in the Potomac between St. Clement's Island, Maryland and Nomini Bay, Virginia as Cockburn set out, in his words, "scaring the militia." He learned of a militia force gathering at Nomini Ferry and launched a raid to break it up. On 20 July Captain John Robyns, RM, led his marines on a standard flanking landing while Cockburn's boats confronted elements of Lieutenant Colonel Austin Smith's Twenty-Fifth Virginia Regiment. The militia defenders were brushed aside and the combined 1,100-man landing force pursued them several miles to Westmoreland Court House, capturing a few Virginians before returning to their boats. They rowed back to the mouth of Nomini Creek where for a second time, they chased away some militia hovering on the riverbank, and burned the Thompson Farm which served as the militia headquarters. The raiders spiked two guns, loaded a large quantity of tobacco on two captured schooners, and allowed 135 slaves to join them for the return to the fleet. One sailor was killed and four wounded by the creekside snipers in the course of the raid. An American taken on board *Albion* recalled the scene: "This great ship lay at anchor like a vast castle moored by the cable; but there were many small vessels, used as tenders to the fleet, that were continually sailing up and down the bay, by night, as well as day, in pursuit of anything they might fall in with." He saw more than thirty American ships brought in, stripped of valuables, and burned in the ten days he was on board.[43]

On 23 July, Cockburn shifted back to the Maryland side of the Potomac, leading the marines up St. Clement's Creek in St. Mary's County where they captured four schooners without opposition. On the way back, someone took a potshot at Cockburn's barge from St. Clement's Island and he ordered the marines to land, sweep the place bare, and burn a farmhouse that was in view. By this time news of his depredations was widespread. On 26 July, Secretary Jones ordered Barney to ready his crews to move to Washington to support the crews of vessels in the Navy Yard. Virginia Brigadier General John P. Hungerford, responsible for the defense of the Northern Neck, tried to meet the crisis with a general militia call-up. Starting on 26 July he had gathered at his headquarters at Yeocomico Church one cavalry, one rifle, two artillery, and six infantry companies representing the ready militia forces from many of the threatened counties. He was discouraged to see the company from the Thirty-Sixth United States Infantry at Yeocomico Church depart for Annapolis to be replaced by an unruly militia unit from Shenandoah County.[44]

That same day, Cockburn's men returned to Virginia. An estimated

---

43. J. Scott, III: 152; Lovell, 151; Norris, 157; James, 171; Ball, 474.
44. Hoge, 1274; Meade, II: 157; Fortner, 277; J. Scott, III: 247; James, 172.

1,200 marines and sailors landed from twenty-two barges on Machodoc Neck, between Machodoc and Nomini Creeks. They were confronted by Lieutenant Colonel Vincent Branham's much smaller Forty-First Virginia Regiment which kept the raiders under observation while avoiding contact. Events moved so fast that Hungerford was unable to bring his Yeocomico force, gathered for just such an occasion, into action. While the marines raided some local farms, the navy rowed up Machodoc Creek and burned six schooners. Before returning to the ships, the ground force burned Nomini Church and made off with its plate, livestock, and over one hundred slaves. This incident prompted the frustrated Hungerford to request authority from Governor Barbour to keep larger militia forces on active status, at least until the end of Cockburn's current threat.[45]

Cockburn continued to keep the Potomac defenders off balance, this time by shifting back to Maryland for his next target. Late on 28 July, the fleet anchored above Blackistone Island and the next day Cockburn led his raiders up the Wicomico River to the villages of Chaptico and Hamburgh. The probe was in response to rumors that substantial amounts of tobacco were stored there. This proved to be true and the British spent three days loading it on captured boats and sending it to Tangier Island. Finally, on 30 July, they purchased some provisions and livestock and departed. The complete lack of opposition encountered in these Maryland raids and the cooperation of the cowed population, reinforced Cockburn's conviction that a land penetration into the region posed little risk. His Patuxent proposal was proving increasingly feasible.[46]

Cockburn's raider's again dropped down the Potomac to Breton Bay where a few sorties were conducted to the Maryland shore before the fleet shifted to the mouth of the Yeocomico River, in response to rumors of Hungerford's large gathering of militia. Starting late on the night of 2 August, he led the sailors and marines on a probe up the river. The distance was greater than estimated and it was well past sunrise on 3 August when the force spotted the camp of Captain William Henderson's Forty-Seventh Virginia Regiment artillery company which immediately opened fire, beginning the Battle of Mundy's Point. A marine in the lead boat commanded by Lieutenant James Scott, RN, was beheaded by one of the first shots and the desperate oarsmen tried to sprint toward the shore to close with the guns. Another shot wounded two other men, and when the boat grounded, two more men were killed getting it refloated. The remainder of Cockburn's force arrived to take

45. Hoge, 1275; Norris, 358; James, 172; J. Scott, III: 247.
46. James, 172; J. Scott, III: 248; Klapthor, 102.

pressure off Scott's battered crew. The fifteen minutes of firing had exhausted Henderson's ammunition and he and his men made a run for it while the redcoats from Cockburn's twenty barges completed their landings.[47]

After burning some houses used by the militia, the raiding force pursued Henderson's retreating force for nearly five miles, compelling him to abandon one of his 6-pounder guns, which the marines led by Lieutenant Athelstan Stephens, RM, found and spiked Henderson's men then headed overland for Lottsburg. The British stayed on the main road for another mile until they reached Henderson's house which they destroyed, along with his neighbor John King's, because they found military goods on the premises. The enemy column then withdrew along its earlier route, destroying houses as it went. A second skirmish erupted when a mounted militia reconnaissance party, led by the regional commander, Colonel Richard E. Parker, ran into the column. The marines formed line and advanced on the horsemen, forcing them to withdraw, but not before Colonel Parker was grazed by a bullet, and he and his aide were unhorsed and forced to hide from British skirmishers. The redcoats resumed the march back to their boats without further incident, other than suffering from the heat. Later in the day another British force entered one of the Yeocomico's estuaries near Exeter Lodge and tried to land. It encountered Major Pemberton Claughton's detachment from the Thirty-Seventh Virginia Regiment which opened fire at less than forty yards. The surprised British immediately pulled off, but not before wounding two militiamen by fire from a barge bow gun.[48]

This event was a diversion for the second part of Cockburn's operation. He learned from the locals that General Hungerford was concentrating his forces at Kinsale, so after a short rest he got his men back into their boats. The town was defended by a blockhouse and earthworks occupied by two militia infantry companies commanded by Captain Henry Travers, and two artillery field pieces supervised by Ensign Kenner W. Cralle also of the Twenty-Seventh Virginia Regiment, Northumberland County Militia. The British tried artillery and rocket fire to dislodge the defenders and two rockets eventually hit the blockhouse and one of the field pieces next to it, killing a militiaman. His comrades ran out of the prepared defenses and rushed to high ground about half a mile further inland, offering little resistance beyond a ragged volley. The marines landed, occupied the earthworks, and spread out into the town where they found eight dead militia and captured five others. They established a perimeter around the town while others ransacked it, loading flour

47. J. Scott, III: 249, 253, 255; James, 172; Norris, 1275.
48. Booker, 2; Niles, VI: 416.

and tobacco onto five schooners captured in the harbor. About thirty residences were destroyed along with several commercial buildings and warehouses, as well as the defenses, before the British withdrew and returned to the fleet early in the morning of 4 August.[49]

Cockburn took his force to the Coan River where on 7 August his marines attacked three field pieces dug in at the river's mouth. Fire was hot and accurate from Captain Thomas Armstrong's Company, Ninety-Second Virginia Regiment, Lancaster County defenders as the marines waded across some mudflats to get at them, but they broke when the redcoats reached dry land. The marines spiked the three abandoned guns, burned the farmhouses on both banks, and departed in three captured schooners loaded with tobacco. Also on 7 August, Royal Navy Captains Edmund Palmer and Sir Peter Parker tracked the admiral down in their ship's barges and reported they had arrived with their frigates *Hebrus* (38) and *Menelaus* (38). They brought with them from Halifax Lieutenant Colonel James Malcolm and his 2nd Marine Battalion staff, who took over Major Lewis's 3rd Battalion, redesignating it 2nd Battalion. On 11 August, the force returned to St. Mary's Creek, Maryland where foragers landed at several points to gather supplies for the new arrivals while the officers enjoyed reunions and began the final planning for the major blow of the season. The continued absence of serious opposition throughout Southern Maryland gave the impression an overland move would be virtually risk free. The vulnerability of the region finally was recognized by the state and federal governments and in the late summer elements of the newly raised Third United States Rifle Regiment were assigned to the Northern Neck to be brigaded with a volunteer battalion from Westmoreland County, Virginia's 111th Regiment. Unbelievably, as soon as the unit was organized, it was transferred to Alexandria, enroute to the northern frontier. The United States authorities seemed intent on allowing Cochrane's plans to succeed. Whatever the case, the increased flow of British reinforcements meant that a new phase of Chesapeake operations was about to begin.[50]

On 14 August, Admiral Cochrane on board *Tonnant* (74) with frigate *Seahorse* (38), arrived with Major General Robert Ross, commander of the army reinforcements, to complete planning for the forthcoming campaign. The general was an Anglo-Irish graduate of Trinity College, Dublin, who entered the British Army at age twenty-three in 1789 where he became a seasoned veteran and infantry leader in the struggle against the French. He had distinguished himself for daring and bravery, earning the first of four gold

49. Booker, 4; James, 173; J. Scott, III: 262; Norris, 358.
50. Norris, 1275; Nicolas, II: 278; J. Scott, III: 265-267; Pack, 177.

medals at the Battle of Maida in Italy in 1806. He rose steadily in rank and was promoted to Major General in 1813 while serving in Spain, where he was severely wounded in February 1814. He was troubled still by his neck wound at the time of his American assignment. Ross had been cited several times for his leadership by the Duke of Wellington, who recommended him for the command. Although he continued to be personally reckless, Ross's normal daring was constrained in America due to orders which enjoined him to undertake nothing unless success was a certainty. His cautious planning was noted by some of his more impetuous subordinates, and he wrote his wife about his fear of the consequences of failure.[51]

Ross's force gathered for embarkation at the village of Pauillac, on the Garonne/Gironde River in southern France. The regiments of foot received orders in mid-May to leave their parent divisions for assignment to the expedition which, although secret, they all presumed to be destined for America. The 4th Regiment of Foot (King's Own) left Major General J. P. Robinson's 5th Division on 14 May for the march to the port. Commanded by Major Alured D. Faunce, its history dated back to the time of the Stuarts, and more recently, it had acquired extensive experience serving in Northern Europe, Spain, and Portugal. Lieutenant Colonel Arthur Brooke's Forty-Fourth Regiment of Foot (East Essex) originated in the 1740s and saw wide service during the Napoleonic Wars in places as varied as the West Indies, Egypt, Holland, and Spain. The unit's first American experience had been at the Battle of the Monongahela (Braddock's Defeat) in 1755. The third regiment to sail was the 85th (Bucks Volunteers Light Infantry) Regiment. Commanded by Lieutenant Colonel William Thornton, Jr., it was raised in 1794 as a light infantry force and fought in campaigns throughout northwest Europe before joining Wellington's army in the Pyrenees. Captain John Mitchell's Number 110 and Captain Lewis Carmichael's Number 94 Companies, Royal Artillery, completed the command.[52]

The regiments marched downriver to Verdon-sur-Mer where they boarded their transports on 31 May. Contrary winds delayed their departure until 2 June after which it was clear sailing to the Azores which were reached in eighteen days. Ross and his staff sailed on HMS *Royal Oak* (74), commanded by Captain Edward Dix and flagship of Rear Admiral Sir Pulteney Malcolm, the fleet commander. The 4th Foot sailed on *Weser* and *Treve*, two captured French frigates reconfigured as troop ships, and on the frigate *Pac-*

51. Smith, (1906), 197; George, 306-308; Cole, 312; Skinner, 343; Pack, 178.
52. Duncan, 395; Chichester and Burges-Short, 213-214, 572-574, 646-647; Anon., Hist. of 4th, 115.

tolus (38). The Eighty-Fifth Regiment was "cooped up" on *Diadem*, an old 64 armed *en flute*, her guns removed to accommodate the troops. The 44th Foot sailed on *Dictator* (66), similarly reconfigured, commanded by Captain Edward Crofton who talked openly about their American destination, although his orders, like those of his colleagues, were sealed. The fleet was escorted by two additional frigates, *Hebrus* and *Menelaus*, three sloops, two bomb ships, five brigs, and tenders. The force stopped at Ponta D'Algada on St. Michaels in the Azores to take on more provisions and fresh water. They sailed for Bermuda on the evening of 23 June, arriving over 21-24 July.[53]

On 29 July, the force was augmented by a convoy from the Mediterranean. This force had left Genoa on 6 June carrying the 28th, 29th, and 62nd Regiments of Foot under the command of Major General Gerrard Gosselin. It picked up an escort of four frigates, *Euryalis* (36), *Iphegenia* (36), *Bacchante* (38), and *Furieuse* (38) at Gibraltar and sailed for Bermuda with barely enough supplies to make the trip. Upon arrival in Bermuda there was some confusion over army command as Gosselin was senior to Ross, but Rear Admiral Sir Edward Codrington, the newly arrived Captain of the Fleet (modern chief of staff), produced sealed orders that clarified the situation for the senior army officers. Gosselin was to take the 29th and 62nd Regiments to Canada while the 21st (Royal North British) Fusiliers Regiment of Foot, along with Captain L. Crawford's Number Ninety-Seven Company (Pyrn's), Royal Artillery, were to join Ross's command. The 21st Foot was another regiment going back to the days of the Stuart kings. Raised in southern Scotland, it spent the first part of the Napoleonic wars there and in Ireland before going to the Mediterranean in 1806. It saw action in Egypt and Italy before its commander, Lieutenant Colonel William Patterson, received orders to take it to America. Although not the 13,000 men originally mentioned, Ross's 4,000 men along with marines and sailors already in the theater were a formidable force. One of its few limitations was the absence of cavalry and the relative immobility of its small artillery force.[54]

Ross joined Admiral Cochrane on board HMS *Tonnant* to help with planning and organizing his command. The admiral gave Ross operational control of the marines in the bay area commanded by Lieutenant Colonel Malcolm, the transport admiral's brother. Ross then organized the force from

53. Brooke Papers, 154; James, 174; Andrews, I: 709; An Officer, 444-445; Cooper, II: 1; Smith, (1906), 189-193.

54. Pack, 13; Mullaly, 79; Chartrand, 182; Chesterton, 112; Buchan, 167; Chichester and Burges-Short, 342; Anon., Narrative of Naval Opns., 470; Brenton, 520; Duncan, 395; Bourchier, I: 310.

Europe into brigades; the First Brigade was composed of the 85th Foot and the light companies of the other regiments; the Second Brigade consisted of the 4th Foot and 44th Foot while the Third Brigade was composed of the 21st Foot and one of the marine battalions. On 2 August he left the troops with Admiral Malcolm and the brigade commanders to sort out last minute details and departed on *Tonnant* with Cochrane for a rendezvous with Cockburn in the bay. The command group, escorted by Captain Charles Napier's frigate *Euryalis* (36), had an unusually long trip because of contrary winds, but finally passed Tangier Island on 12 August and reached Cockburn near Point Lookout late on 14 August. Admiral Codrington's clearest memory of this historic moment was the "very impressive heat" which he did not think boded well for the out of shape troops.[55]

On 3 August, Malcolm left Bermuda with the troop transports and after a calm passage, encountered *Asia* and *Plantagenet* at the Virginia Capes on 10 August, and gave orders for the force to proceed to the mouth of the Potomac and rendezvous with the rest of the command. Many officers had presumed Norfolk was their target and were surprised to be ordered further up the bay. The steady stream of vessels entering the bay was reported by Norfolk coast-watchers who correctly reasoned that the transports and escorts were indications of an upcoming invasion. Most swept right past the Lynnhaven Bay anchorage which clearly meant that some more northern point was the objective. One observer noted that the wind was such that enemy ships could be off Baltimore in less than a day. The Hampton Roads defenses went on full alert and Brigadier General Robert Taylor was recalled to duty, pleasing all who had served under him the previous year.[56]

A naval officer recalled that the day Ross's force joined Cockburn's in the Potomac it received an unforgettable introduction to the American campaign, "On each side of the river, houses were burning with fearful rapidity and when night came on, they resembled signal fires of the Indians." On 15 August, while waiting for the forces to gather, Ross went on a raid with Cockburn up the St. Mary's River in the area last scoured by the admiral's foragers on 11 August. Their target was a warehouse near Leonardtown reportedly used by the militia. After rowing about five miles, the troops landed and Ross supervised their deployment while lecturing Cockburn on the requirements of a successful large-scale amphibious operation. Unopposed, the redcoats reached the cluster of buildings and Ross led a charge into the nearly deserted

55. Bourchier, I: 314; Brooke Papers, 156; James, 174; Anon., Narrative of Naval Opns., 472; M.B. Smith, (1906), 195; Barrett, 1295; Fortescue, X: 140.

56. M.B. Smith, (1906), 197; J. Scott, III: 272; Emmerson, 140; An Officer, 448.

village and supervised the destruction of the warehouse. On the march back, Cockburn spoke of the defenselessness of the country and began to press for the adoption of his plan to use the cover of a thrust up the Patuxent for an attack on Washington. As if to emphasize his point, Cockburn sent a detachment led by Sir Peter Parker to torch a plantation on the creek shore opposite St. George's Island. His July and August raids, plus intelligence on the situation in Washington gained from agents and newspapers, convinced Cockburn that the whole region was at the mercy of the British force.[57]

A final plan was agreed upon when the raiders returned from their Leonardtown foray. Ross's orders from Lord Bathurst told him that the main purpose of his actions were to create diversions which would help British operations on the northern frontier. He was told, "not to engage in any extended operations at a distance from the coast," nor to try to occupy any place permanently, and he was authorized to use his own final judgment when given orders by the admirals. Cochrane felt that his orders gave him any flexibility necessary to contribute to the diversionary objective. He was influenced by the news from Canada of American excesses, and when combined with his personal biases, made him feel that a spectacular success was in order. [58]

The senior officers decided to adopt Cockburn's plan. Ross's support was based on Cockburn's record of successes in using a small force and by the raid on Leonardtown. The plan called for two distracting actions. Captain James A. Gordon, RN, with his frigate *Seahorse* (38) and a few other ships, would raid up the Potomac to Alexandria. His mission was to destroy Fort Washington and open a link to the land force coming from the east. Captain Sir Peter Parker with his frigate *Menelaus* (38), would raid the Eastern Shore and threaten Baltimore and points north, pinning down any militia reinforcements. The officers discussed the best overland route against Washington and selected the Patuxent rather than the Piscataway because of the presence of Barney's fleet. It would serve as cover for the real objective and there were fewer bridges than on the other routes. Once the decision was made in what Admiral Codrington recalled as an incredibly short time, the fleet elements headed for their starting points and were in position by the evening of 16 August. The climax of the campaign was at hand.[59]

---

57. Chamier, 177; An Officer, 449; J. Scott, III: 271; Muller, (1963), 70; James, 174.
58. Pack, 179; Mullaly, 75-76; Muller, (1963), 61; Mahon, (1965), 234.
59. Pack, 181; Chesterton, 113; Robinson, (1942), 279; An Officer, 37, points out that there were four admirals and a general around the table, showing the scale of the operation—V. Adm. Cochrane, OCinC; RAdm. Cockburn, OC Line; RAdm. Malcolm, OC Transports, RAdm. Codrington, Capt. of the Fleet, and Maj. Gen. Ross.

Infantry skirmish line advancing, 1813-16.

Chapter Eight

ટ્

THE BRITISH THREATEN
WASHINGTON: 1814

T HE Madison administration was surprisingly slow in reacting to the renewed enemy activity. The British entry into the bay the previous year
caused considerable initial concern over the safety of the region's cities. However, the successful defense of Norfolk lulled many into a false sense of security and it was difficult to maintain any real sense of urgency. The degree of
complacency was clear when Congress failed to support the July 1813 request
of Maryland Brigadier General Philip Steuart for stronger measures to ensure
the defenses of Washington. Steuart, responsible for the defense of Southern
Maryland, knew the British capabilities first hand, and though he was a member of Congress, still could not get any favorable action from his colleagues.
The change in Napoleon's European fortunes made it plain by October 1813
that a major shift of British resources against the United States was highly
probable. Even with the renewal of British activity in the bay in March 1814,
the capital took little action.[1]

Washington's location made it less accessible than places like Baltimore

113

and Norfolk, with its lack of commercial activity making it an unlikely target. The absence of any serious threat in the 1813 campaign confirmed this view and Secretary of War Armstrong used it as justification for the lack of concrete defense measures. The Secretary brought a large measure of pompous military pedantry to any discussion of the area's defenses. He failed to consider the moral or psychological impact of an attack on the city, presuming that the British would focus exclusively on economic targets. His fixation on the frontier caused him to ignore the local situation, and he hoped military distinction in the northern campaigns would lead him to the presidency. His political ambitions and conspiratorial style made him a liability in the growing crisis of 1814, compelling the president to monitor his actions and to assume an increasing role over the summer.[2]

The lack of a defensive build-up in Washington was cited repeatedly through the Spring of 1814 to both Armstrong and the President by a committee of D.C. businessmen. They urged the formation of a large quick reaction force, but the concept never got beyond the discussion phase. On 27 April, the War Department issued contingency orders to General Samuel Smith in Baltimore to prepare a force which could quickly move to any threatened area in the region. He designated Brigadier General Tobias Stansbury's Eleventh Maryland Brigade, augmented by additional city units, as the force. Satisfied with this gesture, Congress recessed and the President took an early vacation to his Virginia home. Despite the growing crisis, troops continued to pass through Washington on their way to the northern frontier. On 13 June, Lieutenant Colonel Duncan L. Clinch, in Washington training 500 recruits from North Carolina for the Tenth United States Infantry at Plattsburgh, New York, was ordered to march his men northward despite the fact Joshua Barney was under siege by a large British force in the Patuxent. This little force represented approximately one quarter of the Regular Army troop strength in the military district.[3]

On 9 May, Washington received news of the 30 March fall of Paris and of the preparations for British reinforcements for America. Little was done in Washington despite this mounting evidence until on 26 June, the President received news from the American peace commissioners in Ghent, Belgium, of the changes in France and of the growing demands in Britain that the United States be treated severely for its indirect role in delaying the French defeat. The commissioners reported of threats to burn American cities and of the

1. Hadel, 156; Brackenridge, 253; Rutland, (1990), 145; Lossing, 916.
2. Woehrmann, 230; Muller, (1963), 71; Brant (1966), 62-63.
3. Am. St. Papers, I: 535; Rutland, (1990), 149; Pancake, (1972), 111; Hadel, 158.

large numbers of redcoats being marshalled for overseas deployment.[4]

This final evidence compelled the President to call a cabinet meeting on 27 June to address the threat to Washington. A substantial part of the British reinforcements were destined for the Chesapeake, and he reasoned Washington was a likely objective both because of its vulnerability and because of the moral effect such a move would have. The cabinet did not share his alarm. Secretary of the Navy Jones felt Baltimore or Annapolis were more valuable targets while Secretary of State Monroe, in face of all the evidence, still questioned the feasibility of such a large British overseas deployment. Other officials were not as sanguine. Governor Barbour of Virginia wrote his friend Madison for guidance in the growing crisis and got a response to be alert to British actions. Unsatisfied with this vagueness, the governor called up twenty regiments to add to those already sent to the Norfolk defenses. Governor Winder of Maryland, learning of the deployment of the Tenth United States Infantry recruits, reminded the administration of his state's need for help in the defense of Baltimore and Annapolis, particularly the need for trained artillerymen. On 1 July, sensing the growing seriousness of the situation, Madison ordered the creation of the Tenth Military District, consisting of Maryland, D.C., and Virginia north of the Rappahannock, to be carved out of the Fifth Military district with a primary mission of defending the capital.[5]

Concurrent with the creation of the new district, the president urged the mobilization of 10,000 militia and the levying of 90,000 more nationwide. The cabinet discounted his concerns, agreeing only to a general alert. Secretary Armstrong did little, believing that Washington was not the British objective. The President directed Armstrong to review coastal defense preparations and plan for a militia call-up. The basis for the defense plan was a militia levy on all the states. Quotas from Pennsylvania, Maryland, Virginia, and the District were subject to immediate call-up while the remainder were to be on standby. They were subject to Armstrong's orders, although he remained convinced there was no real threat and kept his focus on Canada. Despite these reservations, the new district was announced on 2 July with Brigadier General William Winder named as commander. On 4 July, the President sent a directive to the state governors ordering them to organize their forces for a mobilization. These limited measures seemed sufficient to those who did not consider the British threat serious, and the general mood remained confidently complacent. The paper army spelled out in the levies was

4. Williams, (1917), 32.

5. Brant, (1961), VI: 269-270; James, 173; Muller, (1963), 49; Williams, (1917), 32; An Officer, 450-451.

treated as if it actually existed. This was not the case. Additionally, Armstrong did not approve of Winder's appointment, preferring instead Major General Moses Porter then at Norfolk and in command of what was left of the Fifth District. When his advice was not taken, the secretary lost interest in supporting the new command and focused entirely on the grand strategy of the northern frontier.[6]

William Winder was a protegé of James Monroe involved in a political power play with Armstrong, hence the latter's disappointment when his nominee, Porter, failed to get the job. The new commander was a native of Somerset County, Maryland where he began his legal and political careers. He moved to Baltimore in 1807 and built up a successful law practice while serving as a militia captain in command of one of the city companies, one of Samuel Smith's junior officers. Despite his Federalist sympathies, Winder volunteered for active service and was commissioned lieutenant colonel of the Twentieth United States Infantry which he led to the northern border. Promoted to brigadier general in the Spring of 1813, he performed competently but was captured at the Battle of Stoney Creek in June where he remained a prisoner until June 1814. During his year as a prisoner of war he moved on parole between Montreal and Washington, successfully negotiating the conclusion of a serious hostage crisis between the two warring governments. His dealings brought him in contact with Madison and Monroe, who became a lifelong friend, and being the nephew of Maryland governor Levin Winder was an additional asset. His exchange in June 1814 made him available for the new command. This was his first independent command, but no thought was given to providing him with a staff or any other form of support.[7]

Winder energetically embarked on a tour of his area of responsibility, becoming familiar with the terrain, but lost valuable time better spent gathering his forces and developing a plan of defense. Before going on tour he requested that 4,000 militia be embodied immediately for the defense of Washington. In a 2 July letter to Armstrong, the general pointed out that Norfolk, Baltimore, and to a lesser extent, Annapolis were all reasonably well defended and fortified and thus, by default, Washington was the easiest target. The Secretary rejected his request, saying militia were more effective when called out to an imminent crisis. He rejected Winder's premise that the militia would be useless unless called up early enough to be organized and trained. He continued to downplay the threat to Washington even when he learned from Nor-

6. Woehrmann, 233; Brant, (1966), 65; Lossing, 918; Muller, (1963), 73; Pack, 177; Linthicum, 573.

7. Robinson, (1944), 178-179; Lossing, 919; Muller, (1963), 73.

folk of the arrival of transports carrying the 3rd Battalion, Royal Marines. By then foreign newspapers circulated the names of the ships and the regiments that were arriving or enroute. He gave Winder authority to call out a small portion of the militia force available, but only if invasion was imminent. As a result, Winder was unable to call on even this smaller force until 18 August, at the very moment Cockburn and Ross were landing troops in the Patuxent, and too late to be of much use over the week to come. Armstrong showed no sense of urgency, often sending Winder crucial orders and authorizations through the ordinary mails. One of these took three weeks to reach the general, although he was never more than three or four hours away by mounted courier. Armstrong ignored reports from units in contact such as Steuart's Fifth Maryland Brigade, even rejecting their pleas for supplies, and forcing the President to intervene on their behalf. His opinion that the defense of Washington was a local problem to be dealt with by Winder persisted until the situation was irretrievable.[8]

Despite his shortcomings, Winder correctly believed that the militia was key to the success or failure of his mission. Cockburn's Potomac raids and the obvious British build-up concerned other observers of the situation as well. On 18 July, Washington Mayor James H. Blake headed a Committee of Safety which expressed its concerns for the city's security to Armstrong. The District militia commander, Major General John P. Van Ness, suggested that his two brigades be called up on a rotational basis so at least some force would be on hand in a crisis. The secretary rebuffed the proposal on the premise that the larger deferred call-up authorized on 1 July was sufficient.[9]

Winder's predictions were validated when the British invasion proved a certainty. No state in the region came close to the levies anticipated in the 1 July order. Maryland and Virginia had large numbers of men called up on their own authority and could not mobilize any more without some delay. Governor Barbour of Virginia had activated over 15,000 men, but Armstrong placed only 2,000 of these at Winder's disposal. When the remainder gathered at their rendezvous points, they were sent to the Potomac and Rappahannock to confront Cockburn's raids along the Northern Neck. The federal requisition in Maryland failed to create a mobile force. It was impossible to deploy men from the Eastern Shore due to British raids, and most of the men on the west side of the bay were engaged in semi-static defense missions. When the state was asked to provide a force to assist in Washington's defense,

8. Rutland, (1990), 158; Brant, (1961), VI: 284, 286; U.S. Army Inf. School, 3; Davis, (1832), 169; Williams, 84.
9. Brant, (1961), VI: 286; Byron, 47; Fay, 225.

the only thing available was Stansbury's force, identified earlier for release by Samuel Smith. These represented relatively moderate numbers because of the need to maintain the Baltimore defenses and only a few hundred other enrolled militia were available for immediate duty and Armstrong's policy of deferring further call-ups until actual emergency meant there was little immediate help available from the less committed western counties of Maryland. Pennsylvania was in the midst of changing its militia laws and Governor Snyder was temporarily without the legal authority to call men out except as volunteers. His 14 July appeal raised large numbers, but only after a delay fatal to the defense of Washington. Although the response throughout the region was very impressive, the forces were not available when Winder needed them.[10]

On 9 August, the increased British activity prompted President Madison to return to Washington and call a special September session of Congress. He then accompanied the cabinet to inspect Fort Washington to assuage the concerns of Mayor Blake and his committee over the city's water defenses. On 13 August his growing dissatisfaction with Armstrong led him to write the Secretary reprimanding him for the management of his department, his failure to consult him on major policies, and for exceeding his authority. He ordered the secretary to clear all future decisions with him. The President's ire stemmed from Armstrong's actions dealing with promotions and strategy on the northern border, but the reprimand had a serious affect on the local situation. Instead of resigning, Armstrong became even more passive, effectively impeding the final urgent preparations. As late as 22 August, four days after British landings on the Patuxent, he still was spending most of his time and energy on matters dealing with the forces in New York State. By then events were spinning well beyond the limited American capability to react effectively.[11]

On 17 August, Thomas Swann on lookout at the mouth of the Patuxent, reported to Joshua Barney a huge enemy fleet of at least forty-six vessels anchored off Drum Point. Early the next morning the force headed up the river. The commodore was certain this was the long dreaded invasion and sent a courier with words to that effect to Secretary Jones. The larger British ships anchored off Point Patience and began disembarking troops and artillery into smaller vessels before dawn. Captain Joseph Nourse, RN, of *Severn* had surveyed the river extensively during his June and July operations and took the

10. Brackenridge, 255; Davis, (1832), 168-169; Fauquier Co., 172; Woehrmann, 235; Pancake, (1972), 111.
11. Brant, (1961), VII: 283, 288; Rutland, (1990), 153, 159.

lead as the column of boats, headed by the brig *Anaconda* (18), turned up-river. The trip was remembered by many of the participants as beautiful, with the ships moving between its twisting forested banks, looking from a distance like a fleet moving through a forest. The deeper draft ships had to anchor off Colonel Plater's Plantation opposite St. Leonard's Creek while their marine and naval landing parties joined the single file column in their ships' barges. They landed successfully at Benedict that evening and camped for the night. The next day, 19 August, General Ross organized his force with its Royal Marine additions from Cockburn's command into three brigades headed respectively by Colonel William Thornton, 85th Foot, and Lieutenant Colonels Arthur Brooke, 47th Foot, and William Patterson, 21st Foot.[12]

Late in the afternoon on 20 August, the command set out for Nottingham where its target, Barney's flotilla, was reportedly at anchor. The plan called for Cockburn to parallel the march with his small boats and confront Barney, while the troops isolated Nottingham from the landward side. The commodore had shifted north to Pig Point by the time they got there, but few redcoats would ever forget the march. Each soldier carried three pounds of pork and two and one half pounds of biscuit, as well as eighty rounds of ammunition and his standard arms and equipment. These included his knapsack with extra clothing, a blanket, and a water bottle. Some of the sailors and marines dragged two 3-pounders and a 6-pounder gun. The heat and humidity of the tidewater summer, relieved only by an occasional thundershower, combined with the load and over seventy days inactivity to pose a real hazard. Many of the men collapsed from the strain, a few dying from heat stroke. The column covered little distance that day, camping enroute, and advanced slowly through thick shady woods the following day before reaching Nottingham that afternoon. Contact was made with a small group of riflemen that skirmished with the flank guards, while the main column trudged into Nottingham only to find Barney long gone.[13]

Barney's 18 August messages to Secretary Jones were known throughout Washington, but the ultimate British destination was still debated by American officials. Secretary Armstrong felt the landings were a feint preliminary to an attack on Baltimore, while General Winder first thought they were an effort to attack Annapolis from the landward side. The district commander finally ordered the rallying of the militia authorized weeks earlier, but, just as he predicted, full mobilization would take more time than circumstances al-

12. George, 301; Smith, 195; Shomette, (1981), 89; An Army Officer, 449; Log of *Royal Oak,* 18 Aug.

13. Cowper, II: 3; Brooke Papers, 163; Muller, (1963), 81; Anon., Hist. of 4th, 117; Gleig, 56.

lowed. He ordered the regional on-call militia to rendezvous at Wood Yard, twelve miles east of the District while the militia coming from the direction of Baltimore were to rally at Bladensburg. On 19 August, the Columbian Division gathered at Greenleaf Point with some delay due to a search for weapons for the enrolled militia. Colonial William Dangerfield's Alexandria Regiment was sent to Fort Washington while Major George Peter commanded a temporary light force sent to screen from Piscataway and Upper Marlboro toward Benedict, with cavalry to provide information and create obstacles. The 1st Columbian Brigade under Brigadier General Walter Smith with Lieutenant Colonels George Magruder's First and William Brent's Second Regiments joined the main force at Wood Yard with the D.C. Rifles (Stull's and Doughty's Companies) and the cavalry under Lieutenant Colonel John Tayloe. The division commander, Major General John P. Van Ness, was not mustered into Federal service because he would have outranked Winder. On 21 August the outraged general, a prominent banker in private life, led several hundred volunteers to Bladensburg where they dug trenches for the next few days. Winder set up briefly at MacGowan's Tavern on Pennsylvania Avenue to supervise the start of the call-up then on 21 August, moved to Wood Yard to assume command of the gathering forces.[14]

On 20 August, Major Otho Williams's squadron of Lieutenant Colonel Frisby Tilghman's beautifully uniformed 1st Maryland Cavalry from Hagerstown, Washington County, were among the first units to arrive from outside the immediate area. Winder attached Captain Elias B. Caldwell's Washington Light Horse, D.C. Militia to the Maryland force with orders for the combined organization to join with Major Peter's light battalion to gather information on the British. One of the cavalry patrols was led by Secretary of State and hero of the 1776 Battle of Trenton, James Monroe. He rode with twenty-five men from Thornton's D.C. Dragoons to Benedict, where he observed the British landing of an estimated 6,000 men. He reported on British moves several more times, once from Horse Head and later from Wood Yard, his messages indicating the view that Washington was most likely the British objective. The commander of the Seventeenth Maryland Regiment, Colonel William D. Beall, a fifty-nine year old veteran of the Revolution and former commander of the Fifth United States Infantry, did some scouting as well and told Winder on the night of 21 August, that he estimated the British to number about 4,000 men and that Washington was their target. Secretary Arm-

---

14. Muller, (1963), 98; Pack, 183; Thornton, 50; Brant, (1961), VI: 290-291; Todd, 431; Scharf, (1882), 186. Williams's squadron consisted of American Blues - Captain Jacob Barr, and Washington Hussars - Captain Edward G. Williams.

strong continued to disparage such speculation, repeating his view that Baltimore or Annapolis were much more likely enemy objectives. Nevertheless, others in the city were increasingly alert to Washington's vulnerability and began to evacuate valuable government documents and personal property. President Madison, increasingly dissatisfied, ordered Armstrong to get the Virginia militia to move more urgently to the city's aid, but the secretary remained unmoved.[15]

The militia forces on alert in Baltimore reacted quickly to Winder's levy, with Stansbury's Eleventh Maryland Brigade consisting of the First and Second Maryland Regiments leaving Baltimore on 19 August. On 22 August, the unit reached Bladensburg where it worked on the earthworks east of the village on Lowndes Hill covering the road landing from the direction of Upper Marlboro. At sunset on 23 August it was joined by Lieutenant Colonel Joseph Sterrett's Fifth Maryland Infantry. This unit had left Baltimore on 21 August to a glamorous sendoff full of music, flags, and cheering crowds. In company with Major William Pinkney's Rifle Battalion and Captain Richard Magruder's Artillery Company, they were escorted by a detachment of Captain Harry Thompson's Cavalry Company led by Lieutenant Jacob Hollingsworth and Captain Sterett Ridgely's Hussars. Unlike the federal government, most of the militiamen were not surprised to be ordered out to the defense of Washington. When the men had learned in June of Napoleon's defeat and the shipment of British reinforcements, even the lowest private sensed the increased threat to Baltimore and the bay area, and entire units volunteered for whatever duty was necessary. News of British activities in the Patuxent confirmed their predictions, explaining the quick reaction to Winder's 19 August orders.[16]

On 19 August Secretary of the Navy Jones responded to Barney's news of the British landings by ordering him to move the flotilla upriver to Pig Point near Upper Marlboro, and to bring most of his men to Washington. By 20 August, the flotilla had redeployed and Barney took as much equipment and as many guns as possible before leaving for Washington with 400 of his crewmen. He left behind Lieutenant Solomon Frazier and 120 flotillamen with orders to destroy the ships if the British threatened them, and then to join the rest of the force. On 21 August, Barney left Pig Point for Upper Marlboro with three 12-pounder and two 18-pounder guns, and reached Winder's main force near Wood Yard. The next day he was rejoined by Captain

15. Williams & McKinsey, 170; Davis, (1832), 169-170; Thornton, 49-50; Brant, (1961), VI: 291; Muller, (1963), 96; Shomette, (1981), 90.
16. Byron, 50; Tuckerman, 70-71.

Samuel Miller's 103-man company of United States Marines. During the march from Upper Marlboro, one of the flotillamen noticed that the route passed through both dense forest and cedar thickets and he marveled that no one had prepared ambushes or obstructions to impede the British. The ease of movement in the enemy's country was a wonder to General Ross as well, which ironically made him more cautious.[17]

Barney's Pig Point shift placed him further away from the advanced fleet base at Benedict, but that did not alarm Admiral Cockburn who persuaded Ross to continue in light of the unexpectedly meager resistance. The general agreed to go on so Cockburn could come to grips with the flotilla and resumed the march to Upper Marlboro on 22 August while Cockburn's boats continued up the river. Enroute, the boats were fired on by a cavalry patrol which disengaged as the land forces approached. Cockburn organized his force into three divisions, each headed by a ship's captain under the overall command of Captain John Wainwright, RN, of HMS *Tonnant*. The Royal Marines were commanded by Captain John Robyns, RM, while the Royal Marine Artillery was led by Captain James H. Harrison, RMA. When the frigates *Severn* and *Hebrus* could not go past Benedict, Captains Joseph Nourse, RN, and Edmund Palmer, RN, joined with Cockburn's force at Nottingham. Captain Vincent Newton's brig *Manly* (14) provided support all the way to Pig Point. The waterborne force quickly outdistanced the redcoats and soon sighted Barney's masts. Cockburn landed the marines to create a diversion in Upper Marlboro while he dealt with the flotilla.[18]

As he closed in on the American anchorage, Cockburn realized that the enemy ships were rigged for demolition. He stopped the approach just as the whole American squadron starting with *Scorpion* began exploding in line. Barney's men, now with Winder's force well to the east, heard the explosions, and sadly understood what they meant. Only one of seventeen vessels survived to be captured, along with thirteen merchant ships found nearby. There was some light skirmishing with Frazier's departing demolition teams but it was quickly suppressed by the Royal Marines. The British had to use some rockets to chase away a patrol from Tilghman's Maryland Cavalry which hovered nearby. The British infantry reached Upper Marlboro an hour after the excitement. They had covered thirty-nine miles in two and one half days, reflecting their lack of conditioning and the effect of the high heat and humidity. The veterans in the force were astonished at the lack of opposition. The

17. Andrews, I: 709-710; Fortner, 278; Ball, 467; Muller, (1963), 98.
18. Nicolas, II: 279; James, 175; London Gazette, 27 Sep. 14; Robinson, (1942), 283; J. Scott, III: 275.

exhausted force recuperated in Upper Marlboro until the evening of 23 August while Ross and Cockburn discussed their next move.[19]

After concluding affairs at Pig Point, Cockburn and his staff landed at Mount Calvert and rode on some captured horses to join Ross at Upper Marlboro. The admiral sent Lieutenant James Scott, RN, to Admiral Cochrane at Benedict with an update on the situation, a request for supplies, and a message saying Washington was being considered as the next objective. Cochrane was not enthused by Cockburn's proposal and was supported by Admiral Codrington, the captain of the fleet. They sent Scott back with orders for the raiders to return to Benedict. Cochrane felt any reverse could be disastrous and even a success would have limited strategic significance. On 23 August Scott returned to Upper Marlboro to find the army had shifted its camp to a point three miles from Battalion Old Fields at "Melwood," the home of Ignatius Digges. He reached the new site with the help of a rear guard left waiting for him, after an inconsequential brush with a cavalry patrol. When Scott relayed Cochrane's concerns, Ross was ready to call off further action and reverse course but Cockburn talked him out of it. The admiral argued that not hitting Washington would produce such relief for the Americans that its effect would be as negative as an outright defeat. Consequently, there was nothing to do but go on. Other officers at the conference concurred, and Ross reluctantly changed his mind and ordered an advance on Washington.[20]

Meanwhile, General Winder worked frantically to get his gathering force concentrated at its rendezvous points. As the Washington and Maryland forces mustered, units from south of the Potomac were called as further reinforcements. The Alexandria Brigade of the Columbian Division had reported on 20 August but delays in getting supplies held the division up for two days before it left for Piscataway to support Fort Washington. Brigadier General Hugh Douglass's Sixth Virginia Brigade reported on 22 August and assumed its position in Alexandria while Colonel George Minor's, Sixtieth Virginia Regiment rushed into the District with instructions to coordinate with Colonel Henry Carberry of the Thirty-Sixth United States Infantry for supplies. Minor spent the entire 23rd of August tracking the colonel down. At 9 A.M. on 22 August, Winder sent out a force under Lieutenant Colonel William Scott, Thirty-Eighth United States Infantry, with Lieutenant Colonel Jacint Laval's two companies of United States Dragoons and Major Peter's D.C. Battalion, to reconnoiter toward Nottingham while the American main body

19. James, 175; London Gazette, 27 Sep. 14; Fortner, 278; An Officer, 450; Pack, 184-185; Williams & McKinsey, 170.
20. Lehman, 61; J. Scott, III: 276, 280, 282.

followed from Wood Yard. They were joined by Barney's flotillamen during the march. The cavalry brushed British pickets about three miles from Nottingham and were pressed back to Scott's infantry and artillery drawn up in line of battle. Winder ordered the force to withdraw back to the main body before further contact was made, hoping to lure the British against his whole command. Instead, the redcoats returned to the march and headed for Upper Marlboro, and Winder sent his command back to Wood Yard, then on to Battalion Old Fields (modern Forestville). Winder then joined some cavalry scouts and spent most of the afternoon observing the British in Upper Marlboro, before returning to his camp where he found President Madison and some of the cabinet paying a visit.[21]

There were three roads leading from Upper Marlboro, each eventually reaching Washington. One of these went directly to the East Branch Bridge and could be blocked simply by destroying the bridge. It was however, the shortest distance and promised a quick link to the Potomac while also offering a landward threat to Fort Washington. Another road reached Washington by way of Stoddart's Bridge, while the third wound its way to Bladensburg where the river did not pose a major obstacle. Winder was unable to ascertain British intentions, and pulled his Wood Yard force back to Battalion Old Fields, eight miles from the District. That location covered approaches both to and from Bladensburg and Fort Washington, while the move averted a general engagement before he had all his forces in hand. On the night of the 22nd, the opposing forces had come within eight miles of each other.[22]

On 22 August, President Madison learned of Winder's redeployment and accompanied by Armstrong, Jones, and some other cabinet members, he rode to Old Fields with a cavalry escort. The entourage spent the night, adding to Winder's distractions, and was joined early the next day by Secretary Monroe back from his scouting. Madison reviewed the troops and presided over a staff conference in which Winder opined that Annapolis seemed the most likely enemy objective. Reassured, the President and other civilians returned to Washington. At noon Winder ordered Major Peter to take his battalion eastward to reconnoiter the area. The force encountered the redcoats on the Upper Marlboro road and skirmished with them sharply before withdrawing back to camp with one man wounded. Winder had left the camp in the direction of Bladensburg to confer with Stansbury advancing eastward from there, but soon learned from Major Thomas L. McKenney, D.C. Militia, of Peter's contact and rushed back to Old Fields. Before leaving, he ordered Stansbury

21. Davis, (1832), 174; Lossing, 922-923.
22. M.S. Davis, 846; Byron, 50; Muller, (1963), 99.

to march his forces back to Bladensburg and take up positions there. Once at the main camp he found that Brigadier General Walter Smith had sent the baggage train to the rear and formed the force for battle, expecting the British to follow up their contact with Peter's scouts. Instead, the enemy halted about two miles away and Winder presumed they were preparing a night attack. He did not think his men could deal with such a situation and at about 5 P.M. he ordered a withdrawal into the District. The command marched through the early night and crossed the East Branch Bridge, settling into camps on high ground west of the river by 1 A.M. on 24 August. Few men got much rest because of the dampness and the tension created by the near certainty of battle. Still somewhat confused over specific British movements, Winder was convinced that Washington was their most likely objective.[23]

The situation quickly deteriorated. Winder conferred with Armstrong that night, getting little help and, returning to his quarters at Combs's near the East Branch Bridge, he was thrown by his horse and injured his right arm and ankle. When the exhausted general finally staggered into camp, he sent a group to torch Stoddart's Bridge across the East Branch and posted Captain Burch's Artillery Company at the East Branch Bridge. He ordered an infantry company one half of a mile to the east to provide early warning and arranged with Captain Thomas Tingey, USN, the Navy Yard commandant, for help in preparing it for demolition. At midnight, Secretary Monroe advised the President to order the immediate evacuation of public records and property. The crisis was at hand.[24]

British movements had achieved their first goal. Ross reduced his overhead by leaving all of his artillery except for one 6-pounder gun at Upper Marlboro to await shipment back to Benedict. The artillery drivers were mounted on a variety of captured farm horses and rode as scouts under the supervision of their commander, Captain William Lempière, RA. Captain Robyns, and his Royal Marine company secured Upper Marlboro as a rear base after the main body headed east on the road toward Battalion Old Field at about 2 P.M. on 23 August. Cockburn and Ross selected that route rather than the more direct one to Bladensburg because it obscured their movements and raised the chance for an early confrontation with Winder's force. The redcoats experienced increased sniping and skirmishing with Peter's light battalion which got quite sharp near the road junction leading either to Washington or Fort Washington. But when Ross feinted down the East River

23. Parker 10 Sep.; Rutland, (1987), 160; Lossing, 924; Fortescue, X: 142; Brant, (1961), VI: 293; Anon., Hist of 4th, 118.

24. Brant, (1961), VI: 297; Muller, (1964), 13; Rutland, (1990), 161; Thornton, 50.

Bridge Road against Peter's men, Winder had pulled back to Washington from his Old Field position. The British backtracked to the junction to take the road to Bladensburg the next morning. Although major contact was over for the time being, the camp was continually harassed by small groups of Tilghman's cavalry eager to grab stragglers. The redcoats could see the glow of Stoddart's Bridge in the distant sky as they rested for what they expected would be a climactic next day.[25]

25. An Officer, 451; Gleig, 59-60; Robinson, (1942), 283; Chesterton, 125-126.

Major General Samuel Smith (1752-1839),
commander of the Third Division, Maryland Militia,
defender of Baltimore. (Peale Museum)

Brigadier General John Stricker (1759-1825),
commander of the Third Brigade, Third Division,
Maryland Militia, 1812-14. (Peale Museum)

Capture of the City of Washington. (Library of Congress)

Brigadier General Robert B. Taylor (1774-1834),
Virginia Militia, defender of Norfolk.
(Virginia Historical Society)

Brigadier General William H. Winder (1775-1824),
ill-fated commander of Military District Number Ten in 1814.

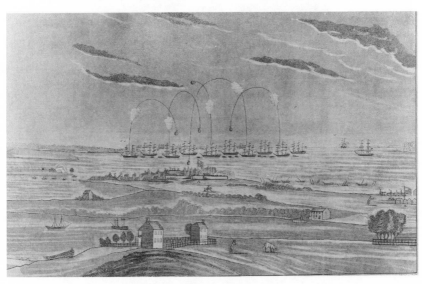

A View of the Bombardment of Fort McHenry, September 13-14, 1814.
(Maryland Historical Society)

Governor Levin Winder (1757-1819).
Governor of Maryland from 1812-14.

Simon Snyder (1759-1819),
Governor of Pennsylvania,
presided over a massive but disjointed war effort.
(Historical Society of Pennsylvania)

*James Barbour (1775-1842), Governor of Virginia
throughout the war and a loyal supporter of James Madison.
(Virginia State Archives)*

*Admiral Cockburn Burning and Plundering Havre de Grace on June 1, 1813.
(Maryland Historical Society)*

Rear Admiral Sir George Cockburn (1763-1847),
scourge of the Chesapeake, master of the amphibious raid.
(National Archives of Canada)

Major General Sir Robert Ross of Bladensburg (1766-1814).
(Lancashire Fusiliers, Lancashire, England)

Commodore Joshua Barney (1759-1818),
Baltimore Privateer, commander of the
U.S. Chesapeake Flotilla. (U.S. Naval Institute)

Capture of the Dolphin on the Rappahannock River, 1813.
(Mariner's Museum)

East view of Baltimore, 1802. (Maryland Historical Society)

Field officers and a dragoon Private, 1810-13.

Chapter Nine

&

BLADENSBURG

A T dawn on 24 August the 85th Light Infantry, "adept pace-setters," led the invading column out of its camps and headed for Bladensburg, twelve miles away. The District of Columbia was less than six miles away on the more direct route, but General Ross reasoned that the one half of a mile long East River Bridge could be destroyed before his troops would use it. Further, he hoped his route selection would confuse his opponents and keep them more dispersed. The heat and humidity soon mixed with the dust of the march to become increasingly oppressive as the day progressed. The conditions further debilitated the tired, out of condition men in the toiling column. Lieutenant George R. Gleig, 85th Light Infantry, remembered the march as the most demanding physical experience of his career. Men straggled and collapsed and many more were at risk of becoming casualties. Consequently, after going about nine miles, the column halted by a stream in a wooded area, closed up and reorganized before proceeding.[1]

1. Gleig, 61; An Officer, 451; Pack, 14.

A large dust cloud soon attracted the troop's attention and just before noon they rounded a bend in the road at Lowndes Hill to see Bladensburg and "thousands" of American soldiers maneuvering on the opposite bank of the river. The American lines were formed to block passage across a narrow 120-foot bridge visible in the distance. Artillery was casually registering on east bank targets and, all in all, the position looked formidable. The column halted briefly so light infantry scouts could clear the village of Americans. A soldier in the 21st Foot Light Company recalled "as soon as the enemy perceived the head of our column halt to draw breath for a moment, they set up three cheers, thinking, I dare say, that we were panic-struck by their appearance." The pause allowed many of the exhausted stragglers to get back to their units before Ross ordered the advance to resume. Once in the village, he climbed the stairs in Colonel Robert Bowie's house to survey the situation. He decided upon an immediate assault.[2]

The British general was observing the massing of most of Winder's forces. Early on 24 August Winder had received confirmation from Jacint Laval's dragoons that the British were headed for Bladensburg. The general sent an urgent message to Madison requesting a conference and alerted Brigadier General Walter Smith to get the troops ready to march in support of Stansbury at Bladensburg. The President and most of the cabinet arrived at Winder's headquarters in Dr. Andrew Hunter's Navy Yard quarters to discuss the situation and "the participants brought many and varied characteristics—but not military perception." The meeting broke up at about 10 A.M. with Winder ordering Walter Smith to march his brigade, the Thirty-Sixth United States Infantry and other regulars and militia to Bladensburg. This force, accompanied by Secretary Monroe, reached the high ground about one quarter of a mile to the rear of Stansbury's lines west of the Bladensburg bridge at noon. Secretary Armstrong made no contribution to the situation, saying it was Winder's problem and he deferred to Madison's 13 August reprimand.[3]

Before leaving for the battlefield, Winder assigned Joshua Barney and his men at the Navy Yard to guard and, if necessary, demolish the East River Bridge. The commodore disagreed with being stationed there with his highly trained men at such a moment and later persuaded President Madison who was passing by enroute to the battlefield, to rescind the order. He made arrangements with Captain Tingey at the Navy Yard to take over the bridge responsibility and rode ahead while his crews and Miller's marine's manhandled

2. Muller, (1963), 121; Gleig, 64; J. Scott, III: 285; George, 302; Horn, 261; Anon., Hist. of 4th, 118; Buchan, 170.

3. Muller, (1963), 114; Rutland, (1990), 161; Parker Ltr., 10 Sept.; Brant, (1961), VI: 297.

three 18-pounders and two 12-pounders the seven miles to the battle site. They joined Smith's brigade after contact had begun and took up a position in Winder's main line overlooking Turncliff's Bridge by the old dueling grounds.[4]

Winder's plan was to deny the British the use of the bridge which marked the head of navigation on the East Branch, and block any crossings at the numerous fordable points above it. The American position was bordered on the east by the low, marshy banks of the river. Low ground sloped gently higher to the west for several hundred yards. The Old Bladensburg-Georgetown Road and the newer Washington Post Road met at a forty-five degree angle about seventy yards west of the bridge to form a single road that ran along a causeway on the river's west bank before reaching the narrow bridge. An orchard and a few farm buildings provided some cover in the "V" formed by the road junction. About one mile from the intersection was a ravine crossed by Turncliff's Bridge on the more southerly road to Washington with a higher north-to-south ridge 600 yards further west. This ridge was cut by several deep gullies produced by run-offs into the ravine. Except for the orchard and brush along the waterways, the area consisted of open fields and fences with very little cover or concealment.[5]

Stansbury's Marylanders were the first to take up positions in what would be the battle area. After meeting Winder on the road to Upper Marlboro, he had pulled his troops first back to Lowndes Hill then west through Bladensburg to a brickyard on the ridge beyond Turncliff's Bridge. He did not think his exhausted and inexperienced men could stand up to the British alone, and he hoped to concentrate his men with the rest of Winder's force to the south. Once on the heights, he learned of the approach of Smith's Brigade and received an order from Winder to return to Bladensburg and establish defensive positions. The Marylanders turned about and set up along the west bank of the river, but did not go into the town, abandoning most of the trenches dug by Van Ness and his volunteers the previous week. Stansbury used an artillery barbette on the road near the river, emplacing the six 6-pounder guns of Captains Joseph Meyer's American Battery and Richard B. Magruder's Franklin Battery to cover the bridge. Although Stansbury gave orders to do so, the bridge was not destroyed. Major William Pinkney's Rifle Battalion occupied the brush along the river to the right of the artillery while Captains Jeremiah Ducker's and Benjamin Gorsuch's infantry companies deployed to the left rear of the guns around some farm buildings. Stansbury placed Lieutenant

4. Fortner, 281; Lossing, 926; Muller, (1963), 128.
5. U.S. Army Inf. School, 6; N.H. Williams, 205; M.S. Davis, 845; Andrews, I: 711.

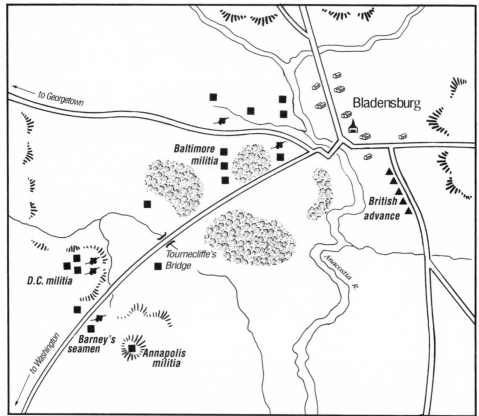

Disposition of forces at the Battle of Bladensburg.

Colonels John Ragan's First Maryland and John H. Schutz's Second Maryland in a supporting position in the orchard to the rear of this first line and ordered the Fifth Maryland Regiment under Lieutenant Colonel Joseph Sterrett behind the artillery as backup.[6]

Winder established a third line on the ridge west of Turncliff's Bridge and sent a mixed force of about 380 cavalry—125 of them Lieutenant Colonel Jacint Laval's United States Dragoons—to a concealed position on the left of Stansbury's second line. Exhausted from constant patrolling and untrained for a conventional mission, they contributed little to the engagement. As the D.C. Militia arrived, Winder directed its elements in support of the Marylanders and to build up his final line. The three 6-pounders in Captain Benjamin Burch's Washington Battery set up on the Georgetown Pike to the left of Stansbury's second line. Winder shifted one of Pinkney's Rifle Companies to

6. Andrews, I: 117; Muller, (1963), 118; Lossing, 926; Brant, (1961), VI: 300-301.

the left of the first line and placed Captain John Doughty's Navy Yard Rifles (D.C. Militia) even further to the left. Colonel William D. Beall's Seventeenth Maryland Regiment, Anne Arundel County, passed through Bladensburg and joined the extreme right of Winder's main line just before the British appeared from the same direction. Smith's 1st Columbian Brigade headquarters and Colonel William Brent's Second D.C. Regiment, many of the men showing the wear and tear of the previous three days, staggered into position around the home of John C. Rives, editor of the Washington *Globe*. Their position was left of the Washington Post Road and slightly to the rear of the main line. Barney's flotillamen with Captain Miller's marines arrived with their guns after Smith's brigade and reached the center of the main battle line near Rive's barn just as the British began their attack. The main line extended to the left with Lieutenant Colonel George B. Magruder's First D.C. Regiment, Colonel William Scott's mixed force of regulars and, finally, Major George Peter's Georgetown Artillery Company. Captain John Stull's D.C. Rifles and Captain John Davidson's Union Rifles took up a position forward of this third line in order to dominate the ravine at Turncliff's Bridge.[7]

Stansbury's troops began to shift in the excitement. Sterrett's Fifth Marylanders pulled back from their supporting position and linked with Schutz's and Ragan's Regiments. They in turn shifted out from the protection of the orchard to a position in the open about one quarter of a mile further back, in full view of the approaching British and well within rocket range. Worse, the regiments were too spread out to support the first line along the riverbank, effectively leaving it on its own. The move was ordered by "Colonel" James Monroe on his own initiative, and neither Stansbury nor Winder were aware of the shift until it was too late. While all this was going on, the President and cabinet arrived to observe the dust and movement from a knoll to the rear of the main line, but would soon depart when the firing became general.[8]

United States outposts in Bladensburg began running to the safety of the river's west bank at about noon. Captain Henry Thompson, a cavalry courier from Baltimore, arrived with messages for Stansbury and reported seeing the British approaching. He was recrossing the bridge as they reached the village and later recalled their advance had hardly slowed as they descended Lowndes Hill. The artillery and rocket exchanges began as he headed north. The American artillery fire rapidly increased in volume and he could hear Winder's men cheering.[9]

7. Parker, 10 Sep.; Todd, 433; Muller, (1963), 120; Lossing, 926.

8. Hadel, 163; Brant, (1961), VI: 301.

9. Andrews, I: 711; Bradford, 344; George, 303.

Thornton's Light Brigade reached Bladensburg long before the other two brigades arrived and he proposed an immediate attack. This amazed the veterans of the Peninsula campaign who were accustomed to probing an enemy's line before committing troops and their surprise angered Thornton. His request for permission to attack was granted by Ross to the astonishment of the remaining officers, who pointed out that the other brigades were not close enough to give support in case of trouble. Undeterred, at 1 P.M. Thornton ordered the light company of the 4th Foot and a company from the 85th Regiment to lead the attack. They were under continual light artillery fire as they trotted through the village and it became devastating once they were in clear view. They rushed the bridge six abreast without being preceded by any skirmishers. Captain James Knox of the 85th later recalled noting the casualties all around him, including three field-grade officers and thinking "by the time the action is over, the devil is in it if I am not either a walking major or a dead captain."[10]

Fortunately for the British, the Baltimore artillery's first rounds were a little over, minimizing their effect. But the cost of reaching the bridge was high with the American riflemen along the riverbank adding their fire to the defenses and Burch's guns west of the first line blasting the charging redcoats. They crossed the bridge and deployed along the west side of the river, unhinging the riflemen who scattered back to their supports. Major Pinkney was severely wounded during the hasty withdrawal and much of the first line collapsed before there was further contact. The Light Brigade deployed into extended order and tried to rush Stansbury's second line but was halted and forced back to the riverbank by a counterattack from Ragan's and Schutz's men. It held until Colonel Arthur Brooke's 2nd Brigade hurried to its relief.[11]

Brooke's Brigade finally staggered in with many of the men showing the physical strain imposed by the heat and their poor conditioning. Ross ordered the colonel to cross the stream and to press both American flanks. He then rushed off to encourage the light infantrymen, leaving his staff with vague instructions to deploy the follow-on forces into action. The general remained in the forefront of the battle while Captain Harry Smith directed the deployment of the brigades. Smith later estimated that the unimaginative tactics caused six times more casualties than necessary. He made sure the Royal Marine Artillery rocket detachment kept up a steady fire on the troops he could see in the middle distance. These were Ragan's and Schutz's regiments which became so unnerved that they were unable to resist the next British moves.[12]

10. Barrett, 153; G.C.M. Smith, 198; Fortescue, X: 143.
11. Parker, 10 Sep.; M.S. Davis, (1937), 847; Cowper, II: 7.

The 4th Foot crossed the bridge and quickly turned for the American right while the men of the 44th Foot forded the river and attacked the other flank which was still engaging the Light Brigade elements. This push forced the last of the riflemen from their positions back onto the shaken second line which briefly held its own and began withdrawing in good order but soon broke under the rocket fire after firing two ragged volleys. Lieutenant Colonel Ragan sustained some brief resistance by rallying forty of his men and joining them with Captain Adam Shower's Company which had stayed on the field. But even this pocket collapsed when he was shot off his horse and captured. The action endangered both flanks of Sterrett's Fifth Maryland Regiment and Winder ordered it to withdraw which it did in increasing disarray and followed by the cavalry. Contrary to Winder's expectations, the men retreated down the Georgetown Road instead of rallying behind the third line on the ridge, thus taking themselves completely out of the action.[13]

The British then shifted their thrust to the American right on the south side of the Washington Road. The riflemen guarding the ravine were quickly scattered back to the protection of Beall's Marylanders but fire from Barney's artillery and Miller's marines first stopped the attack. The British then came under fire from Peter's Georgetown Battery positioned on the American left. Colonel Thornton of the 85th and his deputy, Major William Wood, were severely wounded in this exchange and General Ross's horse was killed. He directed a wider flanking movement which scattered Beall's command after it fired two premature volleys. Miller's marines counterattacked and briefly halted this threat to their and the flotilla's artillery, the anchors of the defense. A British move on the opposite flank enjoyed greater success. Magruder's nervous D.C. Militia engaged the advancing enemy prematurely, firing over the redcoat's heads before scattering. Seeing this, General Winder, shaken by the collapse of his first two lines, ordered Scott's regulars to withdraw back to the regrouping Columbian Brigade, isolating Peter's and Barney's gunners. He rode up to Scott's aide, Captain William D. Merrick, who mutely indicated that Scott, who was on foot, and Winder had repeated the command. When the regular protested, Winder heatedly repeated his order and rode in the direction of Brigadier General Walter Smith's position. Ross saw his chance and directed his infantry against the exposed artillery. The Georgetown gunners got off a volley and skillfully escaped. The immobile flotillamen had no such

12. Robinson, (1945), 3; Smith, (1901), 198, 200; Byron, 52; J. Scott, III: 285; Fortescue, X: 143.

13. Lossing, 929; Cowper, II: 7; Fay, 226; U.S. Army Inf. School, 7; An Officer, 453; Buchan, 170.

luck and continued firing as the British closed in on them. In their excitement, the navy and marine leaders shouted, "Board 'em, board 'em," the only close combat order the men knew. After the ammunition ran out and Barney had been severely wounded in the hip, the sailors spiked their guns and fought their way out.[14]

The fighting died down just as the last of Ross's troops reached Bladensburg. The wounded Barney was found by Lieutenant James Scott, RN, and then by Captain John Wainwright of *Albion*. He was soon surrounded by a cluster of senior officers including Ross, who paroled the commodore and arranged for his evacuation to Bladensburg. Maryland cavalry vedettes north of Bladensburg had reported heavy firing lasting until about 2 P.M. when the battle line passed out of their sight. A single gun had continued firing for thirty minutes followed by silence. They saw groups of redcoats returning to the area of the Bladensburg Bridge soon thereafter. The battle had been lost but the anxious troopers were unable to report on the fate of Winder's men.[15]

Winder hoped to rally his Bladensburg fugitives at some point before reaching the city. He ordered the Baltimore Artillery to withdraw in that direction and presumed Stansbury's brigade also had taken that route. When he discovered it had gone to Montgomery Court House (Rockville) instead, he ordered General Walter Smith to reform his brigade on high ground west of a tollgate on the Washington Post Road. Smith halted his command and linked with Colonel George Minor's 60th Virginia Regiment which was marching to the sound of the guns after a frantic day trying to draw flints and equipment through Colonel Carberry. The two units collected stragglers as the troops drifted back on the road used to reach the battlefield that morning. Just as Smith formed a reasonably satisfactory line, Winder arrived and ordered him to fall back with the unit to Capitol Hill. The militia general protested but complied and brought his men to the vicinity of the Capitol where Winder, Monroe, and Armstrong were conferring. He received orders to move even further west to the heights near Tenallytown, but his brigade dissolved as his soldiers gave up, electing to go home to protect their own families and property. Many of the D.C. militiamen were more concerned over the loyalty of their slaves than they were of any British actions.[16]

The only other organized unit to muster at the Capitol consisted of the 250 flotilla survivors, but Winder did not consider them part of his command.

14. Lehmann, 64; Hadel, 166; Parker, 10 Sep.; U.S. Army Inf. School, 7; Lossing, 930-931.
15. Chartrand, 182; Bradford, 345; Fortner, 283-5.
16. Brackenridge, 260; U.S. Army Inf. School, 20; Netherton, 225; Parker, 10 Sep.; Cassell, (1972), 153.

With Barney wounded and captured, the men had no one to turn to, particularly when nearly all of their officers were wounded or missing. Travelling west, Laval's Dragoons stopped briefly at the White House and helped themselves to something to eat before continuing. Major William G. Ridgely led some District cavalry into Washington, but after finding things in such disarray, stayed only long enough to feed and rest his men before moving westward. Other troops from Virginia and Maryland hovered in Georgetown until the morning of the 25th when those who had not gone home headed for the rallying point at Montgomery Court House. By 26 August General Winder had enough men to begin a march to Baltimore, which he presumed would be the next British target.[17]

The exhausted British pursued the withdrawing Americans for less than one mile when General Ross called a halt until about 5 P.M. The exertion in the ninety-five degree heat caused several men to die from heat stroke and everyone needed rest and a meal. The wounded from both sides were collected and carried to Bladensburg for treatment and the necessary burials were made. The 3rd Brigade had arrived toward the end of the battle and, since it was freshest, Ross and Cockburn took it with them at about 6 P.M. to resume the march on Washington. The Light and 2nd Brigades continued to rest and police the battlefield until darkness when they advanced down the Washington Post Road to a camp site located between the Congressional Cemetery and the Capitol. The 3rd Brigade held up less than two miles from the built-up area, and a 200-man patrol led by Lieutenant George De Lacy Evans, escorted Ross and Cockburn into the city proper. They arrived at about 8 P.M., looking for someone with whom to negotiate. Ross and Cockburn hoped to discuss terms with someone in authority, sparing the city in exchange for ransom. No one was in sight, but as the British van gingerly approached the Capitol it was fired on from a location behind Robert Sewall's house. One soldier was killed and three men were wounded, as was Ross's newest horse. The buildings from which the shots came were torched, lighting the way for the 3rd Brigade to establish camp on Capitol Hill. Many of the British officers feared the worst and still amazed at the lack of opposition, set out to teach "Jonathan" a lesson.[18]

British losses in the battle were reported at fifty-six men killed and 185 wounded while the Americans secured at least 107 deserters and prisoners in

17. Thornton, 51; U.S. Army Inf. School, 20; M.B. Smith, 100; Lord, (1972), 54; Scharf, (1882), 189; Niles, VI: 443.
18. Cowper, II: 7; An Officer, 453, 456; Gleig, 70; Davis, (1937), 847; J. Scott, III: 298-299; Thornton, 50; George, 303; Pack, 16.

the jail at Frederick, Maryland. How many of these prisoners were taken during the battle as opposed to straggling in the heat is unclear. American losses are even harder to estimate because of the confused withdrawal and the informal administration of the militia units. Estimated losses range from ten to forty killed and thirty to sixty wounded with another 120 taken prisoner, many of these wounded. The British spiked ten United States guns on the field. Whatever the cost, neither general deserved much praise for their conduct of the battle. Winder, in his defense, had little support from his superiors and was denied the opportunity to organize and train the men made available.[19]

When Winder was appointed to the new Tenth District, there was no staff or plan and few forces. He was impeded by Armstrong's curious lack of urgency and indifference to the growing crisis. The only thing he had was a surfeit of gratuitous advice and interference from inept government officials. Despite these handicaps, he worked against the growing odds but sensed an impending disaster. He confided to Major John H. Briscoe, one of his aides, "I am but a nominal commander. The President and the Secretary have interfered with my intended operations, and I fear for the success of the day."[20]

He was responsible for the prolonged trips through southern Maryland and the consequent absence of any coherent defense plan, as well as failing to conduct any meaningful delaying actions after the landings. His tentative tactics in the days leading up to Bladensburg reflected his inexperience and lack of faith in the troops under his command. This was further reflected in his uncoordinated deployments on the day of the battle which invited a defeat in detail in "a sad tale of bad guesses, faulty orders, and poor judgment." General Ross was fortunate in such an opponent. The piecemeal commitment of his brigades ironically also risked a defeat in detail had the Americans been able to achieve mass. Sir Harry Smith's criticism over unnecessary casualties was borne out in Thornton's unimaginative frontal assault that far less costly flanking movements could have achieved. The 4th Foot historian concluded, "There was little merit in the generalship, for the British troops were sent into action in dangerous driblets, and the frontal attack of the Light Brigade was pure bludgeon work." As messy as it was, Ross was the victor and had the enemy capital in his grasp.[21]

In 1814 Washington consisted of about 900 buildings scattered in clusters over several miles with the largest group being made up of residences and public buildings between the White House and the Capitol. Civilians began

19. Hendry, Report; An Officer, 453; Williams & McKinsey, 167.
20. E.M. Smith, 45.
21. Rutland, (1990), 162; Buchan, 171; U.S. Army Inf. School, 8; Brant, (1961), VI: 316.

evacuating the city on receipt of the news of the British landings, with most departing when they learned of the British reaching Upper Marlboro. While this was going on, the militia mustered in good spirits, confident they could deal with the enemy. The mood changed as Winder repeatedly withdrew his men closer to the city. State Department documents, including the Declaration of Independence and the Constitution, were readied for evacuation in linen sacks by Chief Clerk John Graham and prepared for transport to Leesburg, Virginia. Wagonloads of government records were shipped to Frederick, Maryland along with specie from Washington and Baltimore banks for storage in Frederick's Central Bank. By the morning of 24 August most civilians had left the city.[22]

Mordecai Booth, a clerk at the Navy Yard, was instrumental in evacuating quantities of government property and military supplies in the days before the British entered the city. He impressed wagons and horses for government service and later got Colonel George Minor to assign men from the 60th Virginia Regiment to guard the material he was stashing in the Virginia countryside. Six of Minor's men watched over artillery pieces and tons of powder eventually placed at Daniel Dulaney's Farm near Falls Church. The tireless Booth continued to scour the city while keeping in contact with Captain Tingey at the Navy Yard even after the British had entered the city. Later, he coordinated the issue of some of the material he had saved in support of resistance to the British Potomac River diversion.[23]

The original evacuation plans called for President Madison to join Secretary of the Navy Jones and the rest of the cabinet at the latter's Georgetown home, "Bellevue," and proceed on to Frederick. The President encountered heavy traffic and decided to change the rendezvous to Wiley's Tavern near Difficult Run on the Virginia side of Great Falls. Mrs. Madison remained at the White House to save some valuables, then left for Virginia where she stayed at "Rokeby," the home of her friend, Elizabeth M. Lee Love and her husband Richard. The President spent the night one mile away at John Moffat's home, "Salona," after fruitlessly searching for his wife. The two reunited the next day, 25 August, at Wiley's Tavern where Secretary Monroe had sheltered. At about midnight that day, Madison and Monroe along with some other officials, rode with a dragoon escort to Conn's Ferry above Great Falls on the Potomac where they rested before ferrying to the Maryland side. They reached Montgomery Court House at 6 P.M. with hopes of meeting General Winder, but he had headed for Baltimore with the troops he had in hand. The

22. Brackenridge, 261; Scharf, (1882), 193; M.B. Smith, 98.
23. Irwin, 22-23; Netherton, 226.

presidential party continued as far as Brookeville where it spent the night at Caleb Bentley's. That night Armstrong and Treasury Secretary George W. Campbell met at the original Frederick rendezvous while Secretary Jones remained in Virginia. Nevertheless, the President and his entourage were poised to resume control of the government.[24]

After the 24 August incident of the ambush on Ross's parlay effort the British embarked on the systematic destruction of public property. Cockburn urged torching the entire city in retaliation for the burnings perpetrated by United States forces beginning with the attack on York in April 1813. Ross declined such an action and compromised by ordering the destruction of all public buildings. Shortly thereafter, Lieutenants George De Lacy Evans, DQMG, and James Pratt, RN, supervised the destruction and burning of the solidly built Capitol. At about 10:30 P.M. Ross and Cockburn led 150 men up Pennsylvania Avenue to the White House which the party thoroughly explored, traditionally enjoying a meal before Captain Thomas Blanchard, RE, and his Royal Sappers and Miners put the building to the torch. Cockburn insisted there be no looting, allowing the men to take only souvenirs of little value, securing just a chair cushion for himself. After the White House, Ross's men torched the Treasury which contained no "treasure" to their great disappointment. They returned to their camps, with Ross setting up his headquarters in Dr. James Ewell's house on Capitol Hill. While this was going on, Captain Tingey at the Navy Yard anticipated the marauders' arrival and directed the destruction of his facility. The Navy Yard and an adjacent rope walk exploded in a spectacular blaze seen as far away as southern Charles County, Maryland. Along with it went the nearly completed frigate USS *Essex* and the sloop USS *Argus*. In the meantime, Admiral Cockburn prowled the city, relishing his role as conqueror. At midnight he came across the office of Joseph Gale's *National Intelligencer* which had been particularly critical of him, but yielded to citizens' pleas not to endanger their homes by burning it. Leaving a sentinel to guard it, the admiral and his party returned to their camp. A late night rainfall contained the fires and prevented chaos.[25]

The next day Ross and Cockburn took the Light Brigade back into the town to complete their work. They supervised the destruction of what remained of the Navy Yard and adjacent rope walks and by 9 A.M., watched the burning of the remaining public buildings, including the State and War Departments as well as the sacking of the newspaper office. Only the patent office survived thanks to the intercession of its director, Dr. William Thornton,

24. Netherton, 226; Brant, (1966), 66; Lossing, 936; Muller, (1963), 167.
25. J. Scott, III: 303, 305; Porter, 358; Lossing, 932; Thornton, 52; Pack, 188; Klapthor, 102.

who argued that it contained private items of value to all mankind. Nervous sentries at both ends of the Long Bridge across the Potomac destroyed it at about noon, each fearing an attack from the opposite side. Although the Americans had done a lot of damage to a fort at Greenleaf's Point, its magazine was still intact and Ross sent the 21st Foot Light Company with orders to complete the destruction and destroy the stores of gunpowder. This was done by throwing the powder barrels down a nearby well which did not have sufficient water in it to cover them. A spark or careless cigar ignited the whole pile, killing twelve redcoats and horribly injuring at least thirty more. The Maryland cavalry vedettes hovering well north of Bladensburg, heard the explosion at 3 P.M. and briefly thought the fighting had resumed. A violent storm swept into the area as the British tried to recover from the tragedy. The winds were so strong, that one officer and his horse were knocked over as they emerged from behind the shelter of a building while thirty men sustained some injury. To add to the British misery, American cavalry could be seen along the Georgetown Heights and some dragoons were probing more and more vigorously. Ross reasoned that they were probably as confused by the storm as his men were and he ordered a night withdrawal before his fortunes got worse.[26]

Ross's experienced staff advised against a night withdrawal from Washington for fear of ambush along the wooded roads. Nevertheless, he persisted and ordered the appropriation of any kind of wheeled vehicle that could carry away the wounded. Some of the casualties could not travel and he left them in the care of his host, Dr. Ewell, while Dr. Thornton agreed to cover the costs of caring for them until government arrangements could be made. The general's urgency was such that the troops did not have time to cook their evening meal. At about 8 P.M. the Light Brigade left its camp fires burning as a deception and joined its sister brigades at the Bladensburg battlefield by 9:30 P.M. The force halted for about one hour to load more wounded. Regimental supply officers collected about twenty more wagons and about fifty horses from local farmers along with sixty to seventy head of cattle, while many soldiers looked in vain for the knapsacks they had grounded during the previous day's fight. The scene was horrible, few of the dead had been buried and stripped corpses dotted the landscape. There were no burials until the next day when George Calvert from Riversdale Plantation two miles north of Bladensburg brought his slaves down to do the job once the British had left.[27]

The nearly one hundred wounded who could not travel were left with

26. Barrett, 148; Lord, (1972), 59-60; J. Scott, III: 313; Thornton, 52; Lossing, 932; Bradford, 346; Dobyns, 66.

thirty tenders in the care of Colonel Thomas Barclay, the British prisoner exchange agent. By fortunate coincidence, he was living in Benjamin Stoddart's Bladensburg home, "Bostwick." Ross gave him some gold to defray the cost of the men's care. Barrels of flour were opened up in the streets and the troops were told to fill their haversacks. Once the column resumed its march, the flour became unwelcome extra weight and the men began jettisoning it, marking the route in the darkness. The column left Bladensburg after one hour. The order of march had the cattle first, then the wounded followed by the brigades. Several slaves joined the withdrawal. Some remained as officer's servants, but most left for Tangier Island to become Colonial Marines or to go on to Halifax.[28]

The march was slow as trees lay across the road as a result of the violent windstorms of the previous afternoon. They blocked the march as effectively as if they had been put there intentionally and required considerable time and effort to clear away. The exhausted force was only three miles east of Bladensburg at sunrise after nearly six hours of marching. At 7 A.M. Ross called a halt until noon to allow the men to rest. They collapsed and were not awakened even by a heavy rain. The disorganization and confusion in the column made it fortunate that the Americans were not in pursuit. The British spread rumors to any citizen they encountered that Annapolis was their next objective, causing most available militia to rally there, clearing the road to Nottingham and Benedict. Once the march resumed, the column proceeded until it reached Upper Marlboro in the dark. It spent the night, confident that it was out of danger. Nottingham was reached the next day and contact made with the fleet. The wounded men and captured flour and tobacco were put on board while the men rested. On 29 August the force arrived in Benedict and completed loading. By 31 August the entire force was back at Point Patience where it remained for the next few days.[29]

General Ross was very pleased with his good fortune. He had led his few thousand men on a one hundred-mile roundtrip journey deep into hostile territory, won a battle, sacked the enemy capital, and destroyed large quantities of military material. In a letter to his wife, he stated he would not have taken the chance if it were not for Cockburn's urging and encouragement. He later confirmed this in a conversation with United States prisoner agent J.

27. G.C.M. Smith, 201; An Officer, 27; J. Scott, III: 309, 324; Callcott, 249, 272; Wallace, 235; Cowper, II: 9.
28. Callcott, 265, 272; J. Scott, III: 309; An Officer, 27.
29. Fortescue, X: 146; J. Scott, III: 313, 324; G.C.M. Smith, 202; Barrett, 150; Logs of *Royal Oak, Severn*, 27 Aug.-1 Sep.

S. Skinner, saying he viewed Barney's flotilla as the main objective. Washington had been mentioned in passing as a target, but he did not take it seriously until Cockburn persuaded him to give it a try. He has been criticized for not attacking Baltimore from the landward side immediately upon withdrawing from Washington. However, the physical condition of his men and the absence of trains, plus the need to transport the wounded made this unrealistic. Additionally, the performance of the American forces up to this point made it unlikely that any formidable opposition would be encountered regardless of the direction of attack. There was no question that the raid and inevitable British delays would have important repercussions in Baltimore and throughout the country.[30]

News of the sack of Washington shocked most of those who heard of it and led many people to reconsider their attitudes towards the federal government. The diehard enemies of the administration gleefully used the incident as evidence of national incompetence and the need to get rid of the Madison administration. They were quickly silenced by an overwhelming outrage at the British actions and a great upsurge of nationalist feeling. Hearing such gloating, Washington Irving retorted, "Every loyal citizen would feel the ignominy and be earnest to avenge it." In another instance, Governor Barbour of Virginia urged a newly raised militia force to avenge the "wound that the character of the country" had experienced. Many Americans recognized for the first time that the government was dependent on popular support to achieve its war aims and could not meet expectations without it. New York Senator Rufus King, a Federalist opponent of Madison's war policy, was converted to supporting it when he heard of the British raid, saying the issue was now one of national rights and dignity. He agreed with Hugh Nelson of Virginia, a fellow moderate Federalist, and Democratic-Republicans that the war was a test for the survival of a republican form of government. This was not the common view before the incident and many had failed to see the connection between broad support and national success. The absence of this feeling was one reason Washington became a British objective. They hoped such a blow might accelerate the fragmentation already noted.[31]

Niles' *Weekly* pointed out that Washington's fate—"worthless as a strategic objective, but a shining target for malevolence"—was relatively insignificant. But, its burning underlined the magnitude of the British threat if all citizens did not put their differences aside and pull together for the common defense. The humiliation brought on by this national disaster had a unifying

30. Mullaly, 82; Muller, (1963), 154; Skinner, 341; Maguire, 8, 9.
31. Woehrmann, 223-229; Brant, (1961), VI: 323; Stuart, 130-133.

effect that earlier, essentially regional, disasters did not have. Regardless of their politics, people felt the need to do anything necessary to defend the country. New York City Mayor DeWitt Clinton stated, "The present inquiry is: Will we defend our country, our city, our property, and our families? Will we go forth to meet and repel the enemy?" The reaction everywhere along the east coast was to call out the militia, particularly around the rest of the Chesapeake Bay where the marauders lingered. The news accelerated the process and made it possible to fully man the Baltimore defenses within days. The Frederick County, Maryland militia mobilized as soon as it learned of the Benedict landings and immediately headed for Baltimore. Enthusiasm was such that after the burning of Washington, more than 3,000 men from western regions of the state volunteered for service and marched through Frederick to Baltimore. New companies were formed in a few hours and completed their organization while on the march. So many men came forward that when General Samuel Ringgold's Second Maryland Brigade mustered on 27 August, the men were issued equipment then ordered home to remain on standby because no more troops could be accommodated at either Baltimore or Annapolis.[32]

Major General James Singleton's Sixteenth Virginia Brigade hastened through Frederick on its way to Baltimore. That state not only sent troops to help its neighbor, but rode the wave of popular momentum and called up even greater numbers of men for the Norfolk defenses and elsewhere. Those not sent to places directly threatened were gathered in camps close to likely points of attack. The Richmond militia went to Warrenigh Church on the York River with all the enthusiasm expected of patriotic amateurs in a moment of crisis. They stayed on high alert throughout the period of emergency, then trained until they were discharged at the end of September. Citizens in unprecedented numbers volunteered their time, services, and possessions for the defense of their communities. The burning of Washington had made the war a personal matter to which everyone could relate. In keeping with this surge, Baltimore civic leaders formed a city Committee of Vigilance and Safety to provide logistical and moral support for its defenders.[33]

The destruction of Washington proved the resiliency of the federal structure. The temporary disruption of the federal government had little practical effect on the already decentralized United States war effort. Generals, governors, and soldiers continued to do what they felt necessary, using local resources or pledging the eventual credit of the government once it had

---

32. Brant, (1961), VI: 284; Commager, 18; Muller, (1963), 171.
33. Williams & McKinsey, 167-168; Scharf, (1882), 190; Woehrmann, 243; Kennedy, I: 335.

recovered. The modest, but important, United States successes on the Niagara frontier in July and August showed that the raid, humiliating as it was, had little military significance. What it did cause was the galvanizing of American defenders into a frenzy of preparations against any such repetition.[34]

President Madison returned to Washington from Brookeville upon learning of the British withdrawal. His quick return and his dignified leadership in the aftermath of the crisis began the restoration of a positive image for the government that increased with a series of military successes over the following weeks. On 29 August the President held a cabinet meeting and the government was back in business despite the presence of a second group of British raiders under Captain James B. Gordon, RN, in nearby Alexandria. Most public resentment for the recent fiasco was lavished on Secretary John Armstrong. Also on 29 August, Major John S. Williams, the inspector general of the Columbian Division speaking for Brigadier General Walter Smith, told Madison that the command would not serve under Armstrong. Consequently, the President eased him from his position, sending him on leave to his New York home. On 4 September during a stop in Baltimore, the disgraced secretary resigned and Madison temporarily assigned the job to James Monroe. As this was going on, efforts were underway to deal with Gordon's Potomac raid and to assist Baltimore in defending itself.[35]

When Captain John Wainwright, RN, and Captain Sir Harry Smith on HMS *Iphigenia* arrived home with the news, the attack on Washington created a sensation in Britain, with celebrations and bell ringing throughout the realm. It was viewed as a great example of military skill and daring and drew enthusiastic praise from Parliament and the Prince Regent. Most people felt that earlier American depredations in the Canadas merited some kind of retribution. When British negotiators at the peace conference in Ghent got the news, they increased their demands that terms include transfers of land occupied or expected to be occupied by British forces. Soon, however, the destruction of public property began to be seen in another light. Samuel Whitbread, a member of Parliament stated Britain "had done what the Goths refused to do at Rome." He was echoed by the London *Spectator* whose editor declared, "Even the Cossacks spared Paris, but Englishmen spared not the capital of America." The *Naval Chronicle* rued the loss of so many public buildings and treasures as smacking of the barbaric and predicted that it would arouse the American population to greater resistance. Captain John Cole, 21st Foot, later wrote "what ought to have been a great war subsided

34. Brant, (1966), 64; Woehrmann, 247.
35. Wharton, 176, 178; Rutland, (1990), 169; N.H. Williams, 105; Brant, (1961), VI: 312.

into a second-rate buccaneering expedition" as a result of the raid and he predicted little of value would come of the campaign. The conduct of Gordon's and Parker's diversionary operations in support of the raid, despite some bright moments, marked a shift in British fortunes.[36]

36. Hadel, 204; Maguire, 9; Cole, 312; Naval Chron., 249.

Earthworks thrown up by Captain David Porter
at White House on the Potomac.

Chapter Ten

૨૭

THE DISTRACTING RAIDS: 1814

T HE two distracting operations under Royal Navy Captains James A. Gordon and Sir Peter Parker opened concurrently with the Benedict landings and met their objective in part, but with equivocal long-term effects. Admiral Cochrane ordered Gordon to go up the Potomac as high as safety permitted and raid both shores hard enough to distract the local forces from aiding their comrades defending Washington. Contact would be maintained with a courier boat so Gordon would know when to break contact and return to the fleet. Gordon's force consisted of his own frigate, *Seahorse* (38), Captain Charles Napier's frigate, *Euryalis* (36), three bomb ships, a rocket ship, and a tender. The ships and most of their crews had come directly from Europe, enroute since early June, and had been in American waters for less than one week before beginning their passage up the Potomac on 17 August.[1]

1. Anon., Narrative of Naval Opns., 473; James, 181; N.H. Williams, 41; Roosevelt, 291. The bomb ships were *Devastation*, Capt. Thomas Alexander, *Aetna*, Capt. Richard Kenah, and *Meteor*, Capt. Samuel Roberts; the rocket ship was *Erebus*, Capt. David E. Bartholomew, and the tender was *Anna Maria*, Capt. Dickson.

The thirty-two year old Gordon was an experienced ship commander with extensive experience conducting the same sort of amphibious raiding in the Adriatic where he had lost a leg and earned a gold medal. He had to use a series of old charts, some dating back to the Revolution, and expected difficulties, particularly on reaching the notorious Kettle Bottoms on the evening of 18 August. The Bottoms were a series of shoals and oyster beds of varying sizes which made sounding very difficult. The ships hugged the Virginia shore where the channel was alleged to be better. But despite every precaution, *Euryalis* ran aground on a small oyster bed undetected by her leadsman or those in *Seahorse* which had preceded her. The force experienced a series of such minor groundings with the ships refloated only after hours of strenuous, frustrating effort before finally clearing the hazard by sunset on 19 August. The wind shifted over the next five days and the crews had to warp and kedge their ships forward with their rowboats until after fifty miles, they reached Maryland Point late on 24 August. Riding at anchor there, they could see the sky aglow from fires in the direction of Washington. Gordon concluded that the army probably was withdrawing, nevertheless, he decided to continue up the river.[2]

On 25 August the crews worked to exhaustion as the winds remained unfavorable and they had to continue rowing the ships forward. The men were beginning to show the strain. Even though there had been no opposition, nightly guard boats had to be manned to protect the ships resting at anchor from any possible hostile action. To add to their distress, at midday on the 25th near Maryland Reach, the force was hit with the same type of violent squalls that made so much trouble for the army in Washington. *Euryalis* lost all three top masts and *Seahorse* had her mizzen-mast sprung while *Meteor* was first run aground, then blown into deep water. The force looked a shambles but Gordon calmly ordered the men to dinner once the storm had passed and then assessed the damage. He considered ending the raid, but his captains skillfully jury-rigged repairs enough to justify continuing. The force even maintained headway as the marines continued rowing in the small boats while the sailors did the carpentry.[3]

On the morning of 26 August the weather became favorable and the ships could use their sail again. They made good time, reaching Mount Vernon at about 5 P.M., and rendered salutes to the first President's memory as they glided by. Their next obstacle was Fort Washington, formerly Fort Warburton, which they anxiously approached and then anchored just out of gun-

2. Anon., Narrative of Naval Opns., 473; Muller, (1964), 86.
3. Anon., Narrative of Naval Opns., 476; J. Scott, III: 314-315.

shot range. The marines judged it impressive but not impregnable. The bomb and rocket ships took up supporting positions for a morning attack and lobbed a few shells into the fort. They were both relieved and amazed to see the garrison withdraw shortly thereafter and to hear explosions from the fort.[4]

The fort could have proven a difficult problem for the British. It was located on high ground above the mouth of Piscataway Creek, clearly visible from Mount Vernon, with armaments capable of dominating the Potomac. Since 1800, the water batteries at the creek's mouth had been augmented so that by 1808 a thirteen-gun fort and six-gun martello tower augmented the initial facility. British raids up the Potomac in 1813 had prompted additional repairs and upgrades and the D.C. Militia made a plan to reinforce the garrison if needed. Colonel Decius Wadsworth recommended some major improvements, to include the emplacement of larger guns, but Secretary Armstrong rejected his proposal as too expensive. On 25 July 1814, Captain Samuel T. Dyson, the garrison commander and a member of the Corps of Artillery since 1796, registered hi s doubts that the fort could withstand any sort of strong attack because its landward defenses were nonexistent and its water batteries could not expect the necessary naval support if attacked by a British fleet. Secretary Armstrong felt that an enemy naval thrust up the difficult Potomac approaches was highly unlikely and authorized only a few superficial repairs. Dyson's complaint was one reason Winder sent the Alexandria Brigade to the fort during the invasion crisis. Winder told Dyson to destroy and evacuate his post if there was any major threat from the land. Down to sixty men the day Gordon appeared, the Alexandria Brigade somewhere in the District, and with no guidance from any of his superiors, the captain lost his nerve, held a quick conference of war, and decided to evacuate the fort after blowing up his magazine. At about 8 P.M. people just returning to Washington heard cannon fire followed by a huge explosion in the direction of the fort and their hearts sank at the prospect of another British attack.[5]

The next morning on 27 August, the marines landed and completed the destruction begun by Dyson's men. The British officers were still at a loss for the garrison's action. After looking it over, they judged it both well positioned and armed and estimated it would have cost at least fifty casualties to capture. The sailors and marines spiked a large number of garrison and field artillery and destroyed the fort's other buildings. A deputation from Alexandria visited Gordon to discuss terms, as they had done earlier in Washington with Ross and Cockburn. Bereft of their militia and with no means of defense,

---

4. Anon., Narrative of Naval Opns., 476; Muller, (1964), 88.
5. Clinton, 236, 242; Lossing, 938-939; J.D. Morgan, 9, 14; Wallace, 235.

the city fathers hoped to avoid a second conflagration. Captain Gordon told the delegation led by Gordon Swift that he would respect private property, but intended to seize any commercial property under terms he would announce once his force reached the port.[6]

That night Gordon's force reached the docile port and he levied his ransom for its submission. All shipping in the harbor was confiscated and all vessels that had been scuttled were raised. Additionally, he required all merchandise in the town brought to the docks to be loaded on the twenty-one various ships ultimately confiscated. The British modified only a demand that evacuated supplies be returned from the countryside. The city fathers pointed out the impracticality of such a requirement. As it was, they already had more than they could possibly haul away. The captured ships were loaded with approximately 14,000 barrels of flour, 800 hogsheads of tobacco, 150 bales of cotton, and smaller quantities of sugar, cotton, and beef. Even then an estimated 200,000 barrels of produce had to be left behind. The only incident during this pillaging was the attempted capture of Midshipman John W. Frazier of *Euryalis* while he was supervising the loading. Gordon dismissed this as some sort of junior officers' prank, but soon learned of more serious opposition building when Captain Henry L. Baker in brig *Fairy* (16) arrived on 31 August with orders from Cochrane for the force to return, and with the news that artillery had fired on him near Mount Vernon.[7]

The two seemingly unrelated events were the first indications that, at last, some sort of opposition was developing. This was indeed the case as Virginia militia and naval and marine groups, directed by Commodore John Rodgers, USN, began to deploy in an effort to stop the raiders from getting back down the river. Rodgers was commander of the frigate USS *Guerriere* under construction in Philadelphia. His duties there extended to providing marine and naval support to the Delaware River area and the adjacent regions of Maryland as well as command of United States Navy Lieutenant Charles W. Morgan's Delaware gunboat flotilla. On 11 July he and his men became involved in the Chesapeake fighting when HMS *Loire* raided Frenchtown and threatened Elkton. Brigadier General Thomas M. Foreman, commanding the First Maryland Brigade in Cecil and Harford Counties, successfully contained the British probe with the artillery companies of the Thirtieth and Forty-Ninth Maryland Regiments but, fearing a repetition, requested help from Rodgers.

6. Netherton, 229; Anon., Narrative of Naval Opns., 476; Byron, 57. The guns spiked at Ft. Washington included two 52-pdrs., two 32-pdrs., eight 24-pdrs., five 18-pdrs. in water battery, two 12-pdrs. in martello tower, two 12-pdrs. and two 6-pdrs. in a land battery.
7. Anon., Narrative of Naval Opns., 477-78; Muller, (1964), 88; Lossing, 939; Porter, 256.

Lieutenant Morgan immediately led a 250-man relief force with artillery on a rapid march from Newcastle to Elkton. The sailors and marines secured sites around Havre de Grace and Cecil Furnace before returning to the Delaware. The expedition proved so successful that the Secretary of the Navy ordered Rodgers to create a quick reaction force for Chesapeake service to deal with future emergencies.[8]

On 22 August Rodgers's Delaware command was ready to march based on receipt of orders dated 19 August to hasten to the Chesapeake area to reinforce the Baltimore and Washington defenses. The force reached Baltimore on 25 August, too late to help in Washington and without contact with the Navy Department. Rodgers decided to make himself useful in Baltimore. He coordinated with the miscellaneous naval forces in the area, ultimately creating a naval brigade with regiments led by Navy Captains David Porter and Oliver H. Perry. Porter had brought part of his USS *Essex* crew from New York City while Perry was already in Baltimore tending to the outfitting of the new frigate *Java* (60). Rodgers's actions and the naval cooperation in the crisis greatly facilitated Samuel Smith's final preparations in getting the city's defenses completed.[9]

On 27 August Secretary of the Navy Jones got back down to business, just as Captain Gordon's British raiders were closing in on Alexandria. On 29 August he sent orders to Rodgers to move part of his force to the Potomac. Anticipating this, Rodgers had already sent Porter ahead with about one hundred sailors and marines and he and Perry soon followed with another 400 men. While the men were forming ranks in Baltimore, Captain Perry's encouragement to them had a particularly nautical air, "My lads, we are going on a service which does not strictly belong to us, but if we go alongside the enemy I hope we shall do our duty." By 31 August, the entire force of 450 sailors and fifty marines with four 12-pounders had gathered in Washington and the officers crossed the Potomac to meet with Virginia militia leaders to discuss tactics.[10]

Brigadier General John P. Hungerford's Fourteenth Virginia Brigade made a forced march from the Northern Neck to help Alexandria, but was stopped well south of the town by city officials who implored them to allow the truce to continue. The brigade halted and took up positions on Shooter's Hill, site of the present Masonic memorial, where the men could clearly see the British loading booty at the Alexandria docks. They were joined there by

8. Paullin, 282; Mullaly, 71.
9. Long, 169; Paullin, 284; Porter, 255.
10. Long, 169-170; Balch, 284; Lossing, 940; Paullin, 284; Byron, 58.

Rodgers and Porter and much of the naval brigade and later by the Secretary of the Navy and Acting Secretary of War James Monroe. After Secretary Jones outlined the situation, Rodgers and the assembled officers decided Porter's and Hungerford's commands should go to White House south of Mount Vernon to build a river battery while Perry would take his men to Indian Head on the Maryland side to do the same thing. Rodgers would go back to the Navy Yard to prepare fire ships and cobble together a naval force to harass the British. When the conference broke up, Porter and Captain John D. Creighton, of *Argus* burned earlier in the Navy Yard conflagration, rode into Alexandria to see what was going on and were the "junior officers" who tried to grab Midshipman Frazier.[11]

By 30 August substantial numbers of regional militia were returning or coming in to join Rodgers's naval brigade and quickly were assigned to the District defenses or to Porter's or Perry's commands. The experience of the Virginia Shenandoah Valley militia was typical. On 22 August the news of the Benedict landings along with orders to muster and head for Washington reached the men. One entire brigade, Singleton's, headed straight for Baltimore by way of Frederick, Maryland. Most of those rallying in the emergency were volunteers as much of the enrolled militia was already on duty in Norfolk. Captain George W. Humphrey's Company from Jefferson County, for example, organized as best as it could that night and left for Harper's Ferry early the next morning. There they were reinforced by local volunteers and issued firearms from the government arsenal. On 24 August they headed by boat for Washington, electing their officers enroute. Throughout the day the men heard gunfire coming from the direction of Washington, followed by explosions in the evening. They learned of the Bladensburg defeat when they put into shore at Seneca Creek, Maryland where a courier from Winder's headquarters ordered them to head for Montgomery Court House. Their night march was illuminated by the glow from Washington and impeded by refugees from the city.[12]

Once at the Court House, they prepared to follow the rest of Winder's force to Baltimore where the British were headed next. They were soon intercepted by a Maryland militia officer who ordered them to join Walter Smith's Columbian Brigade in Washington, where they occupied Greenleaf Point in expectation of an attack from Gordon's force at Alexandria. When this failed to materialize, they shifted to Shooter's Hill south of Alexandria, with part of the District Militia. On the evening of 2 September they joined Porter's force

11. Groene, 14; Pórter, 256; James, 182; Paullin, 286.
12. J.S. Williams, 367-8; Wallace, 236.

setting up at the White House.[13]

The White House, or Heights of Belvoir, was a point south of Mount Vernon also known on the river as Washington's Reach, where bluffs rose thirty to sixty feet above the river, dominating the channel below. It was selected on the advice of Augustus Monroe and Ferdinand Fairfax, local gentlemen, because the channel veered toward the Virginia side of the river, forcing vessels toward it, and Porter assumed guns on the bluffs could fire down on passing ships while the ships would be unable to elevate their guns sufficiently to return fire. On 31 August Hungerford's and Porter's men were enroute when they learned that HMS *Fairy* was headed north. Hungerford rushed two artillery pieces to a point the sailors had just begun to clear of brush and opened fire on the unsuspecting brig, causing some damage, but alerting Captain Gordon to the need for hasty departure.[14]

Gordon ordered *Meteor* and *Fairy* to go downriver and impede the development of the American positions with their fire while he speeded up the loading process and got the force underway. On 1 September the two ships took up position but were unable to prevent Porter's men from emplacing three long 18-pounders which they had brought with them and preparing positions for two 12-pounders which arrived that night. Washington and Virginia militia later added six 9-pounders and two 4-pounders to this formidable battery. On 2 September strong winds delayed the main British force's departure and the crews were compelled to warp their way downriver. *Devastation* ran aground a few miles south of the city, forcing the rest of Gordon's fleet to hold up near Fort Washington. Several ships' boats including a captured American barge with a long 32-pounder, joined *Fairy* and *Meteor* to engage Porter's White House position. The firing went on throughout the day, but little harm was done even after Porter shifted an 18-pounder one mile from his main position to engage *Meteor*, only to have it driven back by British fire.[15]

On 3 September *Etna* and *Erebus* arrived to support their engaged sisters while the rest of the British force and its prizes gathered just opposite Mount Vernon. British fire became increasingly heavy although the rockets soon lost their terror value and the militia learned to dump earth on the sputtering charges to extinguish them before they exploded. Near misses with solid shot compelled Hungerford to shift his command post several times. *Devastation*'s

13. J.S. Williams, 369.

14. Groene, 16; Bushong, (1941), 73; Porter, 257; Lossing, 940-941.

15. Porter, 257-258; Anon., Narrative of Naval Opns., 478; J. Scott, III: 317; Irwin, 26; Napier, 86.

plight was noted by Commodore Rodgers who led a force of three fire ships and four barges against the stranded ship late on the night of 3 September. The fire ships were launched but unfavorable winds and quick British action prevented them from doing any damage. The British turned on the rest of Rodgers's boats and pursued them back to Alexandria where the commodore linked with some Virginia militia and prepared to defend the town. The next day Rodgers tried again, only to have his attackers repelled before they could do harm by a sharp exchange of small arms fire from some British barges hovering around *Devastation*. Rodgers's last action was another fruitless fire ship launch just as *Devastation* freed herself on the morning of 5 September.[16]

Firing continued throughout 4 September while the British worked on freeing *Devastation*. Porter used his militia to snipe at the British crews during the artillery exchanges. Several of Humphrey's Virginians were gunsmiths and expert shots and proved helpful in keeping the British at bay. Many of the riflemen got so excited they rushed down to the river's edge in full view to get a better shot, often suffering the consequences. On 5 September Gordon marshalled his force in preparation for a break-out once he learned *Devastation* was ready to go, ordering increased pressure on Porter's battery in the meantime. One of the American 12-pounders with two of the field guns got in a contest with *Erebus*, doing considerable damage to her, until forced to retire after running out of ammunition. While this was going on, Porter's sailors tried unsuccessfully to mount some new guns which arrived without carriages.[17]

Early on 6 September the British made a break for it with *Seahorse* and *Euryalis*, closing in on Porter's position with the smaller warships while *Fairy* led the prizes past under their cover without any losses. The first indication of the British move was a reduction in the volume of fire as the British ships moved to their new stations. Hungerford ordered three militia rifle companies to march up to protect the batteries in case of a landing. He also prepared to bring forward Lieutenant Colonel Richard Parker's One Hundred and Eleventh Virginia Regiment, Westmoreland County, and Lieutenant Colonel John Dangerfield's Sixth Virginia Regiment, Essex County, as well as detachments from Lieutenant Colonel Enoch Reno's Thirty-Sixth Virginia, Prince William County. While this was going on, Porter's batteries came under intense fire from the enemy ships. Gordon had solved the elevation problem by

16. Muller, (1964), 90; Paullin, 387; Groene, 17.
17. Porter, 258; J.S. Williams, 369; Bushong, (1941), 73. Jefferson County militiaman David Harris was killed while the wounded were Captain David Humphreys, Hugh McDonald, Richard Fielding, Thomas Steadman, and Joseph Blackburn.

ordering his captains to shift their ballast, giving them the angle necessary to deliver nearly forty-five minutes of devastating fire which silenced the American guns and could be heard by fearful crowds in Washington. Porter ordered his battery position evacuated and Hungerford held his main force out of range rather than bring them forward. At Porter's request, he sent 200 men under Major George W. Banks of the Sixth Virginia Regiment to reinforce the rifle companies which had remained along the shoreline to prevent a landing. While this was going on, the enemy slipped southward. They had sprung the trap.[18]

Their relief was short-lived, however, as they came under fire from Perry's battery at Indian Head. This position was manned by many of the Washington and Maryland Militia who had been at Bladensburg and were eager to vindicate themselves. Fourteen guns of various weights were manned by Peter's Georgetown and Burch's Washington Artillery Companies while infantry support came from Stull's and Davidson's D.C. Rifle Companies and parts of Steuart's local militia. *Erebus* ran aground within range and was badly damaged before darkness set in and she could get free. The British expected worse the next day. But Perry had run out of ammunition and the force and its twenty-one prizes sailed safely past.[19]

Gordon's plight was a matter of concern to Admiral Cochrane who diverted his fleet from the Patuxent to the Potomac, sailing twenty miles upriver before rendezvousing with the triumphant Gordon, returning to the bay together on 9 September. Gordon was justifiably proud of his achievement. In twenty-three days he had sailed 200 difficult miles in hostile territory, defeated all opposition, and captured twenty-one prizes full of valuable material. The voyage had cost seven British killed and thirty-five wounded as against eleven United States dead and nineteen wounded. He particularly cited Lieutenant King, RN, of *Seahorse* for exceptional gunnery, saying during the breakout he had disabled two United States guns with two shots. This claim was verified by an American observer who recalled that *Seahorse*'s first shot split a gun barrel to its touchhole while its second shot shattered another gun's wheel and carriage. Most of the junior officers on the expedition were promoted immediately while later all the ship commanders were made post captains, virtually assuring successful careers. Gordon himself was made a Knight Commander of the Bath. Few thought much of the effect the delay waiting for Gordon might have on future operations. They were just glad the Poto-

---

18. Groene, 18; Wallace, 237; Brannan, 409; Porter, 258.
19. Anon., Narrative of Naval Opns., 479; Brackenridge, 263; J.S. Williams, 295; Muller, (1964), 91.

mac diversion had turned out better than Peter Parker's Eastern Shore counterpart.[20]

The jovial and popular Sir Peter Parker was the grandson of an admiral of the same name who had served in American waters during the Revolution. The twenty-nine year old captain had wide experience in blockading and escort duties in the Atlantic and Mediterranean and had been a protegé of Lord Nelson. His force consisted of his frigate *Menelaus* (38), which he had commanded for over four years, and two tenders and its purpose was to commit sufficient mayhem on the Eastern Shore to tie down the militia and keep them from reinforcing either Washington or Baltimore. Cochrane further hoped Parker's northward raid would appear to threaten Baltimore enough so that it, too, would be unable to send reinforcements to the Patuxent area. Pressure on the Eastern Shore was kept up from the base at Tangier Island, whose boats concentrated on raiding from Dorchester County southwards as well as around St. Clement's Bay. Sir Peter's raid began on 20 August when *Menelaus* anchored off Rock Hall in Kent County and the marines landed to burn farms around the mouth of Swan Creek. *Menelaus* then scouted the mouth of the Patapsco, sending one of its tenders, *Jane,* well up the river towards Fort McHenry and capturing a local vessel before returning. Parker's force then entered Worton Creek at the northern end of Kent County and burned Henry Waller's farm, turned south, and committed as much damage along the shore as possible. On 27 August Parker's force anchored of Fairlee Creek and one hundred men landed the next morning to sack John Waltham's farm "Skidmore," burning all the buildings, storing grain, and standing wheat in the field. On 30 August Richard Frisby's farm, "Great Oak Manor," just north of the Fairlee Creek mouth, got the same treatment. One of the slaves there told the raiders of a militia camp nearby at Belle Air, the modern village of Fairlee, and Sir Peter began planning to attack it.[21]

The Belle Air camp consisted of 174 men from the Twenty-First Maryland Regiment organized into a rifle, a cavalry, an artillery, and four infantry companies. They were led by the regimental commander, Lieutenant Colonel Philip A. Reed, a fifty-four year old veteran of the Continental Line who had

20. J.S. Williams, 370; Napier, 86; Fraser & Carr-Laughton, I: 372; James, 185; Long, 171. Of the total casualties 1 American and 23 British were wounded at Indian Head and two British were killed. Capt. Napier reported the prizes as 1 gunboat, 3 ships, 4 brigs, 10 schooners, 3 sloops, and 1 tender.
21. Byron, 59; Chamier, 181; Jones, 255; Beitzell, 5; Andrews, I: 713; Skirven, 23; Lord, (1972), 244. Fox Creek and Norman's Cove in Dorchester Co. and John Kilgour's Farm on St. Clement's Island were especially hard hit from Tangier Island.

served throughout the entire Revolution and was a former United States senator as well. As soon as the enemy raids began, he moved his force to its camp about four miles from the shore and seven miles from Chestertown and trained his men to move immediately if presented with the chance to counterattack. Local coast-watchers kept him informed of British moves, and he had his men on full alert when he learned of Parker's 30 August shift from Frisby's Farm to an anchorage one mile north of modern Tolchester Beach opposite William I. Rasin's farm, "Chantilly."[22]

Parker was about to return to the main fleet, but when he learned of Reed's camp, he thought it too good a target to pass up and decided on leading one final raid to keep the militia intimidated. Starting at 9 P.M. he began landing 104 sailors and thirty marines at "Chantilly" under bright moonlight. The ships were so close to shore that instead of using a bosun's whistle or gong to alert the men for departure, all movement was ordered in whispers by the officers and sergeants. Lieutenant Henry Crease, RN, and Midshipman Henry Finucane, RN, led one division while Lieutenant Robert Pearce, RN, and Midshipman Frederick Chamier, RN, led the other, both under Sir Peter's overall command. After going about one quarter of a mile, the advanced guard tried to capture a vedette by approaching to within ten paces and opening fire. None of the startled cavalrymen were hit and they all galloped off. The disappointed British heard a series of pistol shots fading in the distance to which a distant cannon responded, alerting the countryside.[23]

Despite this, Sir Peter decided to continue and the column advanced down a road from the beach, the marine's rifles glittering in the moonlight and revealing their movement. Shortly afterward, they captured a mounted militia officer heading from his home to his unit's rendezvous point. Parker expropriated the man's horse but again, failed to consider that the man was responding to a general militia call-up and that the column might be taking on more than it could handle. They marched three more miles before making contact with American skirmishers deployed in the trees forward of a clearing known locally as Moorefields, behind which the main militia line could be seen.[24]

Colonel Reed had learned of the British landing at 11:30 P.M. and presumed that they intended to ravage "Chantilly" as they had other farms. He ordered his troops to advance across "Tulip Forest," "Eccleston," and "Everest" farms in the direction of the landings. Enroute, he learned from his ve-

22. Andrews, I: 714; Skirven, 25; Lossing, 945.
23. James, 186; Chamier, 183; Skirven, 25.
24. Chamier, 185; Skirven, 30.

dettes that the British were coming inland, apparently heading for the militia camp. He quickly ordered his supply officers to evacuate the camp. He halted and formed his command into line on a slight wooded ridge at Moorefields on Isaac Caulk's farm, adjacent to the road on which the British were advancing. The road ran west to east and hit the ridge's southern side at a ninety degree angle. The north side of the ridge was protected by a thick forest while to the front was a large fifty-acre clearing.[25]

Reed placed Lieutenant Aquila M. Usselton's and Lieutenant Henry Tilghman's Artillery Companies in the center of his line with state senator Captain Ezekiel F. Chambers's Company to their left covering the road. Reed's second-in-command, Major Joseph Wickes, placed the remaining infantry companies to the right of the battery, extending the line into the forest. The colonel personally led Captain Simon Wickes's Rifle Company and Second Lieutenant John Beck's rifle detachment forward to form a picket line along a slight hollow in the woods beyond the cleared field. The riflemen opened fire on Reed's order when the advancing British got to within about seventy yards. The Royal Marines instantly attacked the outposts and Reed slowly withdrew his men to the right of the American line, contiguous to Chambers's Company. He then took up a position in the center near the artillery.[26]

The American artillery fire forced the British off the road and away from the center toward the defenders' flanks. Sir Peter headed toward the American left with the marines while Lieutenant Pearce led the sailors to the opposite flank. He had a four-man rocket team which he hoped would offset the American artillery, however, the marine carrying the staffs was killed early in the engagement, rendering the weapons useless. Some of the American riflemen on the left fought a delaying action back to their main line, causing the marines to lose momentum. Sir Peter waved his sword and ordered them forward, prompting a blast of fire from Ezekiel Chambers's Company which wounded the Englishman. He was hit by buckshot and ball in the femoral artery and bled to death before his comrades could find the wound. His death ended the attack on that flank and the marines began to withdraw. The firing had been so intense that the artillery had run out of ammunition. Consequently, Colonel Reed ordered a withdrawal to some earthworks closer to camp where the remaining ammunition was redistributed. Lieutenant Pearce attempted to rush the withdrawing Americans only to find they were safely ensconced in their second, even more formidable position, and he ordered his

25. Byron, 60; Andrews, I: 716; Skirven, 25.
26. Chamier, 187; Skirven, 30; Andrews, I: 715.

men to withdraw. The British left on the field the bodies of Midshipman John T. Sandes and eight others killed, while the militia collected nine enemy wounded of whom six died soon afterwards. Substantial numbers of small arms were picked up the next day.[27]

In the meantime, the remainder of the raiding party managed to evade cavalry pursuit by moving with twenty-two wounded and Sir Peter's remains cross-country through ripe cornfields and woods. At one point, the party carrying Parker and wounded marine Captain Benjamin G. Banyon exchanged fire with one of the cavalry patrols. The group stopped at "Mitchell House" about one mile from the beach to use its well water in a hopeless effort to revive Sir Peter before reaching the ship's stay-behind party where the surgeon pronounced him dead. British casualties were ten dead and twenty-five wounded while the Americans lost three men wounded. Late on 31 August Lieutenant Crease, now senior officer, sailed *Menelaus* to an anchorage in the middle of the bay near Poole's Island to avoid being harassed by American gunboats. He sent his sad report of the Battle of Caulk's Field to Admiral Cochrane.[28]

Eventually, Captain Parker's remains were sent to Bermuda where he was temporarily buried in an elaborate funeral. Later, his remains were sent for final burial in London. News of his loss saddened Cochrane's fleet but was a morale booster for the Americans at a time when they needed it most. But his reports on the apparent vulnerability of the Patuxent were of greater long-term significance. The fact that no Eastern Shore regiment reinforced any of Baltimore's or Annapolis's defenders may have been mute testimony to the effectiveness of his diversion, whatever the outcome of Cochrane's next major effort.[29]

27. Skirven, 25; Chamier, 189; L.H. Tucker, 191.
28. Andrews, I: 715; Lord, (1972), 210, 244.
29. James, 186.

General and staff officer, 1815.

Chapter Eleven

ڒ

BALTIMORE PREPARES

A DMIRAL Cochrane was very concerned over the safety of Ross's Washington raiders and was extremely relieved when the command returned safely to the Patuxent on 29 August. He and Ross decided to accept their string of successes and, after giving the troops a few day's rest, left the bay for the Long Island area where raids promised the greatest potential to divert enemy forces from the northern border. All the senior officers agreed that their objective remained taking the pressure off Canada. The question was where that could best be done. Cochrane was aware of the need to begin massing troops for the operations planned for the Gulf of Mexico and did not think he had sufficient forces in the interim to take on any further major targets in the bay. Additionally, he wanted to get out of the Chesapeake before the advent of the malaria season. Admiral Cockburn, on the other hand, argued that the momentum of the earlier successes should be capitalized on with an attack on Baltimore.[1]

---

1. Mahon, (1965), 236; An Officer, 29; Muller, (1963), 173; Rutland, (1990), 166.

There was a bitter feeling amongst the British against Baltimore because of its aggressive and damaging support for the war and its notorious pro-French, anti-British attitude. Royal Navy officers were painfully aware that it was the most active privateering base on the American coast. Ships from the city began taking prizes within a month of the declaration of war and this symbolized to the British all of the costs and frustrations of this kind of war. Although ships and crews from many other ports participated, Baltimore's successes made it the center of privateering and most richly deserving of chastisement. Its destruction was one of the most desirable objectives considered in the naval officers' planning. They were supported by similar views back home where a London paper declared, "The truculent inhabitants of Baltimore must be tamed with the weapons which shook the wooden turrets of Copenhagen." In addition, they knew Perry's frigate *Java* (60) and the sloops-of-war *Erie* and *Ontario* (both 22) were being completed in the port. Their destruction and that of the large quantities of naval stores in Baltimore would be an important blow, not to mention the profits from prizes such a wealthy port would provide in the event of a success.[2]

General Ross initially agreed with Cochrane's assessment, believing the raid on Washington would have alerted Baltimore and allowed it to fully prepare for its defense. The rumors his withdrawing column deliberately spread on the way back to Benedict could come back to haunt them if they had achieved the desired effect and larger numbers of militia had been lured to Baltimore and Annapolis. He also pointed out that the shallow Patapsco prevented the navy from giving full support to a ground force. His aide, Captain Sir Harry Smith, strongly opposed to Cockburn's proposal, pointed out the poor physical condition of the men and stressed the negative effect a defeat would have on the news of the Washington success. Admiral Codrington added that there was little reliable information on the Baltimore defenses, making an attack highly risky. As late as 2 September Ross seemed to agree with these views and assured Sir Harry when he departed for Britain with the Washington raid dispatches, that he would not make the effort.[3]

Cockburn and Captain George De Lacy Evans, Ross's deputy quartermaster-general, continued to press Ross for a reconsideration and the general,

2. Hunter, 31; Brackenridge, 266; Colston, 111-112; Scharf, (1881), 89, 104, 112; Scharf, (1874), 355; James, 188; Buchan, 172. Fifty-eight of the approximately 250 privateers licensed came from Baltimore with 55 from New York City and far lesser numbers from several other seaports. The British lost about 2,000 ships in all categories throughout the war as a result of privateering.

3. G.C.M. Smith, 206; Robinson, (1942), 287; Bourchier, I: 320; Fortescue, X: 146-147.

without Smith to support him, gradually came around to their view. As the debate was going on, Admiral Cochrane continued plans to leave the bay. By 2 September all the ships had completed watering and those ships carrying wounded to Halifax and messages home were on their way. On 4 September Cochrane ordered Cockburn to take his force to Bermuda while he and Ross proceeded on *Tonnant* to Tangier Island to transfer troops and supplies to the vessels designated to continue the bay blockade once the main fleet headed for Long Island or the Gulf. By then Ross must have been in agreement with Cockburn as he got Cochrane to change his plans and approve an attack on Baltimore. Admiral Codrington later characterized his superior as too affable and amenable to pressure and attributes the change to Cockburn's, then Ross's, arguments. Cochrane later claimed it was his concern for Gordon's Potomac force which caused a delay followed by contrary winds which mandated staying longer in the bay, thus requiring something useful to do until the weather cleared.[4]

Cockburn and Codrington had heard unfounded rumors that Gordon was in trouble. On 7 September he ordered Cockburn, who had not made it very far due to the contrary winds, to turn about and rendezvous off the mouth of the Potomac while he went up that river to contact Gordon's returning ships on 8 September. Gordon's successful experience, newspaper reports bemoaning the city's alleged weaknesses, plus the late Sir Peter Parker's report of the vulnerability of Baltimore Harbor, all could have been the final factors in his decision to attack Baltimore. Whatever the case, on 9 September the reunited fleet gathered just off the Patuxent and the shipboard marines and sailors organized landing parties to support the ground forces. The next morning, leaving *Royal Oak* off the Patuxent to guard the unneeded transports and administrative vessels, it scudded northward to reach the Patuxent's mouth on Sunday morning, 11 September. As the fleet progressed, those on board saw activity in every little village or port on the way. Alert guns fired at each lighthouse and signal station they passed. The British took this as panic and fear when they should have seen it as preparation and determination. All the way to Baltimore people knew of their movements long before they appeared. The debate and indecision over what to do next had granted Samuel Smith and Baltimore eighteen precious days to get ready for a last ditch defense.[5]

Baltimore had been stunned by the news from Washington. The glow of

4. Bourchier, I: 319; Robinson, (1942), 290; Lord, (1972), 62.
5. George, 305; Fraser & Carr-Laughton, I: 273; Pack, 200; Robinson, (1942), 290; J. Scott, III: 326; Andrews, I: 717; Barrett, 167; Scharf, (1971), 90.

the fires raging in the capital brightened Baltimore's night sky and convinced its citizens that they would be next. Initially there was great concern over the fate of the local troops who had fought there. That was soon replaced by a sense of pride after news of their overall performance was received. Many persons evacuated their families and valuables but Samuel Smith's iron control mitigated panic and instilled a will to get the city ready for defense. Suspense turned to determination and each day without a British attack lessened people's fears and inspired greater efforts at preparedness. Smith's peremptory manner had not set well with some residents before the emergency, however, his past performance marked him as just the man for the moment. His Revolutionary War record, long prominence in state and local politics, and impressive performance during 1813, led to great public confidence in his leadership and assured him the widest connections to draw on for material support.[6]

Baltimore was particularly well suited to react effectively to the British threat. The city's prewar experience as a rising commercial power held it in good stead as its leaders and citizens considered the risks inherent in taking on the British. Its tradition of popular participation and rough egalitarianism made the appearance of emergency committees and their requirements quite acceptable as the crisis grew. Growing commercial success meant that considerable funds were available which could be called on to finance defense costs in the event of federal default. Leadership, starting with General Smith, came from a group of wealthy merchants, lawyers, and manufacturers, many of them self-made men risen from the city's artisan classes, who dominated local politics, assuring strong support from the voters of their former class. These hardheaded men were not surprised when their city became the main British target. Memories of British probes during the Revolution were still fresh in many minds. The federal government's focus on the northern frontier became apparent as soon as war was declared and this was confirmed repeatedly by the lack of federal help during British threats in 1813. The lack of support from Washington and Annapolis convinced most citizens that they would have to rely on their own resources to defend their city. They knew that British officers in Washington talked of attacking Baltimore next and they took the threats seriously.[7]

Mayor Edward Johnson reacted quickly in the crisis, assuring unity of command in Baltimore with his strong support for General Smith and galvanizing civilian support for defense with the formation of a new Committee of

6. Cassell, (1971), 199; Cassell, Response, (1971), 265; Brackenridge, 262, 265; Piper, 379; Lord, (1972), 62-63; Fortner, 290.
7. Brugger, 181; Cassell, Response, (1971), 261-263; Piper, 377; M.B. Smith, 103.

Vigilance and Safety. The old Committee of Supply formed during the 1813 crisis had done yeomen's work up to this point, dispensing nearly half a million dollars in support of the city's defenses. But, it was not structured to deal with the kind of situation confronting Baltimore in August 1814. Mayor Johnson continued to serve as chairman while Theodore Bland was secretary. Unlike its predecessor, its members were elected, thus assuring broad popular support for the extraordinary measures it had to take in the emergency. On 23 August each of the city wards voted for their representatives who met for the first time as a committee the next evening. The members were merchants and businessmen with social and professional access to every person who could somehow help in the crisis. The committee dealt with state and federal support issues and got involved in virtually all aspects of logistical support for Smith's men, security against espionage, and support for soldiers' families. At the first meeting James Buchanan, Theodore Bland, and Henry Payson prepared an address to the population describing the danger and outlining the requirements to meet it.[8]

On 27 August, the new group sent a subcommittee composed of Colonel John Eager Howard, one of Smith's old political foes, Richard Frisby, and Robert Stewart to request Samuel Smith to assume overall charge of the defense efforts. They did this on the urging of Brigadier General Stricker, Major George A. Armistead, USA, Commodore Oliver H. Perry, USN, and Captain Robert T. Spence, USN, perhaps in an effort to achieve unity in the crisis by avoiding interservice and intercomponant rivalries. The problem lay in the fact that Tenth District commander William Winder, as a regular army brigadier general, outranked Smith as a major general not in federal status. Smith had vainly tried to clarify the relationship with the War Department once he heard of his former subordinate's appointment. He does not appear to have encouraged the unusual cooperation amongst his fellow officers, but they seem to have colluded to assure stability and continuity at such a critical time. Smith would agree to the arrangement if Governor Winder concurred. In response, the governor appointed Smith to the command of Maryland troops in federal service, thus indirectly giving him federal status and arguable seniority over Brigadier General Winder.[9]

On the same day, the committee responded to Smith's request for manpower to complete the modest number of entrenchments on Hampstead Hill and on the Patapsco Neck. The city was divided into four districts based on groupings of voting wards. The free black and exempt white men from each

8. Andrews, I: 716; Cassell, (1971), 200; Scharf, (1971), 89; Hunter, 32.
9. Scharf, Balto. Co., 89; Andrews, I: 716; Cassell, (1971), 200-202.

district were directed to muster with their rations for a day's labor on the city fortifications in rotation, working one day in four. The committee requested owners to have their slaves report on the days their districts were required to work. Persons from outside the city were encouraged to come in and work any day they could. All the workers were asked to bring shovels, spades, wheelbarrows, and any other digging equipment and to leave them at collecting points for use until the labor was completed. On 31 August Smith's quartermaster Paul Bentalou announced he was out of funds. The committee successfully secured a $100,000 loan from local banks to pay for the costs of construction while it also received smaller contributions in cash and kind from public spirited citizens. Local banks continued to make loans and donations throughout the emergency, ultimately providing over $660,000, while persons without cash continued to provide for the care and comfort of the workers and soldiers.[10]

On 2 September the committee expanded its activities by forming a relief group to help the families of the soldiers and workers called away from home, and to establish hospitals in anticipation of battle with the British. It dealt with a growing food shortage by contracting with a local bakery to produce bread for the growing numbers of troops rushing to the city's aid. The committee issued a call to farmers in the region to bring in supplies for sale to the population and garrison. In its plea, it guaranteed that horses and carts performing such a task would not be confiscated, apparently a fear which had curtailed the flow of produce into the city. The popular response to the calls for work and help was overwhelming. Virtually everyone stopped their normal pursuits and gave whatever services and material they could afford. Women rolled bandages, farmers responded to the call for food, and residents donated building materials and military equipment in a final burst of preparation. Baltimore seethed with activity as large numbers of militia from all over arrived to help their local comrades, mixing with the citizens moving through town on any variety of errands and duties. Everyone felt that they had a part to play in perfecting the city's defense. The citizen's committees relieved Smith of nearly all major logistical concerns, allowing him to focus on the reception of the incoming manpower and completion of fortifications.[11]

The men serving in the militia made many sacrifices as a consequence of their service. The time away from their jobs greatly curtailed business activi-

10. Cassell, Response, (1971), 276; Saffell, 69; Scharf, (1881), 89; Lossing, 948; Brugger, 183; Lord, (1972), 60.
11. Cassell, Response, (1971), 277; Scharf, (1881), 90; Byron, 64.

ties in Baltimore, already slowed by the effects of the blockade. However, the frequent presence of British ships lurking at the mouth of the Patapsco served as a strong motivation for the city militia to take their duties seriously. The many alerts and drill requirements made the men increasingly confident and proud of their discipline and growing proficiency. At any one time, several thousand men were in some kind of duty status, often spending week-long tours in support of the regulars at Fort McHenry. When on duty, the routine involved a 6 A.M. reveille parade followed by three hours of drill after which the men were given some free hours to meet their civilian obligations before returning to barracks for several more hours of evening drill.[12]

Tension increased with news of the British Patuxent landings and the departure of Stansbury's force for Bladensburg. On 18 August General Smith ordered Brigadier General John Stricker's Third Maryland Brigade from the city on active duty and directed it to undergo a full field inspection the next day to assure it was as well equipped as possible. On 29 August he ordered all of Stansbury's Eleventh Brigade units not at Bladensburg to report to Hampstead Hill to be organized and assigned duties in the preparation of the defenses. He directed unattached officers from the Eleventh Brigade to scour the city for draft evaders. Drilling increased to six or seven hours daily in addition to the fatigue work and all militia were expected to attend on penalty of heavy fines. The news of the sack of Washington was followed by reports of Parker's raids on the Eastern Shore and of a clash on the West River between local cavalry and some of Parker's men. As a result, the tempo of drills and duties increased and Smith began sending units on extensive patrols along both banks of the Patuxent. These served as vigorous physical conditioning exercises, but also got the men and their officers familiar with the terrain. By 1 September the entire city began to assume the appearance of a huge garrison and the men became increasingly confident they could deal with any British threat. This confidence was due in part to their awareness of the sizeable forces coming to their aid from the hinterland.[13]

As soon as the British raids had begun on the Patuxent in July, Governor Winder had ordered militia from the western counties of the state into active service to reinforce the bay's defenders. On 23 July Lieutenant Colonel John Ragan took elements of his Twenty-Fourth Maryland Regiment from Hagerstown to Baltimore where they merged with local units to form the First Maryland Regiment under his command. On 11 August, two companies from Allegheny County arrived and joined them to become part of Stans-

12. Saltonstall, II: 549; Piper, 378-379; Tuckerman, 65, 67.
13. Bradford, 349; Tuckerman, 69; Moody, II: 559; Cassell, (1971), 199.

bury's brigade sent to Bladensburg. Their availability made it possible for Smith to retain most of his highly trained City Third Brigade manning Baltimore's defenses while meeting the government levy to defend Washington. Many of the survivors of Bladensburg returned to participate in Baltimore's defense where they were joined by additional units from Washington and Frederick Counties, formed in response to news of Bladensburg and Washington. Many of these came together spontaneously within hours of learning of Washington's fate and headed for Baltimore, getting organized enroute.[14]

The surge of manpower into Baltimore's neighboring counties was similar. News of Washington's plight persuaded Revolutionary War veteran Samuel DeWee, long past any legal obligation, to attach himself as a fifer to a company of the Thirty-Sixth Maryland Regiment being raised in Westminster and to go with it to Baltimore. His knowledge of military calls coupled with his musical ability, made him invaluable and he became the principal musician in the center part of Smith's fortifications on Hampstead Hill, not only playing the daily routine, but also fifeing the piquet guards out to Patapsco Neck and beyond. Brigadier General Thomas Foreman's First Maryland Brigade from Cecil and Harford Counties manned positions along the bay shore north and south of the mouth of the Patapsco in order to observe any British approach and to repel enemy scouting probes. Lieutenant Colonel William Smith's Forty-Second Regiment, Harford County placed a team at Gunpowder Neck which had a view as far south as Kent Island. Of Smith's three brigades, the First was the least experienced in drill and combat, but this duty helped reduce this disadvantage. General Smith ordered Foreman, in addition to his brigade duties, to assume control of any troops coming in from Anne Arundel and Prince George's Counties or from out of state. He also directed Foreman to work with Colonel Richard Waters, the state quartermaster, and Major William Bates, the assistant state adjutant general, to provide for the logistical needs of the gathering troops. Foreman was to work with Major George Armistead at Fort McHenry to redistribute supplies of ammunition stored at the fort.[15]

Smith ordered all the newly arriving forces to undergo the same drill regimen as his own men as soon as they arrived, both for their training and his assessment of their quality. Martin Gillette, a native of Connecticut and a Baltimore merchant, served in the city militia throughout the war. He wrote his father that starting in the middle of August, every militiaman in or coming into Baltimore was expected to perform the two or three hours morning and

14. Scharf, (1882), 186, 191; Williams and McKinsey, 167, 169-170.
15. DeWee, 343; Mullaly, 71; Preston, 245; Bradford, 349.

evening daily drills. At least 1,000 of them every day worked on the batteries or earthworks forming the city's defenses and every man from privates to officers was increasingly confident that the city could not be taken. Although the sack of Washington concerned everyone, he did not think it "so dishonorable to us nor the results so disastrous as first represented." He saw no real change in the war effort nor reduction in Baltimore's determination to defend itself. By 5 September he estimated there were at least 15,000 troops from all over the state, as well as from Pennsylvania and Virginia, in or around Baltimore.[16]

On 22 August the Sixth Virginia Brigade under Brigadier General Hugh Douglass had mobilized from its homes in Loudoun and Fairfax Counties in response to Winder's call for help. General Douglass ordered Lieutenant Colonel George Minor's 60th Virginia into Washington to search for equipment while the rest of his brigade gathered at Alexandria. When the Washington defenses collapsed, Douglass led his men to Montgomery Court House, then on to Baltimore where Minor's regiment caught up with him. On 31 August, Brigadier General James Singleton's Sixteenth Virginia Brigade from the Northern Shenandoah Valley left for Baltimore by way of Frederick, losing some of its units enroute to the reviving defense forces around Washington. On 5 September when the Valley men reached Baltimore, there was an insufficient number of Virginia troops to justify two general officers and in an embarrassing readjustment, General Singleton was relieved in favor of Douglass who assumed command of the troops. Douglass merged the Valley companies into a single unit under Lieutenant Colonel Griffin Taylor and designated it as First Virginia Regiment. Major General Smith assigned the Virginians to positions southeast of the city and along the banks of the Patapsco.[17]

Baltimore's defenders were encouraged even more by the return of Commodore John Rodgers, his sailors, and marines from the Washington area. As early as 3 September, as Rodgers was trying to deal with the British in the Potomac, Secretary of the Navy Jones grew concerned over enemy intentions for Baltimore. He alerted Rodgers to prepare for an immediate return to the city as soon as the threat to Alexandria was over. On 6 September the sailors and marines, with Captains Perry and Porter, left Washington in a wagon convoy to the cheers of citizens who lined the streets. Their presence back in Baltimore added a reassuring tone of calm professionalism which acted as a tonic

16. Brugger, 182; Van Why, 81.
17. Balch, 284; Butler, 28, 30; Valley regiments represented in the 1st Va. were 31st, 51st (Frederick Co.), 55th (Jefferson Co.), and 67th (Berkeley Co.).

to many of the worried militiamen. A citizen-soldier on duty in Light Street recalled the naval brigade preparing for a march, "Then there was a company of marines drawn up in array, stout hardy, weatherbeaten, jolly tars who seemed strangers to every fear, who had met danger in its every form, cool collected, indominatable. They were of nearly all colors—badly dressed, and apparently reckless and indifferent to life." With men like these, particularly with their artillery skills, the city seemed to be in increasingly good hands.[18]

Rodgers assumed command of the naval elements in Baltimore upon his return and cooperated with Smith in making the final defense preparations. Naval personnel supervised the completion of the waterside batteries while others looked to the placing of hulks in the Patapsco to thwart any water advance past Fort McHenry into the inner harbor. Other sailors learned the rudiments of infantry drill, much to the amusement of their militia and army counterparts, as barefooted tars bellowed, "Aye, Aye, Sir," to commands or screamed "Board, Board," when ordered to charge. Rodgers lost the services of David Porter who was ordered back to New York and of Oliver Hazzard Perry who became so ill he could perform no duties.[19]

Smith also added the United States Sea Fencibles to Rodgers's control. These were local men who had volunteered for federal service to augment the defensive forces of their home port. They were mostly unemployed mariners stranded by the British blockade. Two companies were raised in Baltimore to supplement the garrisons at Fort McHenry and its dependencies. Captain Matthew Simmones Bunbury left Stiles's Marine Artillery of the city militia to assume command of one of the companies destined for assignment to Fort Babcock. The second company was assigned to Captain William Addison, formerly an ensign in the Thirty-Eighth United States Infantry, and ordered to garrison Fort Covington (formerly Fort Patapsco), another one of Fort McHenry's dependencies. Bunbury's Company was fully operational by February 1814, followed by Addison's in May. Prior to the emergency, the units spent most of their time working on gun batteries and maintaining and operating the harbor boom which Smith ordered closed nightly starting in June. Addison's Company became so weakened by illness that it was replaced at Fort Covington on 12 September by sailors under Lieutenant Henry Newcomb, USN, and its remnants were attached to Bunbury's Company which had transferred to the water batteries of Fort McHenry.[20]

Volunteers from Pennsylvania began arriving concurrently with the sail-

18. Paullin, 289; Balch, 284; Muller, (1963), 180.
19. Paullin, 290-91; Mullaly, 74.
20. Sheads, (1982), 160, 162.

ors and Virginians. Governor Snyder's authority to call out the militia was hampered by some legislative changes not yet in effect. As early as 22 July he tried to respond to the initial federal levy by calling out his volunteer companies. On 26 August, he learned of the threat to Washington and ordered mobilization of all volunteer, rifle, and flank companies in southeastern Pennsylvania. He designated York as the rendezvous point for all Susquehanna Valley troops and Marcus Hook for men in the Delaware Valley, and ordered the movement of military equipment from Philadelphia to the sites. By 5 September, the men in York were organized into the Third Division, Pennsylvania Militia consisting of two brigades commanded by Major General Nathaniel Watson with Brigadier Generals John Forster and John Addams leading the brigades. Watson judged the threat to Baltimore so serious that he directed Colonel Archibald Jordan, one of his inspectors general, to rush volunteer and flank companies to the city as fast as they were ready, regardless of the condition of their parent regiments. He told these units to report to the headquarters of whomever was the senior officer in Baltimore and to take their orders from him. On 29 August Captain Michael Spangler's York Volunteers was the first such company to depart. It was an elite unit equipped and uniformed by the unit members themselves and as soon as General Smith took their measure, he judged them to be of the same quality as Sterrett's Fifth Maryland Regiment and attached them to it. Watson continued forwarding reinforcements to Smith until ordered on 19 September by the War Department to stop and shift his focus to the Delaware River. By then several thousand Susquehanna Valley men were in the Baltimore area and would remain until December.[21]

General Winder at Montgomery Court House organized the survivors of Bladensburg and those who had joined them after the defeat as quickly as possible. At 7 A.M. on 26 August cavalry vedettes scouting Bladensburg notified him that the British were headed back to the Patuxent, not overland to Baltimore. Relieved that he had some time, Winder started his men for Baltimore on the correct assumption that the British were preparing to attack it from the direction of the bay. He sent orders ahead to Smith and Stricker to hold all troops in the city as he expected it to be hit next and directed rations and munitions be gathered for Stansbury and the other reinforcements on the way. Once his column reached Snell's Bridge on the Patuxent, he left Stans-

---

21. Niles, VII: Suppl., 3; Gibson, 167, 165; Ellis & Evans, 76; Egle, 119. The Pennsylvania militia at Marcus Hook were also charged to support Maryland forces in Cecil Co. Two of the Pa. volunteers sent to Baltimore were James Buchanan and Henry Shippen, destined for greater fame in national and state politics; Scharf, (1881), 97.

bury in charge and raced ahead to the city expecting to assume overall command. He was stunned to find that although he was commander of the district of which Baltimore was a part, he had been preempted by the Committee of Vigilance and Safety and the governor who subordinated him to Smith.[22]

After a heated discussion with Smith, Winder wrote to Secretary Armstrong, protesting the situation and suggesting that he be commissioned a major general, where, as a federal officer, he would outrank Smith regardless of dates of rank. The disgraced Armstrong was on his way out and Acting Secretary of War James Monroe was too busy taking over his post to become embroiled in a command controversy at such a critical moment. He confirmed Smith's status as overall commander to Winder and directed his friend to subordinate his interests to what was best for the plans for defense. The disappointed general recognized the inevitable and had the loyalty and sense to yield. Smith assigned him to command a temporary division composed of Douglass's Virginians, the regulars of the Thirty-Sixth and Thirty-Eighth United States Infantry Regiments not in the fixed defenses, and Laval's United States Dragoons. Recognizing his secondary status, he wrote one last letter seeking to clarify his responsibilities as Tenth District commander and then gracefully put aside his hurt feelings by doing whatever he was asked to do for the city's defense.[23]

General Smith intended to make the defenses so formidable that capturing the city would not be worth the price to the British. As soon as he learned they had headed back to the Patuxent from Washington, he recognized that they had given up any consideration of conducting a landward assault from the southwest with secondary support from the bay, or east, side. Their move had committed them exclusively to an amphibious assault from the east. The shallowness of the Patuxent precluded their making a rush in full force against the heart of the city, and they would have to land a force to move against the city with lighter naval support using the river. The approaches to the city south of the Patuxent were dissected by creeks and estuaries flowing into the river that made any rapid movement of a large force impossible. The configuration of the land pointed almost exclusively to North Point as a place for a landing, explaining Smith's insistence that his officers became familiar with the terrain there. The Long Log Lane axis from North Point seemed the most likely approach to the city proper and such a land attack could be expected to be made in conjunction with some sort of naval thrust at Baltimore Harbor.[24]

22. Bradford, 347-348; Robinson, (1944), 179; Lord, (1972), 65.
23. Robinson, (1944), 183-4, 187; Pancake, (1972), 113.

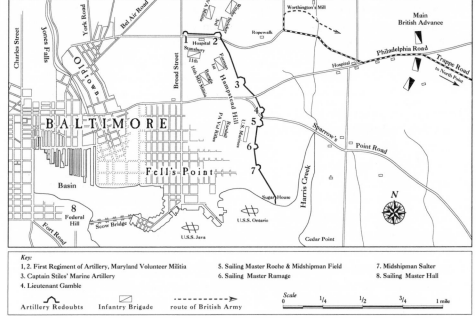

Rodgers' Bastion: September 13-14, 1814.

Smith decided to focus his mens' efforts on covering the eastern land approaches while improving the defenses in the harbor area. He designed a line figuratively anchored on Fort McHenry on Whetstone Point and the waterfront opposite it. This would anchor and protect the right flank of a heavily fortified line running along the crest of Hampstead, or Loundenslager's, Hill. Harris, or Collett's, Creek running along the base of the hill presented an enemy with another obstacle. Supporting batteries for the fort had to be completed to protect its south rear along Ferry Branch, and at Lazaretto Point across from the fort, to assure blocking the entrance into the harbor.[25]

Fort McHenry had not been well maintained before the war and the federal government did little to improve it once war was declared. As late as April 1813, many of its guns had not been mounted due to a lack of gun platforms. Colonel Decius Wadsworth, prodded by Smith, worked hard that spring to rectify the situation by emplacing the thirty-six 42-pounders and smaller guns from the broken up French ship of the line *L'Eole*, giving the fort considerable strength and greater range than its original guns had allowed. The entire tip of Whetstone Point was fortified with water batteries containing thirty-six guns, fifteen of them the big 42s from *L'Eole*, and trenches built to protect

24. Pancake, (1972), 118.
25. Pancake, (1972), 108; Scharf, (1882), II: 40; Sanford, 357.

the fort from amphibious assault and to better link with the Lazaretto battery in blocking the harbor entrance. The big guns were manned by fifty-four flotillamen led by Sailing Master Solomon Rodman and were provided infantry support by Steuart's regulars. The City Battery, also called Fort Babcock, one and one quarter miles west of Fort McHenry, was begun near Winan's Wharf in late April 1813 and was completed in the late summer as a crescent-shaped earthwork with six of the French 18-pounders and a hotshot furnace. Located near where Hanover Street Bridge crosses the Patapsco, it was manned by Sailing Master John A. Webster and fifty-two flotillamen at the time of the battle and was sometimes identified as "Fort Webster" in reports. Fort Covington, one quarter of a mile west of Fort Babcock slightly below Spring Gardens, was completed in December of 1813 and possibly contained ten guns. The Thirty-Eighth United States Infantry under Lieutenant Colonel William Steuart continued to work on Fort Covington until June, turning it over then to Addison's United States Fencibles who occupied it until September. Manned by eighty *Guerriere* sailors under Lieutenant Henry S. Newcomb, USN, it was built to dominate the Ferry Branch approaches into the city and support Fort Babcock. A seven-gun Circular Battery commanded by Lieutenant George Budd, USN, was built to the rear at the foot of Light Street, or present day Battery Square, to provide cover and support. A small earthwork right at Ferry Point manned by some of Douglass's Virginians during the battle completed the system of the Ferry Branch side of Whetstone Point.[26]

When the British threatened Baltimore the previous year, General Smith ordered construction of a boom across the harbor mouth as a supplement to Fort McHenry's fire. State Sea Fencibles under Lieutenant Solomon Rutter began work in May and finished in August, making a barrier that extended between both shores as well as 450 feet in front of Fort McHenry's water batteries. The boom consisted of a chain fastened to masts laid end to end and bolted together, while the part in front of the shore was made of timber laid end to end and anchored on piles. Smith ordered hulks prepared which could be sunk behind the chain boom. These were anchored in readiness until the fall of 1813 when they were taken to a wharf for maintenance before being brought out and sunk when the enemy fleet appeared in September 1814. These barriers were sustained by eight of Lieutenant Solomon Rutter's flotilla barges, armed either with an 8 or 12-pounder gun and each with a crew of thirty-four men. Additional flotilla barges patrolled the mouth of the Patapsco for added security. The three-gun battery with forty-five men at Lazaretto

26. Bradford, 199, 201, 207, 208; Walsh, 298-299; Mullaly, 64; Scharf, (1881), 90; Lossing, 949.

Point commanded by Lieutenant Solomon Frazier of the flotilla, could fire down the line of hulks as well as in support of Fort McHenry. The battery was secure from landward attack by positions occupied by 114 more flotillamen.[27]

Smith delegated these naval preparations to the recently returned Commodore Rodgers while he focused his energy on the completion of the landward defenses on Hampstead Hill and Patapsco Neck, and integrating the growing numbers of incoming manpower. Construction of the more than one mile of earthworks and gun positions was supervised by J. Maximilian M. Godefroy, a French émigré, engineer and architect, assisted by militia officers with some engineering or construction experience. It was expedited by the zealous support of nearly every able-bodied resident working in the daily dawn to dusk shifts mandated by the Committee of Safety and Vigilance. A Baltimore paper later quoted one of the workers saying, "They are throwing up trenches all around the city, white and black are all at work together. You'll see a master and his slave digging side by side. There is no distinction made whatsoever." On 3 September, General Smith ordered construction of a floating bridge across the inner harbor to alleviate the terrific congestion caused by the movements of the large numbers of workers and soldiers. It was in use on 5 September.[28]

The flurry of activity completed the eastern defenses by 10 September. The hard work of the relays of diggers had developed a system which would be manned by 10,000 troops in trenches interspersed with battery positions which contained sixty-two guns. Additional battery positions were prepared on the high ground behind the lines while even more had been built north and west of the main line along with breastworks and trenches. The line began at Harris's Creek, or Sugar House, where Midshipman William D. Salter, USN, of *Guerriere* and twelve men manned a single gun. It ran slightly northwest to Salter's left, to a point just off the right of the Sparrow's Point Road where there was an eighty-man five-gun battery commanded by Sailing Master James Ramage, USN, also of *Guerriere* Sailing Master George F. de La Roche, USN, of *Erie* with Midshipman Robert Field, USN, of *Guerriere* commanded a two-gun battery and twenty men that fronted the Sparrow Point Road. Further west at the junction of the Sparrows Point and Philadelphia Roads Lieutenant Thomas Gamble, USN, of *Guerriere* commanded one hundred men and seven guns situated to provide crossfire to adjacent batteries as well as dominate the roads. The marines from *Guerriere* under Lieutenant Joseph L. Kuhn, USMC, occupied earthworks that ran from Gamble's

27. Bradford, 206; Mullaly, 61-62; Scharf, (1881), 90.
28. Piper, 378; Sheads, (1989), 21; Cassell, (1971), 204; Andrews, I: 717; Lord, (1972), 65.

battery to Ramage's position. This part of the defenses was under the command of Commodore Rodgers and was known as Rodgers's Bastion. His mobile infantry force, stationed to the rear of the batteries, was composed of the local First Maryland Regiment now commanded by Captain Henry Steiner, who had replaced the fallen John Ragan, and a battalion of Pennsylvania riflemen led by Major Beale Randall, the Eleventh Brigade major.[29]

The line extended westward from the Philadelphia Road to the Belair Road, modern Broadway, where it ended except for a detached work on the west side of the road. It was built around positions manned by seven companies of the Maryland First Artillery Regiment, each with its own four 6-pounders and sixteen heavier guns from federal sources. Foreman's and Stansbury's Maryland brigades provided the infantry support and had cleared the area forward of the earthworks for more than one mile. They also manned a detached earthwork on McKim's Hill on the east side of the York Road (modern Greenmount Avenue). Another earthwork was being built about where today's Broadway crosses Gay Street. General Smith was so determined to continue the fight even if these formidable works were breached, that he ordered his engineer, Captain Samuel Babcock, to prepare the recently built cathedral to be used as a fort and to make arrangements to barricade the streets.[30]

As soon as he had learned of the British return to the Patuxent, Smith had established an early warning system under the supervision of Major William Barney, USMC, with observation stations along the shore from the Patuxent north to Baltimore, each linked to the other by mounted couriers. The major's effective intelligence system not only kept Cochrane's fleet under observation, but acquired information from deserters and released prisoners, keeping Smith fully informed of enemy movements and plans. On 10 September Barney notified Smith that the fleet was heading north and early morning sightings at Herring Point on 11 September reported at least fifty vessels headed for the northern bay. Later outposts confirmed these initial sightings just as the first enemy ships appeared off the mouth of the Patuxent. Some of the lighter ships immediately headed into the river after small craft, while the larger ships hovered off North Point. The time was at hand to test Smith's intuition and to validate the hard work of so many thousands of anxious Baltimoreans.[31]

29. Andrews, I: 729; Mullaly, 65; Scharf, (1881), 90; Lord, (1972), 66.
30. Piper, 378; Mullaly, 66, 102; Colston, 113.
31. Cassell, (1971), 279; Scharf, (1881), 346.

Rifle corps in action, 1813-21.

Chapter Twelve

✺

THE ATTACK ON BALTIMORE

L ATE on 10 September a few small British ships were noted scouting the mouth of the Patapsco. They were followed the next day by a growing number of vessels which aggressively probed upriver. By noon on 11 September, the appearance of men-of-war escorting troop transports through the haze, marked the beginning of the enemy attack. General Smith ordered three cannon stationed at the courthouse to announce the British arrival and alert the troops to report to their stations. Many of the men were caught attending church services and at one, the Reverend John Gruber of the Light Street Methodist Church dismissed his congregation with the benediction, "The Lord Bless King George, convert him, and take him to heaven, as we want no more of him." The entire city burst into intense, controlled activity as congregations poured out of dismissed services, drums beat, and mounted couriers raced about with messages. The militia gathered at their rendezvous points and drew a day's rations and thirty-six rounds of ammunition. Everyone was steady, although many of the men not unexpectedly were apprehensive as they went about their tasks. Private Martin Gillette later wrote his father about the strange feeling he had when "for the first time in my life I took my musket and entered a regiment" and headed for battle.[1]

The appearance of the British fleet on 11 September coincided with events on the northern frontier that together determined the outcome of the war. On 31 August Governor General Sir George Prevost with 12,000 red-coats had opened the main British effort of the summer with an advance up Lake Champlain, intended to secure the North Country to British control. Brushing aside New York Militia, he reached the Saranac River at Plattsburgh on 6 September where he encountered Brigadier General Alexander Macomb and a smaller American force. Both groups awaited the outcome of a parallel naval contest to determine control of the lake. On 11 September, even as Admiral Cochrane was reaching North Point, Lieutenant Thomas McDonough's United States squadron defeated a British force in Plattsburgh Bay, forcing Sir George, bereft of control of the lake, to withdraw his large force northward. The full effect of this defeat on the Ghent peace negotiations would depend, unbeknownst to the defenders of Baltimore, on their success or failure.

General Smith directed a small number of units to reinforce the light forces already on the south side of the Patapsco and, correctly judging the enemy fleet's deployment meant landings at North Point, he began his Patapsco Neck contingency plan by ordering Brigadier General John Stricker to get his city Third Brigade ready to march. The fifty-five year old native of Frederick, Maryland commanded the best trained unit with the most at stake of any in the city. Stricker himself was an experienced veteran of the Revolutionary War having served as a company officer in infantry and artillery units. He and Joshua Barney were brothers-in-law, married to sisters, and business partners. He had remained active in militia affairs while pursuing his mercantile interests and had been second in command to Smith when Maryland troops took to the field during the 1794 Whiskey Rebellion. He quickly had his brigade in hand and at 3 P.M. led it down Baltimore Street accompanied by bands and the cheering crowds, then out the Philadelphia Road and Long Log Lane to Bear Creek on the Patapsco Neck where it had occupied positions during the alarms of 1813. By sending Stricker to Bear Creek, Smith adopted an active defense, unlike the passive performance of Winder during the Bladensburg incident. His seizing of even this much of the initiative was good for morale and bound to make it more difficult for the British.[2]

At about 8 P.M. on 11 September Stricker's Brigade of about 3,000 men,

1. Van Why, 63; Brugger, 183; Sanford, 359; Mullaly, 82; Bryon, 65; Scharf, (1881), 92.
2. Sanford, 363; Brugger, 183; Scharf, (1881), 92; Cassell, (1971), 205.

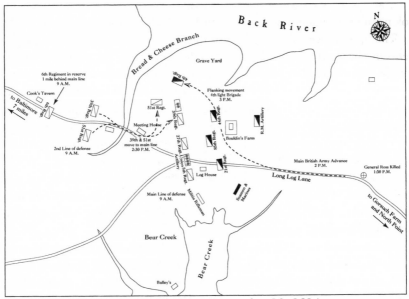

Battle of North Point: September 12, 1814.

reached the position on Long Log Lane below Trappe Road where a neck of land less than one mile wide is bounded to its north by Bread and Cheese Creek and by Bear Creek to its south. A wooded rise to the rear provided concealment and the marsh adjacent to Bread and Cheese Creek's source added to the left, or north, flank's security. The woodline was delineated by a strong zigzag fence fronted by open fields which any attacker from the direction of North Point would have to cross. The only cover in the fields was the house and buildings of the Bouldin Farm and some haystacks. Food and fodder had been placed at the site for just such a contingency as this. Stricker established his camp near a Methodist Meeting House behind the cleared area. More Pennsylvania and the Hagerstown, Maryland companies joined the command and were attached to various regiments. Meanwhile, Captain William B. Dyer's Fell's Point Riflemen marched an additional two miles east to a blacksmith shop where they set up a skirmish line. Lieutenant Colonel James Biay's Fifth Maryland Cavalry, about 140 strong, went with them and rode one mile further to Gorsuch's Farm where its vedettes screened possible landing points.[3]

3. Andrews, I: 717; Lossing, 951; (1972), 124; Scharf, (1881) , 92; Spaulding, 325. The new foreign units were Dixon's Marietta, Pa. Co. attached to 6th Md., Metzgar s Hanover, Pa. Co. and Quantrell's Hagerstown, Md. Co. both attached to 39th Md.

The landing place the British selected was an open area on the west side of North Point, at modern Fort Howard, as there was no place closer in the shallow Patuxent that the big ships of the line could advance to provide fire support to units going ashore. Early in the evening of 11 September, the fleet completed gathering off North Point and the order went out for the troops to prepare a light pack, cook three day's rations, and draw eighty rounds of ammunition. The actual landings began about 3 A.M. on 12 September. Gun brigs came in close to shore to provide fire in case of resistance, while the landing boats came in groups, each led by a barge armed with a carronade. The shadows of the big ships and the movement of their small craft were discernible in the moonlight from Baltimore. This display of military power and efficiency was daunting to the citizens and defenders alike, many of them with fresh memories of Bladensburg, nevertheless all but a few remained grimly determined to resist.[4]

General Ross was aware of some kind of American position three miles from the landing point. As soon as the Light Division was organized, he set out to investigate at 7 A.M., leaving Colonel Arthur Brooke in charge of the landing with orders to advance as soon as the artillery was ready to move under escort of the 21st Foot. The Light Brigade, consisting of the 85th Regiment and the light companies of the foot regiments, all under Major Timothy Jones of the 4th Foot, set out at a brisk pace.

The six field pieces and two howitzers, all horse drawn, were landed at 8 A.M. and Brooke decided to advance even as other units were still unloading. The conditions were stifling and several soldiers collapsed from the heat. Landings continued until by noon about 4,000 men were ashore. While the landings progressed, Admiral Cochrane led the shallower draft vessels upriver to serve as a distraction and to later provide support for the anticipated assault on the city.[5]

The troops advanced four miles from North Point in about an hour to unfinished earthworks dug at the narrow neck between Humphrey Creek and Back River (Greenhill Cove) before halting for a rest. Although far from complete, the works indicated that their architects knew what they were doing and led Ross to anticipate imminent contact. He ordered a halt so the column could close up. It was here Colonel Brooke found Ross and Cockburn resting on the steps of the nearby Gorsuch farmhouse and briefed them on the state of the force. The general ordered him to go back and keep things moving, as

4. Scharf, (1881), 90-91; Andrews, I: 718; George, 310; An Officer, 30; Anon, Hist. of 4th., 121.

5. Scharf, (1881), 90; J. Scott, III: 332; Byron, 66; Brooke Papers, 180-181.

he wished to get close enough to Baltimore to launch an early morning attack. While this was going on, a patrol captured three cavalrymen from Captain James Sterrett's First Baltimore Hussars as they tried to evade the column. Upon interrogation, the men told Ross there were 20,000 men in the city defenses, prompting Ross to comment, "I don't care if it rains militia." He concluded from the interview that his advance would face little more than light forces anywhere on the Patapsco Neck and that he would encounter nothing substantial before reaching the Hampstead Hill earthworks. He had no inkling of the relative nearness of Stricker's whole brigade.[6]

Meanwhile, at 7 A.M. General Stricker learned of the British landings from the cavalry. He immediately sent back his baggage and formed a mile-long battle line across Long Log Lane just inside the woods line. The Fifth Maryland moved to the south of the road with its right contiguous to Bear Creek and Captain John Montgomery's Union Artillery formed across the road itself. Lieutenant Colonel Kennedy Long's Twenty-Seventh Maryland took up positions to the left with its flank anchored on the Bread and Cheese Creek marsh. Stricker formed a second line 300 yards further back with Lieutenant Colonel Henry Amey's Fifty-First Maryland on the right and Lieutenant Colonel Benjamin Fowler's Thirty-Ninth Maryland on the left. Lieutenant Colonel William McDonald's Sixth Maryland took up a reserve position about one half of a mile to the rear on Perego's Hill near Cook's Tavern. Stricker's plan called for the front two regiments to hold as long as possible, then leapfrog behind the two to the rear and form on the right of McDonald's regiment in reserve.[7]

The cavalry kept Stricker well informed of the British advance. He hoped as they came closer that Dyson's riflemen to the front would create an extended delay. This was not to be, however, as they overreacted to a rumor that a second amphibious landing on the Back River was about to cut them off, and they hustled back with the cavalry. Disappointed, Stricker placed them and the returned horsemen along Bear Creek to the right of the Fifth Maryland. He soon learned of the British halt at Gorsuch's and, after some hesitation, he decided to deploy another force under Major Richard K. Heath of the Fifth Maryland to try to develop a fight before darkness put his less experienced infantry at risk. Heath advanced with the 150 Fifth Maryland men in Captains Aaron Levering's and Benjamin C. Howard's Companies as well as

6. Andrews, I: 720; Mullaly, 85; Spaulding, 323; Morgan, 9; Scharf, (1881), 89; Brooke Papers, 181. The captured cavalrymen were Sgt. William B. Buchanan, Pvt. James C. Gettings, and Pvt. Richard Dorsey.

7. Andrews, I: 725; Colston, 114; Muller, (1963), 189.

Captain Edward Aisquith's seventy-man Rifle Company and a 4-pounder gun supervised by Lieutenant John S. Stiles. At about 1 P.M., just after Major Heath deployed his flankers, they unexpectedly contacted the British advance guard one half of a mile from their main line and entered into a brisk skirmish. This lasted but a few minutes before they were forced back after some losses, including the major's horse.[8]

The British advance resumed from Gorsuch's Farm at about 9 A.M. and proceded for two miles until the light infantry advanced guard bumped into Heath's men in dense woods. Firing began immediately, with Ross and Cockburn riding forward to join the point element when they heard the gunfire. Although the Americans were falling back, the British estimated Heath's numbers to be almost double what they actually were and Ross decided it was time to get the main body forward quickly. He turned about saying, "I'll bring up the column" and was hit through the arm and chest with a combination of buckshot and ball and fell from his horse. The animal raced to the rear just as the main body was coming forward, causing the men to fear the worst. Their fear was confirmed as they saw the little group of men gathered around the dying general. Others coming forward knew something was wrong by the sudden increase of galloping aides. As the men of the 85th Regiment marched past the point where Ross was being treated along with five other British wounded, they saw three dead Americans nearby and stoically continued their advance. Later, a naval work party carried Ross's remains back to the landing point as the forces became fully engaged.[9]

Colonel Arthur Brooke was to the rear of the column, hastening it forward in accordance with Ross's orders when he learned of the general's wounding from Lieutenant George De Lacy Evans. Brooke rode two miles ahead of his marching column until he encountered the light infantry engaging what seemed to be the main American force, complete with artillery. The fallen general had not informed Brooke of his intentions but there seemed little choice but to engage the enemy. Brooke ordered his artillery forward to engage his opponent's artillery while he made a reconnaissance and waited for the infantry to move forward. He commanded the light troops to screen the

8. Andrews, I: 726; Scharf, (1881), 347; Mullaly, 85.

9. Lingel, 144; Scott, III: 333; Colston, 114; Byron, 66; Andrews, I: 720; Barrett, 169; An Officer, 30. Privates Daniel Wells and Henry G. McComas of Asquith's company, killed in the battle, are credited by some as having fired the fatal shots. A British sergeant in Ross's headquarters group later reported that three Americans were caught in the act of gathering peaches. One of their number in the fruit tree jumped to the ground and all three men fired, mortally wounding Ross. Colston, 115, says none of the three could have been Wells or McComas. Ross's remains were buried at St. Paul's Churchyard, Halifax on 29 Sept.

entire front while he observed the American position across what he judged to be a 500 yard wide clearing. He directed his men to get something to eat while he developed his plan and got the regiments into position. From their perspective, the American line with each of its flanks anchored on water looked strong. Across the field they could see a line of infantry and artillery in the woods behind fence palings, and a reserve line in the brush behind that.[10]

The British Light troops advanced into the open field, sniping as they could at Captain Philip B. Sadtler's Baltimore Yeagers occupying the farm buildings. Brooke quickly deployed the 2nd Brigade behind this screen to form his main line and kept the 3rd Brigade in reserve further to the rear, with orders to support the main battle line or head for the American right as the situation developed. Brooke was careful in his deployment as he credited Stricker with nearly three times more men than the approximately 3,000 he had on the field. Seeing a weakness on the Bread and Cheese Creek side of the American line, he ordered Major Alured D. Faunce to take his 4th Foot along a concealed route and turn that flank. This move took fifteen minutes and in the interim, he used rocket and artillery fire to keep the Americans distracted. The rockets began sailing into the American left at about 2:30 P.M., at first doing little more than alerting Stricker to the attack. Captain John Montgomery's full six-gun battery immediately replied, drawing British artillery fire which pounded the United States center and left. Noting the probe to his left, Stricker ordered Montgomery to stop his counter-battery action and to change to canister.[11]

The British light infantry quickly made for the farmhouse occupied by Sadtler and his Yaegers, rushing it under the protection of an increasing volume of rocket and artillery fire. The Americans torched the buildings and withdrew even as the flames spread to the nearby haystacks. British observers credited their rocket fire with the damage. The 2nd Brigade troops deployed right and left as they reached the field and formed line behind the skirmishers. The naval detachment under Captain Edward Crofton, RN, formed in the center of the main line with the 21st Foot in column on the road behind them while the marines under Captain John Robyns, RM, deployed left toward Bear Creek and the 44th Foot moved to the left of the sailors. Admiral Cockburn seemed to be enjoying the experience as he rode along the line, conspicuous on a white horse and in a gold-braided blue uniform. He drew fire wherever he went to the strained amusement of the infantry. The United States artillery concentrated their fire on the 21st Foot and the sailors in the

---

10. Brooke Papers, 182-183; J. Scott, III: 336; Fortescue, X: 148; Andrews, I: 720.
11. Andrews, I: 726; Mullaly, 85; Muller, (1963), 188; An Officer, 31; Brooke Papers, 183.

center, as well as the British guns. The blazing farm and the exchange of fire and rockets made a spectacular scene which the disciplined British troops endured until the 4th Foot reached its positions on the American flank.[12]

Seeing the continued British interest on his left, Stricker ordered the Thirty-Ninth Maryland and two guns to move to the left of the Twenty-Seventh Maryland and extend the American left further across Bread and Cheese Creek marsh. He ordered the Fifty-First Maryland to march from the right side of the road to behind the main line, and to establish a new line perpendicular to the Twenty-Seventh's position and connect to its left flank, hopefully making it impossible for the maneuvering British to turn the position by way of the marsh. Lieutenant Colonel Amey botched this maneuver and Stricker's aides rushed to get the Fifty-First into its proper position while under heavy enemy artillery and rocket fire. Unfortunately for the disorganized Americans, the 4th Foot had reached its jumping off position and Major Faunce signalled his readiness to Colonel Brooke. The colonel rode down his line to assure everything was ready and at about 2:50 P.M. gave the order to advance.[13]

The 4th Foot musicians blew the charge, the call was quickly taken up all along the British line, and the redcoats and sailors began to cross the yards of open space between them and the defenders. The American volume of fire increased at once as Montgomery's gunners let loose with scrap and canister and every infantryman who could, blazed away with his rifle. Cheering, they fired first a volley and continued with heavy independent fire. The pressure was too much for the confused Fifty-First Maryland which panicked, firing a volley over their comrades at the advancing 4th Foot before dissolving in confusion under the British fire. Their disarray caused a battalion of the Thirty-Ninth Maryland to collapse as well, and both groups ran away. But the rest of the United States line held. Stricker was focusing on the attack on the center of his line and was unable to take action before the collapse. The sailors in the center of the British line, less disciplined than their marine and army counterparts, were understandably eager to end the torment of the American fire and moved ahead of the rest of the line. Brooke ordered the whole line, then about twenty yards from the Americans, to deliver a volley and charge with the bayonet. There was a climactic ten minute struggle during which the rest of the American left fell apart and Stricker ordered his line to break contact and fall back. The American right held briefly and inflicted considerable damage to the 21st Foot, but soon withdrew to the protection of Mc-

12. Andrews, I: 722; James, 188; Scott, 337; Spaulding, 325.
13. Andrews, I: 722, 726; Byron, 68.

Donald's regiment on the reserve line at Cook's Tavern.[14]

Once everyone was gathered at Cook's Tavern, Stricker allowed the men a short rest while organizing to repel any British pursuit. The British probed briefly, capturing a few United States stragglers. But Brooke was deterred by his overestimation of the size of Stricker's force and wanted to get the 4th Foot extricated from the marshy area and the rest of his exhausted force in hand before making any further commitment. Consequently, he recalled his men to police the battlefield and get reorganized while the light infantry engaged the few American marksmen remaining in the area. The British set up on the battlefield and used the partially burnt farm and the nearby Meeting House as a hospital. Twenty-six Americans wounded and captured on the battlefield were treated by the British and paroled into the care of United States surgeon James H. McCulloh to be exchanged for a like number of British casualties being treated at Bladensburg. Early on 13 September, after the previous day's intermittent showers had turned to steady rain, a courier came up Bear Creek and pronounced it navigable. The British wounded were loaded on confiscated local carts and sent to the creek for evacuation to the fleet. It had been a bad day, perhaps worse for the British who at this Battle of North Point had lost the popular Ross with thirty-eight others killed, 251 wounded, and fifty missing to Stricker's twenty-four killed, 139 wounded, and fifty captured.[15]

Some desultory skirmishing continued even after Brooke's recall order and Stricker decided a further withdrawal was necessary to avoid nighttime fighting. He led his men down Long Log Lane to some high ground designated earlier by General Smith at Worthington's Mill, east of the Belair Road and about one half of a mile forward of the left flank of the main defenses. They were joined from positions south of the Patapsco by General Winder with Douglass's Virginia Brigade and Captain John Burd's Company of United States Dragoons. The wet, exhausted men continued to ready themselves for more contact, then got what rest they could. Smith kept his most reliable units mobile by placing Stricker's and Winder's men in a position to maneuver on the flank of the Hampstead earthworks instead of taking up positions in them. With few exceptions, the earthworks were manned by the enrolled militia units on the assumption that even untried, untrained men could do reasonably well fighting from a protected position.[16]

The British spent a miserable night on the old battlefield in heavy rain

---

14. Lingel, 145; Brooke Papers, 184; Andrews, I: 722, 727.

15. Spaulding, 326; Byron, 69; Saffell, 77; Chesterton, 147, 150; Brooke Papers, 201-202; Barrett, 178.

which began about midnight, soaking everything and rendering many weapons inoperable. The courier from the fleet had arrived in the darkness with word that the navy was taking up bombardment positions against Baltimore harbor to support the ground attack. Brooke aroused the command at dawn, about 5:30 A.M., and ordered the men to ground their packs and blankets and carry only their knapsacks and weapons for the final approach to Baltimore. The advance was greatly slowed by the number of trees felled across the road by Stricker's men, and the need for the point guard to stop and deploy at nearly each barrier in case it was an ambush. The rain and the necessity for the flankers to plow through the wet brush on either side of the route soaked the lightly clothed men before the column came in sight of the Hampstead Hill defenses at about 10 A.M. The march was accompanied by the sound of the naval bombardment of Fort McHenry which began at 6 A.M. and continued throughout the day and night. Emerging from the forest into cleared fields on the Philadelphia Road just south of its junction with Long Log Lane, the British were stunned by the scale of the American defenses. Brooke had assumed Stricker's command was the main enemy force. He established his headquarters in the Kell House south of the junction and tried to form an attack plan.[17]

One look at the position and Brooke realized it could not be taken in a daylight frontal attack. He credited Smith with having even more than the approximately 11,000 men and one hundred guns he did have massed in the defenses. The area between the two forces had been cleared, offering little cover or concealment. The rainy weather added to the defense by softening the soil and making the approaches to Hampstead Hill slippery and boggy. Brooke had received a message from Admiral Cochrane, who had studied the American positions from his vantage point in the harbor and suggested that he try to turn Smith's north flank. Brooke headed west toward the Harford and York Roads where he hoped to make his turning movement. Earlier, Winder and Stricker had formed their brigades in line with the trenches and skillfully advanced to form a line on high ground west of the Belair Road and perpendicular to the main American position. This compelled Brooke to turn around and regroup opposite Smith's center where at about 1 P.M. his skirmishers advanced down the Philadelphia Road to within one mile of the American line, probing the defenses in preparation for a possible night attack. Smith, in turn, ordered Winder and Stricker to advance closer to the Belair

16. Van Why, 83; Robinson, (1944), 195; Fay, 247-248; Saffell, 79; Cassell, (1971), 206; Brackenridge, 268-269; J. Scott, III: 338; Andrews, I: 727; Scharf, (1881), 95.
17. Gleig, 101; Anon, Hist. of 4th, 122; Brooke Papers, 193; Spaulding, 327; Scott, III: 343.

Road to threaten Brooke's rear and cut off his avenue of escape if he moved closer to the main line. The British troops took over William Bowley's house, "Furley Hall," as well as Joseph Sterrett's estate, "Surrey," and waited for their leaders to decide what to do next.[18]

General Smith observed Brooke's efforts from a command post at the highest point of Hampstead Hill where he could view his entire force as well as the British to his front and the harbor to his right. The men in the trenches watched the British maneuvers with interest as they stood thigh-deep in the water and mud-filled earthworks. John L. Dagg, a young enrolled Loudoun County, Virginia militiaman in Captain James Cochrane's Company, Fifty-Seventh Virginia Regiment, recalled that his unit's position gave them a clear view of Fort McHenry, the British fleet, and the road to North Point. They saw smoke from the battle on the 12th and advanced from their trenches to support Stricker's withdrawal and assist in dragging the wounded back from that encounter. When Brooke's force appeared, they shifted position several times to conform with British movements, always with the enemy in sight and within earshot of the ferocious bombardment of Fort McHenry. At 3 P.M. British attempt to close with the fort and the fort's response provided background sound to the British maneuvers against the American center.[19]

Admiral Cochrane had shifted his flag to the frigate *Surprise* commanded by his son, Captain Thomas Cochrane, RN, to supervise the attack on Baltimore harbor in support of the ground force. He anticipated the quick reduction of Fort McHenry followed by a thrust into the harbor to intimidate the city itself while dominating the water flank of the Hampstead Hill defenses, allowing the army to defeat Smith's defenders and occupy the city. Fort McHenry was the first objective, but could not be approached by the larger ships because of the river's depth.[20]

A total of sixteen shallow draft vessels led by the frigate *Seahorse* took most of 12 September to work their way up the Patapsco, a number of them running aground in the process. By about 3:30 P.M. *Seahorse* and her sister frigates *Surprise* and *Severn* anchored with the brigs and tenders five miles away from Fort McHenry. The bomb ships *Meteor, Aetna, Devastation, Terror,* and *Volcano,* the latter two just joined from Europe, and the rocket ship *Erebus* continued to within about two and one half miles of the fort. The bomb ships posed a potent threat to the fort as each could fire the equivalent

18. Brooke Papers, 311; Barrett, 172; Colston, 119; Mullaly, 95; Carroll, 245; Fay, 248; Andrews, I: 727.
19. Cassell, (1971), 206; Dagg, 15; Piper, 382-383.
20. Cassell, (1971), 207; Mahon, (1965), 326; Skinner, 344.

of ten inch and thirteen inch shells at the rate of about one every five minutes. *Volcano* had some big 190-pound incendiary shells used to support night attacks by providing light from their fires. While the ships assembled, Cochrane was dismayed to see Rutter's flotillamen completing the barrier of hulks behind the harbor boom, with gunboats deploying behind them, ending any chance at a dash into the harbor. Nevertheless, he readied the bombardment as the fall of Fort McHenry was essential to success. Preparations continued through the night while the marines and some of the crew manned small boats against fire ships and torpedoes.[21]

Major George Armistead had completed the manning of Fort McHenry's defenses over the preceding days and it was as ready as possible. On 10 September, Lieutenant Colonel William Steuart and Major Samuel Lane combined four companies of the Thirty-Eighth United States Infantry with one from the Twelfth and two from the Thirty-Sixth United States Infantry Regiments to make a 527-man composite unit which they led into the outer ditch. Their mission was to repel any landings while supporting Rodman's flotillamen, Captain John Berry's Washington Artillery Company, and Captain Charles Pennington's Baltimore Independent Artillerists from the First Maryland Artillery Regiment as they worked the thirty-six guns in the lower works or water battery. The regulars joined Bunbury's Sea Fencibles already in the lower works who in turn were reinforced by Addison's Fencibles on 12 September. The artillery in the fort itself included The Baltimore Fencibles Artillery led by Captain Joseph H. Nicholson, a local judge, and was under the overall command of Captain Frederick Evans, United States Artillery, with his regulars. The Lazaretto Battery and the gunboats guarding the hulks protected one flank of the fort while Forts Covington and Babcock guarded the Ferry Branch side of Whetstone Point. Late in the afternoon of 12 September, the news of Stricker's withdrawal from Patuxent Neck reached the city and the Committee of Vigilance and Safety ordered a blackout while newspapers reminded persons to be ready to douse any fires caused by rocket fire. It was obvious to the defenders of Fort McHenry an attack was imminent.[22]

At 5 A.M. on 13 September the British rocket and bomb ships, escorted by the brig HMS *Cockchafer*, approached Fort McHenry. From a distance of over two miles, Captain David Price's *Volcano* heaved to, fired a few shots for range, and moved closer. By 7 A.M. the ships were at a distance of under two

21. James, 190; Fraser & Carr-Laughton, I: 273; Sheads, (1988), 172; Lossing, 954; Lord, (1972), 69.

22. Pancake, (1971), 126; Mullaly, 62; Andrews, I: 730.

miles when *Cockchafer* and all the other vessels fired a broadside. Building foundations in the city trembled from the blast and many civilians raced to the same rooftops from which they had seen the glow of Washington burning only three weeks before. The fort's guns quickly returned the British fire, but when a round damaged *Cockchafer*'s rigging at about 8:40 A.M., Admiral Cochrane ordered a slight withdrawal, getting the British ships out of the fort's range a little after 9 A.M. The firing from that position could be done only by the bomb ships. To boost morale, Major Armistead allowed his gunners to fire until 10 A.M. when he ordered a cease-fire to conserve ammunition. The crews endured the British fire, remaining calm and steady, looking for a chance to participate. By the time of the American cease-fire, Cochrane experienced his first doubts about his chances of success. He sent a note to General Ross expressing his concerns over the apparent ineffectiveness of the bombardment and his fear that the cost of seizing Baltimore might be too high. His confidence was undermined further when the unopened note was returned with news of Ross's death and he readdressed it to Colonel Brooke.[23]

From his position inside the fort, Captain Frederick Evans described the bombardment as overwhelming. When three big mortar rounds crashed into the fort, one of his men was so stunned that he began to shake uncontrollably. Evans told him to take cover under one of the guns, only to see the man and a nearby soldier killed by shrapnel from another explosion. Food was scarce throughout the attack because of difficulties in bringing it in and distributing it. Evans remembered a female water carrier disintegrating from a direct hit. Soon after, a round he described as big as a flour barrel landed near him but failed to explode. Inscribed along its side were the words "a present from the King of England." Black humor was not restricted to the British. Amid all the chaos, a very confused local rooster took cover in the rear ditch of the fort, and began crowing defiantly. This broke the tension and one of the militiamen promised the bird a full meal if they both survived. Happily, the bird got its rations later.[24]

At about 2 P.M. a British round hit one of the 24-pounders under Nicholson's command in the fort's southwest bastion, dismounting it while killing Lieutenant Levi Clagett and Sergeant John Clemm and wounding several others. An eyewitness said the sergeant was killed when "a piece the size of a dollar, two inches thick passed through his body in a diagonal direction from his naval, and went into the grounds upwards of two feet." Evacuating the

---

23. M. Morgan, 10; Lord, (1972), 71; Fay, 252.
24. Linn, 420; Brugger, 183; Cpt. Evans kept the round as a souvenir and took it home with him after his discharge.

wounded and remounting the gun caused a flurry of activity which led Cochrane to believe that his attack was having an effect and he ordered three bomb ships to close in for the kill. At 3 P.M. they came within range and the fort responded with a devastating fire as the gunners unleashed their frustrations from nearly six hours of inactivity. Two rounds hit *Devastation*, causing no casualties, while *Volcano* was hit five times at the cost of one man wounded. The unlucky *Erebus* was hit so badly that she had to be pulled out of range by boats from the frigate *Severn*. Her sister ships wisely backed out of the fray and the incident was over within thirty minutes.[25]

The bombardment continued at long range, imposing additional strain on Major Armistead, the only man aware that his powder magazine was not bombproof. It had a capacity of 300 barrels of powder but was merely a brick structure with a shingled roof and could be destroyed by a lucky hit. One British shell did land in the unprotected magazine but miraculously, failed to explode. Soldiers quickly redistributed the powder barrels throughout the fort to reduce the chance of a massive explosion. The experience alleviated the garrison's concern for their safety and the men rested against the barrels and detachedly observed the effects of the bombardment. The shelling went on into the night with few intermissions. A British midshipman recalled, "All this night the bombardment continued with unabated vigor; the hissing of rockets and the firey shells glittered in the air, threatening destruction as they fell; whilst to add solemnity to this scene of devastation, the rain fell in torrants— the thunder broke in mighty peals after each succession of lightening." At about 1 A.M. the chaos died down as Cochrane switched tactics.[26]

Admiral Cochrane was not certain that Colonel Brooke had gotten his messages urging caution because the harbor defenses had not been penetrated and the navy could not support any land offensive. Consequently, he decided some effort was required to divert the defenders in case Brooke tried an attack on his own. He considered a small boat attack on the Lazaretto site, but ruled it out as too hazardous, deciding rather to probe at a more vulnerable point which might threaten Fort McHenry or Baltimore itself. He ordered Captain Charles Napier of *Euryalis* to lead twenty boats with 1,200 men up the Ferry Branch to Ridgely's Cove to threaten both the city and the fort's dependencies while making a credible diversion for Brooke's possible benefit. There was a lull in the firing as the boats set out in single file into the darkness and driving rain. The last eleven boats lost contact with their leaders and, disoriented, headed for the inner harbor where they were spotted by the

25. M. Morgan, 12; Fraser & Carr-Laughton, I: 275; Andrews, I: 270; James, 190.
26. M. Morgan, 8, 12; Walsh, 300; Lossing, 955.

Lazaretto Battery. The defenders, presuming they were the objective, sent for a company of Randall's Pennsylvania Riflemen. The British realized their error and withdrew before any firing began, but could not regain contact with Napier.[27]

Meanwhile, Napier and the other nine, consisting of a rocket boat, five launches, two pinnaces, and a gig manned by a total of 128 men, proceeded as planned. He got by Fort Babcock and almost reached Fort Covington before he was detected by Sailing Master John A. Webster at Babcock. The twenty-seven year old Harford County native, disturbed by the change in the bombardment rhythm, was straining to detect anything unusual when he spotted the little force. Both forts immediately opened fire and the British gunboats responded, wounding one man at Fort Covington. Instantly, every American gun began blazing away. The "concussion was tremendous." Houses throughout the area were shaken and many citizens feared the worst. Not only were the forts engaged, but some ships in the harbor began firing as well, and even the Lazaretto Battery got into the act as the British came within range. Everyone assumed that devastation to the harbor would be complete based on the noise, flashes, and explosions. By coincidence, this was occurring at the time of Brooke's withdrawal.[28]

Napier had no choice but to withdraw. Opposite Fort McHenry an ill-advised crew member fired a signal rocket and the entire fort again burst into a frenzy of fire. One of the boats was seriously damaged and had to be abandoned and one sailor was mortally wounded. Napier's force regained the safety of the fleet at about 2 A.M. He had created quite a diversion, but Brooke's men were already well away from Hampstead Hill and Admiral Cochrane had given up on breaking the city's defense. Silence fell over the harbor until Napier was out of harm's way. The ships then resumed a desultory heavy shelling which became increasingly intermittent by 4 A.M., tapering out at 7 A.M. on 14 September. The British ships waited another two hours before slipping back to the fleet at North Point.[29]

Private John Dagg on Hampstead Hill who observed Brooke's camp fires as the firing was going on, recalled the experience as the worst night of his life, made even more tense when the shooting in the direction of Fort McHenry stopped. He and his companions feared the fort had fallen, allowing the British to get in their rear, and were relieved when they saw the stars

---

27. Mullaly, 98; Pancake, (1972), 130.
28. Beitzell, (1958), 1; Scharf, (1881), 97; Scharf, (1874), 349. Mr. Webster had been 3rd Mate on the *Rossie* before joining Barney's flotilla.
29. Fay, 252; Napier, 90; James, 191.

and stripes still flying over the fort in the early morning light. The citizens of Baltimore were equally grateful, but amazed, to discover that their men remained in control and that relatively little damage had been done. Major Armistead estimated that 1,500 to 1,800 rounds were fired by the British during the twenty-four hour bombardment. A few of these fell short or "over" but many were accurate airbursts and at least 400 detonated on contact inside the fort, damaging two buildings with four men killed and twenty-four wounded.[30]

Brooke's land force had an eventful time as the navy fruitlessly tried to provide support. The colonel concluded that a night attack on the American left coupled with a diversionary attack on the right might be successful, but since the American left was at the water's edge, naval support was essential. He sent Lieutenant James Scott, RN, through the thin American piquets with a summary of his plan and a request for a waterborne diversion. Scott returned while attack preparations were underway with a message from Admiral Cochrane saying that the fleet had failed to neutralize the harbor defenses and could not provide the substantial support as hoped. Meanwhile, the troops made a miserable bivouac in the rain and tried to cook their rations. Admiral Cockburn urged Brooke to attack anyway, with or without naval support, but the colonel declined, and withdrew that night.[31]

The withdrawal began at 1:30 A.M. on 14 September. Preparations for the night attack were almost complete and the force first thought that it was advancing. Midshipman Gordon G. McDonald, RN, from HMS *Diomede* (50) recalled, "We soon found out we were in retreat, at which (to tell my good friends the truth) I was not sorry. These Americans are not to be trifled with." The rain continued as they marched and after going about seven miles, the column halted until daylight. Brooke hoped the Americans would pursue and attack, giving him the chance to achieve a success and exploit the confusion. There was no pursuit, however, and at daylight the column continued back to the old battlefield, still littered with corpses. It held there for three hours while Brooke exchanged his wounded being treated at the Meeting House before marching another three miles. From there, Brooke notified the navy to prepare for reembarkation at the landing site.[32]

The night of 13 September had been a tense one for the troops on Hampstead Hill. They stood their vigil in the fog and mist observing the faint glimmer of the enemy camp fires left blazing for their benefit and, like John

---

30. Dagg, 16; Byron, 72; Scharf, (1881), 97.
31. J. Scott, III: 344; Brooke Papers, 187; Fortescue, X: 149; Andrews, I: 723.
32. Brooke Papers, 187; J. Scott, III: 345; Lingel, 145; Gleig, 106.

Dagg, listened to the firing in the harbor. Major George Timanus of the Thirty-Sixth Maryland moved along the trenches issuing bread and whiskey to the men, accompanied by a squad of fifers and drummers who played patriotic tunes. It was a tense, miserable night brightened only by the dawn and Fort McHenry's success, along with the realization that the enemy had slipped away during the night. As soon as this became apparent some of Smith's officers suggested a general counterattack. But Smith rejected this proposal with the comment, "Yes...but when you fight our citizens against British regulars you are staking dollars against cents." Instead, he kept the men in the trenches but allowed Winder to take part of his mobile force in pursuit. Winder set out down Long Log Lane with Burd's Dragoon Company and Lieutenant Colonel Griffin Taylor's First Virginia Regiment while Major Beale Randall's light troops took a route closer to the Patuxent shore. The troops were sluggish after three days of hard work and got off to a slow start. They made no contact except for a dragoon patrol under Sergeant Keller which encountered the British rear guard and captured six men from the 21st Foot Flank Company. The entire British force deployed to take on the dragoons and they wisely withdrew. The British avoided any further harassment by occupying the abandoned earthworks at Humphrey's Creek until the force completed its reembarkation by 1 P.M. on 15 September. The men on board looked up the Patapsco that night to see Baltimore lit up and celebrating its victory.[33]

The fleet remained at anchor off North Point until early on 17 September when it slipped anchor and headed back to its former position off the Patuxent. *Hebrus* and *Euryalis* continued straight to Tangier Island to escort prize vessels taken at Alexandria, some of which carried the prisoners taken at Baltimore to either Halifax or Ireland, and to carry away the remains of General Ross and Sir Peter Parker. Midshipman Richard J. Barrett of HMS *Hebrus* recorded, "And as the last vessel spread her canvas, the Americans hoisted a most superb and splendid ensign on their battery, and fired at the same time a gun of defiance." Major Armistead is said to have raised the big flag first on 14 September while the fort's musicians played "Yankee Doodle" which served as the inspiration for Frances Scott Key's famous poem. Key was detained with the British fleet while negotiating the exchange of Dr. William Beanes of Upper Marlboro and witnessed the naval battle from the North Point area.[34]

33. Chesterton, 152, 158; Buchan, 173; Fay, 249; Andrews, I: 728; DeWee, 345; Van Why, 84; Pancake, (1972), 130.
34. Lord, (1972), 66; Gleig, 109; Barrett, 464; Tucker, 192; M. Morgan, 13.

Admiral Cochrane told J. S. Skinner, Key's fellow negotiator, that the sunken hulks had prevented a dash into the harbor which led to the British failure. Their presence made flanking Fort McHenry impossible and denied the land offensive any substantial naval support. Both he and Brooke knew that New Orleans and other Gulf targets were still on their agenda and they could not afford any substantial losses on what was really only a diversionary raid. Ross's telling remark about raining militia reflected the contempt he and Cockburn had for the militia. This bred an overconfidence which caused them to overextend themselves while never considering the possibility of meeting a competent, determined opponent with adequate resources. Fortescue, the historian of the British Army, considered the attack a pointless operation aimed at gathering prizes for the navy, the prospect of which, he said, frequently clouded sailors' judgement when coordinating amphibious operations.[35]

There were rumors that the British were regrouping in preparation for a second attack, and work continued on the fortifications as reinforcements poured in. General Smith took no chances. He considered the British dangerous as long as they remained in the area and, accordingly, continued to adjust the defenses on 14 September to meet any second attack. He shifted troops from Hampstead Hill to Fort Covington to further strengthen the Ferry Branch positions. This shift was not without incident as a runaway wagon team crashed into the Third Maryland Regiment causing a brief panic until steadied by some of the Frederick County troops. Smith transferred Winder with Douglass's Virginians back to the south side of the city in case the British tried another approach. On 13 September Commodore Rodgers had exercised informal command over a large part of the Hampstead Hill line during the climax of the battle. When Major Armistead collapsed from fever and exhaustion the next day, Rodgers assumed command of Fort McHenry at Smith's request until 19 September when the Secretary of the Navy ordered him and his men back to the Delaware in case the British shifted their attention there.[36]

When the British ships eased into the bay on 16 September the city went delirious with relief and celebrations, but soon had to face a sadder task. General Smith ordered a convoy of wagons to return to the Meeting House battle area to police the battlefield and recover the dead. News of the expedition spread through the city and several thousand people left for Patuxent Neck in search of fallen soldiers. As many of the dead as possible were brought back

35. Skinner, 344; Spaulding, 328; Fortescue, X: 151.
36. Anon., War's Wild Alarm, 221; Mullaly, 102; Paullin, 295, 298.

to the Hampstead Hill trenches where they were laid out for identification. One grieving old man told Paris M. Davis that he had lost his father and two brothers in the Revolution and had just seen the bodies of his two sons, "but (said he) they have died in a good cause." Those whose remains were not claimed were buried in a nearby "potters field."[37]

Large numbers of Pennsylvania troops continued to pour into the city, setting up in a camp at Fairfield two miles from the city. Organized under their own officers, they took their direction from Smith. News of the British departure was interpreted by the Keystoners to mean they had gone for reinforcements and this inspired even more intense drilling and training. On 19 September the War Department ordered Governor Snyder to send his remaining forces to the defense of the Delaware, however, those Pennsylvanians already at Baltimore remained until the first week of December when they headed home for an 8 December discharge. A large force of Virginia militia stationed at Camp Springfield south of the city also gathered during this time and was organized into a division under Major General John Pegram, to which the remaining regulars were attached.[38]

The new forces and leaders arrived just as the original cast was changing. On 21 September General Winder led his regulars and Douglass's Virginia Brigade back to Washington as Secretary Monroe wanted him to be available for any inquiries into Bladensburg. When these did not materialize, Monroe ordered Winder to the Niagara frontier to replace the convalescent Major General Winfield Scott who was scheduled to take over the Tenth Military District as soon as he was well enough. With Scott's arrival in Baltimore in late October, General Smith requested relief and was replaced by Major General Robert G. Harper. On 18 November, Scott signed the order discharging the Third Maryland Division from federal service with the thanks of the nation. On 10 October the still ailing Joshua Barney resumed command of his flotilla in Baltimore after escorting a prisoner exchange boat to Hampton Roads with most of the Bladensburg British casualties. He spent the rest of a frustrating fall and winter hanging on to control of his force and jousting with Congress to get his men paid and compensated for their losses. The danger now gone, politics prevailed over gratitude and it took until February 1815 to squeeze out the earned benefits. Regardless of their treatment at the hands of Congress, every man in Baltimore at the time of the attack knew he had accomplished something of great significance. In the words of William Wirt, "The invincibles of Wellington are found to be vincible" and the reason for

37. DeWee, 347; Davis, 180-181.
38. Egle, 121; Ellis & Evans, 77; Pomeroy, 169; Crain, 129, 146.

British continuation of the war had been undercut on the Patapsco. But it would be several more months before the achievement bore fruit.[39]

39. Robinson, (1944), 196; Colston, 121; Scharf, (1881), 98; Fortner, 292; Kennedy, I: 336.

EPILOG

O PERATIONS in the Chesapeake were anticlimactic after the departure from North Point. Admiral Cochrane had learned of the dispatch of 7,000 more troops to Jamaica for the proposed Gulf operations even before the ill-fated attack. He wasted little time lingering in the bay after the rebuff on the Patapsco. Most of the fleet gathered off the Patuxent to take on water and supplies while a few ships proceeded to the Tangier base where the eccentric local minister, Joshua Thomas, reminded them of his prediction of disaster in a sermon given before the Baltimore expedition. Cochrane began immediate plans for operations against New Orleans and on 19 September left for Halifax aboard *Tonnant* to supervise planning and preparations before heading for the Gulf. Admiral Cockburn left on *Albion* for Bermuda the same day, with most of the ships of the line to be refitted at the docks there. Coastwatchers in Princess Anne County, Virginia reported an uninterrupted trickle of ships coming from the north and heading out to sea over 22-28 September. Rear Admiral Sir Pulteney Malcolm remained off the Patuxent with *Royal Oak, Asia, Ramillies,* the frigates *Hebrus* and *Havanah,* the bomb vessels, and all the troop ships and transports. The faithful *Dragon* accompanied by some tenders, resumed its patrol in Lynnhaven Bay. Leaving only the frigate *Diadem* to watch the Patuxent until his move was completed, Sir Pulteney shifted his anchorage to the Potomac by 27 September.[1]

The fleet maintained daily contact with the land forces which had returned to Tangier Island to rest and recuperate. Before going to Baltimore, Admiral Cochrane had ordered the establishment of another marine battalion—designated "3rd,"— composed of three companies from the old 2nd Battalion and three companies of Colonial Marines. A few of the latter deployed with the fleet to North Point and acquitted themselves well. The battalion was placed under the command of Major George Lewis, RM, and returned to strength quickly with the addition of ex-slaves inspired to enlist after the news of Washington and the offer of of an eight dollar bounty. The three marine battalions under the overall command of Lieutenant Colonel James Malcolm, RM, were designated the stay-behind land force to support raids after the withdrawal of the army troops. The marines decided to make their stay at Tangier as comfortable as possible and set about improving the island's facilities even further. When not on raids, the men harvested local timber and completed the troop barracks and officers quarters begun in the summer and refurbished Fort Albion.[2]

Meanwhile, Admiral Malcolm and Colonel Brooke planned to keep the troops still on board ship occupied while they awaited orders for deployment to the Gulf. On 19 September, when Admiral Cochrane left for Halifax, Brooke shifted his quarters from *Tonnant* to Malcolm's *Royal Oak* and accompanied Sir Pulteney to the new anchorage on the Potomac off St. George's Island. The island was the primary source of water for the fleet and remained under British control until 25 January 1815. While conducting the reprovisioning, the officers observed considerable militia activity at the mouth of the Coan River on the Virginia shore and decided to give the troops some exercise. Two diversionary operations were launched while Brooke led the main effort against the Coan positions.[3]

On 4 October Captain Robert Rowley, RN, with the frigates *Brune* (38) and *Melpomene* (36), the brig *Thistle* (16), and the schooner *Hornet* landed a battalion of marines at Nomini Bay, fifteen miles upriver, while the 4th Foot hit Mundy Point on the Yeocomico River, both having light contact. Colonel Brooke himself led the 44th Foot and part of the 21st Foot with one six-pounder to Black Point on the Coan River. His objective was to attack a force of 500 militia with eight guns rumored to be at Northumberland Court House. The troops left the ships at 8 P.M., reaching Black Point at about 4:30

1. Emmerson, 144; Brenton, 527; Park, 207; Mullaly, 103; An Officer, 182; Byron, 81; Footner, 97.
2. Nicolas, II: 282; Field, I: 301; Fraser & Carr-Laughton, I: 275.
3. Fortescue, X: 149; Rowley, 249.

A.M. on 5 October where they came under small arms fire from Lieutenant Colonel Thomas D. Downing's Thirty-Seventh Virginia Regiment, Northumberland County. Captain Richard Kenah, RN, of *Aetna* was killed and two men were wounded during the landings. The British fired a volley and the militia hastily withdrew five miles to Northumberland Court House where there was another brief skirmish in which the colors of the Virginia Regiment were captured. The invaders destroyed some military supplies and burned a few small ships before reembarking early on 6 October, ending what one British Army officer called "an ill-managed, unmeaning, and unnecessary affair."[4]

The fleet continued preparing for its long voyage and, as each ship completed its requirements, it headed south to Lynnhaven Bay. By this time the growing sick list convinced everyone of the wisdom of an early departure and on 9 October there was great relief when a dispatch boat arrived from Bermuda with orders for Malcolm and Brooke to take their force to Point Negril, Jamaica to rendezvous with the reinforcements from Europe. Beginning on 11 October, coast-watchers in Princess Anne noticed a sudden increase in the number of ships in Lynnhaven Bay, peaking at thirty-three transports and tenders and five 74s. The big fleet hoisted sail on 15 October and by sunset all except for *Dragon* and *Euryalis* had left the bay. The veterans of Baltimore and Washington were off to try their fortune at New Orleans.[5]

The attenuated British force in the bay remained active, keeping the Eastern Shore militia at a high state of readiness. The militia commanders assumed that the British might vent their frustrations over Baltimore on easier targets and expected the worst. Captain Barrie shifted *Dragon* from Lynnhaven Bay back to Tangier Island while *Euryalis* continued the blockade against Hampton Roads. The Tangier position allowed his smaller force to impede movement on a line between the Patuxent and the Choptank River at one of the bay's narrowest points. On 19 October, eighteen barges and a schooner entered the Choptank River and moved as far up as Castle Haven, five miles from Cambridge, where the marines landed and pillaged Kemp's Farm, carrying off livestock and provisions, before shifting to do the same to Alexander Hemsley's property to the west on Tilghman's Island. Brigadier General Perry Benson alerted the Dorchester and Talbot County militia and called out Lieutenant Colonel Hugh Auld's Twenty-Sixth Maryland Regiment. He was especially concerned that Easton might be the ultimate enemy

---

4. Brooke Papers, 204, 206; Hammett, 108-109; Rowley, 251; An Officer, 182-183.
5. Rowley, 249; An Officer, 183; Emmerson, 146; Brooke Papers, 211. The last of the fleet put into Point Negril on 1 Nov.

objective and directed the emplacement of artillery at Fort Stokes on the Tred Avon River to block that avenue of approach to the town. An attack was building to come down the Avon River, a tributary of the Choptank, but some of the barges grounded on Benoni Point at the mouth of the Avon. A burst of severe weather dissuaded the British from continuing and they withdrew to Tilghman's Island. Nevertheless, Benson kept his men on full alert until the British fell back to Tangier Island on 2 November.[6]

Captain Barrie continued to use his marines for what he called his "shooting parties" intended to augment the half-rations diet his crews were compelled to follow. The day after the Choptank raid, 20 October, eight of *Euryalis's* barges raided the Atlantic side of Princess Anne County to destroy some saltworks but were driven away before they could do more than burn three small vessels and carry off some livestock. A few days later, members of the same crew aboard five barges entered Hampton Roads and captured some local cargo craft, continuing attacks "in which small gains and no honors were to be won." Captain Robert Rowley, RN, wrote home that "wherever we move in ships they collect and move after us. When we know they are there then we move off to another spot. This is a harassing system carried on. Many have died from fatigue." By early November, he was tired of the work and of what it was doing to his crew.[7]

Captain Barrie became so concerned over his supply situation that he sent a courier to Bermuda describing the health of his crew and asking for help if his superiors expected the blockade to continue. At the same time he needed to uphold the discipline and morale of his small stay-behind force. A particularly notorious case involved a 30 October raid by a foraging party from Captain Alexander Dixie's frigate, *Saracen*, against the Catholic mission farm and chapel at St. Inigoes in St. Mary's County, Maryland. The raiders carried off quantities of clothing, bedding, kitchen equipment, and sacred vessels from the chapel then desecrated the altar. Farm employees herded surviving livestock away in an effort to avoid losing it in another raid, only to have the animals taken by a second foraging party from Barrie's *Dragon*. When Barrie offered to pay them, they complained to him about the conduct of *Saracen*'s crew. Outraged, Barrie ordered Captain Dixie, then at the Tangier base, to have those responsible return the sacred vessels and pay the priests for the vandalized property. On 18 November a chastened Lieutenant William Hancock, RN, landed under a flag of truce and made restitution, saying his career had been ruined by the affair.[8]

6. Emory, 439; Byron, 81; Tilghman, 178.
7. Rowley, 253; Emmerson, 147, 148; Lovell, 164; Tilghman, 180.

On 1 November, Barrie's problems were partially resolved with the arrival of the frigate *Dauntless*, Captain James Pierce, escorting four troop transports enroute from Halifax to Jamaica. The new arrivals shared some of their rations and helped scour the Hampton Roads area so energetically that for a brief moment, Norfolk thought it faced another attack. Fears increased with the return of Admiral Cockburn on 30 November which allowed Barrie to reinforce a raid up the Rappahannock River to Tappahannock beginning the same day. Lieutenant Colonel Archibald Ritchie of the Sixth Virginia Militia deployed Captain Richard Rouzee's Artillery Company with one gun to defend the place. On the morning of 1 December, the British barges shelled the village, damaging several houses, and when an estimated 500 marines and sailors landed, Rouzee's forty-six men prudently withdrew with their gun and helplessly observed the ransacking of the town. The raiders rowed more than twelve miles beyond Tappahannock and scoured the countryside for provisions before withdrawing on 4 December after destroying the docks and several commercial buildings.[9]

Enroute to the bay on 5 December, the raiders encountered opposition from Captain Vincent Shackleford's Artillery Company of the Forty-First Virginia Regiment, Richmond County. The militia had set up at a narrow point interdicting the Rappahannock's mouth near Farnham Church but it was broken up after a landing supported by rocket fire in which Shackleford was badly wounded and captured. Having acquired supplies, Cockburn sent the frigate *Ceylon* escorting the transport *Queen* to remove the First Marine Battalion from Tangier Island. On 11 December, the frigate *Regulus* took off the other two marine battalions and the last redcoat cleared the island two days later. The admiral's fleet began leaving Lynnhaven Bay on 17 December to create a diversion off the Georgia coast in support of operations in the Gulf. The last sail was out of sight by sunset the next day with *Dragon*, *Euryalis*, and their tenders left once more on their own.[10]

The dreary winter weather made it difficult and frustrating to stop blockade runners, let alone maintain any level of comfort, and ship's crews spent most of their time in small boats searching for provisions or prizes. The last major incident of the war in the bay occurred as *Dauntless* patrolled along the Eastern Shore in January 1815. The frigate was unusually successful throughout the month, using her long boat commanded by Lieutenant Matthew Phipps, RN, to capture on average one substantial vessel per week. On 6 Feb-

8. Anon, Robbery of St. Inigoes, 553-57; Beitzell ms.; Rowley, 252.

9. Hoge, 1278; Emmerson, 149, 152; Butler, 27.

10. Lovell, 166, 171; J. Scott, III: 350, 352; Fraser & Carr-Laughton, I: 279; Butler, 186-187.

ruary when *Dauntless* anchored off James Island, Phipps hoped to continue his success with a raid up the little Choptank River in Dorchester County to capture three schooners rumored to be somewhere along its banks.[11]

On 7 February he took the brig's long boat and jolly boat and forayed up the river, stopping first at Mose Gaohagen's farm to take on some provisions. This alerted the companies of the Forty-Eighth Maryland Regiment who headed to prearranged rendezvous points near the river to await further orders from their commander, Lieutenant Colonel John Jones. The raiders, in the meantime, torched a ship near Tobacco Stick (modern Madison) and then headed downriver only to run aground off the mouth of Parson's Creek. The winter weather worsened during the night and by morning, Lieutenant Phipps's two stranded boats were immobilized by ice. A patrol from Captain Thomas Woolford's Company spotted the boats and sent to Cambridge for a cannon. As they day wore on, it became obvious to the waiting militiamen that no help could reach the trapped boats and some of the men developed a plan. The wind and tide had caused the ice to buckle, forming a mound about 150 yards from the British which concealed an approach from the shore.[12]

Private Joseph F. Stewart led nineteen men across the ice floes to the mound from where they could fire accurately on the British. This fire forced the boat crews to shelter below deck and prevented their responding with their deck guns. After two hours all hands surrendered. Stewart gathered together Lieutenant Phipps, Midshipman Galloway, twelve sailors, three marines, and a black man and woman and turned them all over to the county marshall who sent them to Easton. The militia also secured a 12-pounder carronade, swivel gun, and the small arms of the crew which they kept as trophies of this so-called "Battle of the Ice Mound." They were later awarded $1,800 prize money for the two little vessels eventually retrieved from the ice, while the two British officers were placed on parole and became the center of Easton's winter social season. On 27 February *Dauntless* left the bay, wondering about Phipps's fate which remained unknown until his exchange in May 1815.[13]

Most British activities were restricted to the Virginia Capes and Hampton Roads areas where an occasional boat was captured, but little else took place. It got so boring that Captain Charles Napier aboard *Euryalis*, sent a 28 Jan-

---

11. Stewart, 373-4; Byron, 83.
12. Stewart, 374; E. Jones, 255.
13. Stewart, 376; Tuckerman, 68. The black woman was Lt. Phipps's cook, Rebeccah - her name and his are on the gun, "Becca-Phipps", taken from the long boat. It is still on display at Taylor's Island, near the point of capture.

uary challenge to Captain Charles Gordon, USN, to bring his USS *Constellation* out of Norfolk for single combat. The American captain accepted the challenge, but news of the Peace of Ghent thwarted their plans. Christopher Hughes, a native of Baltimore and secretary to the United States peace commissioners, reached Annapolis overland from New York on 13 February with news of the peace agreed upon in the Belgian city the preceding 24 December. Formal notification reached the Norfolk area on 18 February and *Constellation* left Norfolk unmolested and headed to New York on 16 March. The war in the Chesapeake was over.[14]

The British negotiators at Ghent had gone there with every intention of punishing the United States for declaring war on their country while it was embroiled in the European conflict. On 19 August 1814 they presented a series of demands in which the United States was expected to give up large parts of Maine and New York, as well as most of the Old Northwest, while also agreeing to unilateral disarmament on the Great Lakes and free British navigation on the Mississippi. The harsh demands were an extreme position and reflected Britain's confidence in their forces and lack of respect for their opponent. On 27 September, London learned of the sack of Washington and Lord Bathhurst pressed for the territorial changes while making a few minor concessions. The belief was that the longer the discussions took, the more successful British forces would be and the more difficult the American negotiating position would become.[15]

The American negotiators learned of Washington's fate three days later while they were considering the British territorial demands and desperately tried to hold their position. On 10 October, the British raised the ante by questioning the legality of the Louisiana Purchase. On 17 October the British learned of the twin failures at Plattsburg and Baltimore and the modest American success on the Niagara frontier, all of which undercut their hopes for winning territorial gains by force of arms and encouraged their American counterparts to resist any pressure. Lord Castlereigh said the news "materially counteracted" the effect of the burning of Washington and stimulated British public opinion to end the war. The Chancellor of the Exchequer, Lord Vansittart, reported that most people were tired of conflict and "were very indifferent...to the final issue of the War, provided it not be dishonorable." Castlereigh felt the outcomes at Baltimore and Plattsburg boded no further hope of British advantage, and believed it was time to end "the millstone of an American war" so he could deal with the unstable European situation

14. Emmerson, 152; Napier, 91-92; Scharf, (1881), 98.
15. Perkins, (1964), 89; W.D. Jones, 486-7; Dangerfield, (1963), 67.

without distraction.[16]

The sudden shift in attitude was directly attributable to the dashing of British hopes at Baltimore and in New York State and the consequent bolstering of the United States commissioners' resolve at Ghent. Learning of Samuel Smith's success at Baltimore, William Wirt perceptively noted that such a loss would erode British will to continue the war and, further, would negate any strong demands at Ghent, ending the only British motive for continuing the war. The victories also ended the Federalist's politics of protest in a wave of national pride while strengthening popular support and sympathy for the Madison administration. The success at Baltimore, in particular, was seen as a vindication of republican institutions, proving that a people schooled in self-rule could find the means to resist without compromising their political values. Baltimore's performance confirmed the hope that a republican government could survive the stress of war intact. Shortly after the war, Decius Wadsworth expressed this relief in a letter to a friend, saying, "Hereafter, we can look confidently in the Face of any Nation which may feel a disposition to trample on our rights."[17]

In retrospect the Chesapeake operations did not bode well for British strategy. The policy of pinpoint raids proved counterproductive, driving growing numbers of bay residents into active opposition while consuming large amounts of British military resources with minimal return. William Cobbett commented that British acts "would only tend to unite the Americans and, in the end, produce such a hatred against us as would tend to shut us out ..." England had forgotten the size of her former colonies and the impossibility of finding any vital point for a decisive thrust in such an undeveloped country. The British Chesapeake campaign ultimately failed because of the absence of any clear-cut objective, beyond that of harassment, which diverted military resources that could have been used to greater advantage in the Canadas. They could have perhaps achieved more by seizing a single point and using it as a base to lure American forces, while alienating fewer civilians. As it was, they achieved very little after a prolonged, spectacular effort. But the opponents developed a new, albeit grudging respect for each other that ended in a mutual preference for negotiation rather than war. The struggle in the Chesapeake contributed substantially to this new relationship, showing in the words of Henry Clay that "our character and Constitution are placed on a solid basis, never to be shaken."[18]

16. Perkins, (1964), 99, 152; Engelman, 84.
17. Perkins, (1964), 155; R.C. Stuart, 144; Brynn, 25; Kennedy, I: 336; Cassell, (1971), 209.
18. Perkins, (1964), 150; Dudley, II: 56.

Appendix A

≈

CHESAPEAKE CHRONOLOGY 1812-15

1812

18 June	War is declared. Regional militia units deploy to defense of key sites. Baltimore Militia start town defenses.
	Two Baltimore companies and one from Hagerstown reinforce U.S. troops at Annapolis.
	Norfolk, Virginia Militia is reinforced by Greensville County Militia.
22 June	Mob destroys Baltimore *Federal Republican* newspaper office.
12 July	The first seven Baltimore privateers depart to prey on British shipping.
26-27 July	Baltimore mob attacks newspaper supporters being held in city jail.
26 Dec	British declare blockade of Chesapeake Bay.

1813

4 Feb	Adm. George Cockburn, on HMS *Marlborough* (74), anchors off Hampton Roads with fleet of four ships of the line, six frigates, plus smaller vessels (1,800 men). Real blockade of Chesapeake Bay begins.
8 Feb	British fleet establishes base on Lynnhaven Bay, captures privateer *Lottery*.
11 Mar	Gov. Winder directs Maj. Gen. Samuel Smith to assume command of the Baltimore defenses. U.S. engineers begin improvements to Fort McHenry.
16 Mar	British capture *Arab*, *Racer*, *Lynx*, and *Dolphin* in raid fifteen miles up the Rappahannock.
24 Mar	Adm. Warren with HMS *San Domingo* (74) joins Adm. Cockburn.
26 Mar	British raid Sharpe's Island, off mouth of Eastern Bay (entrance to Choptank River, Maryland).
28 Mar	Alarm over British ships off the entrance into the Choptank River leads to militia call-up in Talbot County and construction of "Fort Stokes" on Easton Point.
30 Mar	Royal Marine infantry battalions and artillery companies leave Plymouth, England for Chesapeake operations.
3 Apr	British raid up the Rappahannock River into Lancaster County, Virginia and capture six ships.
4 Apr	Lancaster County Militia, Col. John Chewning, repulse a British attack at Chewning's Point on Carter's Creek.
6 Apr	British destroy small ships along the Rappahannock River in Essex County, Virginia, threaten Urbanna, land at Carter's Creek, Lancaster County after a sharp skirmish.
	Three sites in Westmoreland County, Virginia are hit.
7 Apr	British ships probe into the Potomac. In response the Westmoreland County, Virginia Militia establish a base below the mouth of Nomini Creek.
11 Apr	British establish temporary base on Tangier Island and conduct small raids in area.
12 Apr	British occupy Sharpe's Island.

13 Apr	Baltimore City Council appropriates funds for defense of the city.
16 Apr	British fleet appears at mouth of the Patapsco; efforts continue on the Baltimore defenses, early warning signal system is developed. Fort McHenry is reinforced with additional heavy artillery, hulks are positioned to block harbor channels.
20 Apr	Queenstown packet is captured between North Point and Fort McHenry. Cross-bay travel curtailed.
23 Apr	British occupy Spesutie Island (now Aberdeen P.G.).
26 Apr	Fleet scouts mouth of Severn River, returns to Baltimore, blockades Patapsco for one week.
29 Apr	British raid Frenchtown and White Hall, Maryland against some resistance from local and Elkton Militia.
3 May	Havre de Grace, Maryland is sacked. Principio Foundry is destroyed.
5 May	Fredericktown and Georgetown, Maryland are sacked. Charlestown on Northeast River surrenders.
23-24 May	Partial mobilization of D.C. Militia to guard Potomac approaches.
26 May	Maryland legislature votes $100,000 for defense of state to compensate for lack of federal help.
1 June	Adm. Warren returns from Bermuda preceding his additional forces.
8 June	British reinforcements leave Bermuda for Chesapeake Bay.
12 June	HMS *Narcissus* captures U.S. Revenue Cutter, *Surveyor* in York River.
18 June	British reinforcements join forces already in Chesapeake Bay.
20 June	British scout Norfolk area, skirmishing. Norfolk command crews unsuccessfully attack HMS *Junon* near mouth of Elizabeth River.
22 June	British attack on Craney Island is repulsed.
26 June	British attack Hampton, Viriginia; town is sacked.
27 June	British depart Hampton.

29 June	Crutchfield's Virginia Battalion reoccupies Hampton.
1 July	British raid up James River—Hog Island, Four Mile Creek, Lower Chippokes, and Jamestown Island. They were opposed by Virginia Militia led by Maj. Gen. William B. Chamberlyne which was based at Hood's Point (Fort Powhatan).
	Part of British fleet explores into Potomac.
10 July	British raid Loun's Creek, Isle of Wight County, Virginia.
11 July	A large British force probes up the Potomac as far as Kettle Bottom Shoals. Another attacks up Yeocomico Creek, Virginia, captures USS *Asp*, Lt. James B. Sigourney, USN is killed.
12-14 July	Adm. Cockburn with four ships of the line and tenders attack Ocracoke, North Carolina.
15-31 July	Full D.C. Militia is mobilized, deploys to Potomac shore of Charles County, Maryland.
7 July	A large British force anchors at mouth of Mattox Creek, Virginia.
18 July	Col. Richard E. Parker repulses British attack at Rozier Creek, Westmoreland County, Virginia.
19 July	U.S.P.O. courier system begins operation from Point Lookout, Maryland to D.C.
	British occupy Blakistone and St. George's Island, Maryland, land force two and one half miles from Point Lookout and begin raids along Potomac and Patuxent.
	Activity reported by Capt. Forrest, Leonardtown Maryland Horse.
	British raid on Mattox Creek, Westmoreland County, Virginia, is repulsed by local militia led by Capt. Henry Hungerford of Col. R. E. Parker's Regiment.
21 July	British probe at Swan's Point, Maryland is repulsed.
	British raid Hollis's Marsh and withdraw before militia at Mattox Creek Bridge can react.
27 July	British depart Point Lookout, move up Chesapeake, touch on Sandy Point.
6 Aug	Royal Marines from HMS *Marlborough* occupy Kent Island.

British headquarters is established at Belleview Plantation.

8 Aug British fleet threatens Baltimore again; militia elements occupy approaches from North Point and familiarize themselves with the terrain. Other militia occupy Hampstead Hill or reinforce Fort McHenry.

10 Aug British land at Parrott's Point, Maryland, make unsuccessful attack on St. Michaels, repulsed by Talbot County Militia; Adm. Cockburn's nephew is killed.

13 Aug British launch unsuccessful attack from Kent Island against Queenstown on the Chester River. Queen Annes County Militia, Maj. William H. Nicholson, resist.

23 Aug British evacuate Kent Island.

26 Aug British land at Wade's Point, Talbot County, Maryland, advance toward St. Michaels. A second landing behind Capt. John Caulk's defenders forces his withdrawal, sixteen U.S. prisoners are taken at Harris Creek, British withdraw.

30 Aug British fleet leaves Tilghman Island area for Hampton Roads.

30 Aug Fleet moves to point off the mouth of the Rappahannock by end of the month.

13 Sept Beckwith's force reaches Halifax, Nova Scotia.

22 Sept British raid Pleasure House, Princess Anne County, Virginia. Virginia Militia stations detachments at Pickatone, Lynch's Point, Ragged Point, Hague, Sandy Point, and Kinsale to confront raids for the remainder of the year.

2 Nov British make small raid on St. George's Island, St. Mary's County, Maryland.

7 Nov British depart St. Mary's County with about 170 slaves.

Most of the fleet goes to Bermuda; Capt. Robert Barrie, HMS *Dragon* (74), remains with a small force based on Watt's Island in Tangier Sound.

1814

Feb-Mar Spring raids cause heavy damage at Carter's Creek and Windmill Point in Lancaster County, Virginia, extend as far north as Tilghman's Island, Kent County, Maryland.

7 April	Royal Marine reinforcements depart Plymouth, England for Bermuda and service in Chesapeake.
14 Apr	British reoccupy Tangier Island and Watt's Island.
22 Apr	British raid Carter's Creek, Lancaster County, Virginia.
23 Apr	British raiders at Windmill Point on the Rappahannock are attacked and driven off by Col. R. E. Parker's Westmoreland County Militia.
27 Apr	HMS *Dragon* raids both sides of the Potomac.
2 May	British reported in Westmoreland County, cruise around St. George's and Blackistone Islands, St. Mary's County, Maryland. Col.
	Henry Carberry, 36th U.S. Infantry, sends Maj. Alexander Steuart with a battalion to try to confront.
31 May	HMS *Dragon* and fleet rendezvous off Point Lookout.
	British repulsed at Pungoteague Creek, Accomack County, Virginia.
1 June	British raid St. Jerome's Creek, St. Mary's County, Maryland, encounter Barney's U.S. Flotilla, engage it off Cedar Point and force it up the Patuxent.
	British (Capt. Barrie) establish blockade and begin shore raids to lure out Barney.
3 June	British raid Mr. Sewall's at Cedar Point. Three hundred 36th U.S. Infantry troops sent from Leonardtown, but arrive too late.
6-7 June	Main British fleet arrives, eases up to Somervell's (now Solomon's) Island.
8 June	U.S. Flotilla moves up St. Leonard's Creek. British make first probe.
9 June	British make second probe up St. Leonard's Creek.
10 June	First Battle of St. Leonard's Creek.
	U.S. reinforcements cross from west bank of Patuxent at Col. George Plater's house, "Sotterly."
	0800, RN and RM troops advance up Creek; 1400, commit main force; 1900, battle ends.
11 June	British resume Patuxent raids.

12 June	Broome's Island raided.
14 June	St. Mary's County areas opposite St. Leonard's Creek raided.
15 June	Benedict is raided by Capt. John R. Lumley with 180 Royal Marines and thirty Colonial Marines from HMS *Narcissus*.
16 June	Lower Marlboro, Hall's Creek are raided.
17 June	Magruder's Landing is raided.
18 June	Cole's Landing is raided. Col. Carberry shifts 36th U.S. Infantry north from Flotilla to cope with raids. 31st Maryland (Calvert County), Col. Michael Taney, deploys units under Maj. Stephen Johns and Capt. John Broome.
	Maj. Gen. John P. Van Ness is ordered to send D.C. Militia force to assist, Maj. George Peter is put in command of the detachment.
19 June	Peter's D.C. Militia force reaches Nottingham. Lt. Thomas J. Harrison, U.S.
	Artillery, is attached to the 36th U.S. Infantry with a battery, he successfully discourages a second British raid on Benedict and coordinates with D.C. Militia. Peter's force returns to D.C., 30 June.
20 June	Peter's force engages a British landing near Benedict. Br. Gen. Philip Steuart, 5th Maryland Militia Brigade, participates with a mounteddetached. Gallant struggle with Sgt. Maj. Mayo, RM.
21 June	Peter's D.C. Militia camp at Benedict.
24 June	Flotilla is reinforced with one hundred Marines (Capt. Samuel Miller) and 600 U.S. troops with artillery (Col. Decius Wadsworth).
26 June	Second battle of St. Leonard's Creek.
	Flotilla is able to escape up the Patuxent.
29 June	British raid Deep Creek, Accomack County, Virginia.
30 June	Royal Marine reinforcements depart Bermuda.
1 July	President Madison issues call for militia.
2 July	Military District Number Ten activated.

4 July   British burn Leonardtown, Calvert County, Maryland.

16 July   Royal Marine reinforcements join Cockburn's command.

18 July   Large British force anchors off Blackistone Island.

              Capt. John Davidson's D.C. Militia Detachment is ordered to Wood Yard (now Forrestville), Maryland.

19 July   British raid Leonardtown, St. Mary's County, Maryland, with Maj. George Lewis's battalion of RM and RMA; they are opposed by 36th U.S. Infantry.

20 July   British raid Nomini Creek, Virginia, accuse Americans of leaving poisoned whiskey.

22 July   British advance on Westmoreland C.H. (now Montross), Virginia, and scatter the King George and Stafford Counties Militia. Maj. Gen. John Hungerford orders in troops from Richmond, King George, and Essex Counties.

23 July   British capture several small vessels and burn property at Clements Bay, Virginia.

24 July   British reinforcements arrive in Bermuda from Europe.

26 July   British land at the Narrows between Machadox and Nomini Creeks. Nomini Church and Plantation are sacked.

              Col. Vincent Branham marches from Hague but has insuffient forces to engage.

30 July   British raid Chaptico, Virginia on the Yeocomico River.

2 Aug   Fleet with British reinforcements enters Chesapeake Bay.

3 Aug   British defeat Virginia Militia at Battle of Mundy's Point, burn Henderson's Plantation and shift to Coan River.

              A secondary British raid at Cherry Point is repulsed by Capt. Henry Traver's Infantry Co. and Capt. William Henderson's Artillery Co., Westmoreland County Militia.

              Kinsale is threatened by British actions.

5-6 Aug   British raid up Coan River to Northumberland Court House, are contested unsuccessfully by Lancaster County Militia and British burn shipping and houses along both riverbanks.

7 Aug   Royal Marines complete Coan River raid by destroying a battery at river's mouth after a sharp skirmish.

12 Aug	Royal Marines forage along both banks of St. Mary's River, Maryland.
14 Aug	British reinforcements led by Adm. Cochrane and Maj. Gen. Ross rendezvous with Adm. Cockburn's fleet off the mouth of the Potomac; decide strategy.
16 Aug	British enter Patuxent in force.
18 Aug	U.S. Cabinet learns of British move into the Patuxent.
	Br. Gen. John Hungerford's Northern Neck, Virginia forces are ordered to march from Nomini Bay to Alexandria.
	Br. Gen. William Madison's Militia Brigade is mobilized to cover the southern Potomac.
	Small British force raids mouth of Eastern Bay, Talbot County, Maryland.
19 Aug	British fleet reaches Benedict, Maryland.
	War Department directs full mobilization of D.C., Maryland and Virginia Militias.
20 Aug	Capt. Peter Parker's HMS *Menelaus* crew raids Rock Hall and Swan Creek, Maryland.
	Baltimore, Maryland Militia under Br. Gen. Tobias Stansbury reaches Bladensburg.
	British troops disembark at Benedict.
21 Aug	British troops march to Nottingham during very hot weather.
	Lt. Col. George Minor's Fairfax, Virginia Militia ordered to D.C.
22 Aug	British troops reach Pig Point at Upper Marlboro; flotilla is destroyed.
	Br. Gen. Hugh Douglass's 6th Virginia Militia Brigade is ordered to Alexandria.
23 Aug	By afternoon, British advance reaches to twelve miles from Bladensburg. 5th Maryland, Lt. Col. Joseph Sterrett, flotillamen, and other U.S. troops gather at Bladensburg and D.C.
24 Aug	Baltimore Committee of Vigilance and Safety is formed and Maj. Gen. Samuel Smith is appointed OIC.

Battle of Bladensburg.

25 Aug   Hungerford's men reach Neabsco (Prince William County, Virginia) and learn of Bladensburg.

Burning of Washington. British withdrawal begins.

26 Aug   Alexandria officials ask Hungerford to stay out of the city. He occupies Shooter's Hill and sends detachments to Mason's (now Roosevelt's) Island and Aquia.

27 Aug   Capt. James A. Gordon's fleet reaches Fort Washington on the Potomac.

28 Aug   British occupy Alexandria.

29 Aug   Br. Gen. John B. Hungerford's Virginia Militia go to White House south of Mount Vernon to assist Commodore Porter's Naval gunners.

Main British force reembarks at Benedict, departs next morning.

30 Aug   Battle of Caulk's Field, Kent County, Maryland. Sir Peter Parker is killed.

31 Aug   Maj. Gen. James Singleton's 16th Virginia Militia Brigade marches to Montgomery C.H. (now Rockville) and is ordered to Baltimore.

1-5 Sept   British fleet in Potomac engages U.S. forces at White House, Virginia and Indian Head, Maryland.

6-8 Sept   Capt. James A. Gordon's fleet escapes, heads out of Potomac. British fleet exits Patuxent.

7-8 Sept   British fleet sails up Potomac until contact with Gordon's ships is achieved.

9 Sept   British fleet beats northward for the Patapsco.

11 Sept   British fleet anchors of North Point. Baltimore forces mobilize.

1500, Stricker's 3d Maryland Brigade advances to Patuxent Neck.

12 Sept   0300, British forces land at North Point.

0700, Stricker learns of British landings, deploys his brigade for battle on Patuxent Neck near Bear Creek.

1300-1700, Battle of Long Log Lane (North Point),

Stricker withdraws to Worthington's Mill.

13 Sept	British advance toward Hampstead Hill line, reach it by 1000.
	0630, fleet begins bombardment of Fort McHenry.
14 Sept	0100, British small boat attack is repulsed by Fort Covington and surrounding batteries.
	0130, British land forces begin to leave Hampstead Hill.
	0600, Fleet ceases bombardment.
15 Sept	British reembark.
16 Sept	Fleet returns to Potomac and begins improving a semipermanent base at Tangier Island. Bulk shifts to Lynnhaven Bay.
Oct-Nov	Small fleet under Capt. Barrie, HMS *Dragon*, patrols a line from Patuxent to Choptank.
6 Oct	Br. Gen. Joel Leftwich's 2d Virginia Militia Brigade, and Br. Gen. John Breckenridge's 3d Militia Brigade are ordered to Baltimore.
19 Oct	British raid up Choptank River to Castle Haven, five miles from Cambridge, Dorchester County, Maryland.
	Talbot and Dorchester County Militias are mobilized. Stormy weather ends the raids.
	Main British fleet departs for Gulf Campaign.
2 Nov	British depart the Choptank River and hover in the vicinity of Poplar Islands and Thomas's Point to raid local shipping.
9 Nov	Virginia Brigades at Baltimore are concentrated near Ellicott's Mills and are formed into division commanded by Maj. Gen. John Pegram.
18 Nov	3d Maryland Brigade is mustered out of service.
1 Dec	Tappahannock, Virginia is seized after heavy shelling; the Essex County Militia, Lt. Col. Archibald Ritchie, is scattered.
4 Dec	British hit Tappahannock again then depart Rappahannock.
5 Dec	Royal Marines land near mouth of the Rappahannock, advance to within twelve miles of Warsaw where they are repulsed by Richmond County Militia at the Battle of North

Farnham Church.

Virginia governor orders a large mobile militia force to be at Urbanna to deter further raids.

11-13 Dec   British evacuate Tangier Island.

1815

7 Feb   Lt. Phipps, RN, leads a raid on a shipyard at Tobacco Stick (now Madison), Maryland via Parson's Creek, is counterattacked successfully by Dorchester County Militia (Battle of the Ice Mound).

13 Feb   News of Peace of Ghent reaches Annapolis.

15 Feb   Baltimore holds a grand illumination to celebrate peace.

18 Feb   Last reported hostile incident.

10 Apr   Congress ratifies Peace of Ghent.

Special Baltimore committee sends a congratulatory message to President Madison.

Appendix B

⪼

CHESAPEAKE OPERATIONS, 1812-15
U.S. ORGANIZATIONS

1812

Baltimore defenses are manned periodically by Baltimore City Militia starting when war was declared.

Fort Madison, Annapolis, commanded by Lt. Col. Jacob Small, 39th Maryland Militia, is garrisoned by:
    Union Artillery of Baltimore—Capt. George C. Collins
    Independant Co.—Capt. Samuel Sterrett

Frederick and Washington County Battalion —Maj. Ezra Mantz
    Capt. Stephen Steiner's Co.
    Capt. Henry Steiner's Co.
    Mountain Rangers—Capt. Daniel Marker
    Washington Rifle Greens—Capt. Robert Gatzendanner
    Homespun Volunteer Co. of Hagerstown—Capt. Thomas Quantrill

Alexandria Volunteers, D.C. Militia—Capt. James McGuire assigned 10 September - March 1813.

1813

18 Feb Columbian Hussars, D.C. Militia—Capt. William G. Ridgely, ordered to patrol Prince George and Charles Counties shore of Potomac.

8 Apr D.C. Militia Artillery reinforces Fort Washington.

20 May-19 Aug Provisional D.C. Militia battalion is activated to reinforce 36th U.S. Infantry (Col. Henry Carberry):
    Maj. Adam King, Commanding
        Capt. Richard John's Co.
        Capt. William McKee's Co.
        Capt. William Minor's Co.
        Capt. Stephen Parry's Co.

24-30 May D.C. Militia Cavalry is activated.
    Lt. Col. John Tayloe, Commanding
        Columbian Hussars—Capt. William G. Ridgely
        Washington Light Horse—Capt. Elias B. Caldwell
        Alexandria Dragoons—Capt. John H. Mandeville

8 Aug Approach of the British fleet to Baltimore.
    U.S. artillery garrison at Ft. McHenry is reinforced with Capt. George Stiles's Marine Artillery.
    Maj. Joseph Jameson, 1st Regiment Maryland Artillery, with Baltimore County Militia develops positions on North Point.

10 Aug British attack St. Michaels—500 Talbot County men from 12th Maryland Brigade, Maryland Militia under Br. Gen. Perry Benson oppose.
    26th Regiment, Maryland Militia—Lt. Col. Hugh Auld
        St. Michaels Artillery—Capt. William Dodson
        Capt. William Jordan's Co.
        St. Michaels Patriotic Blues—Capt. Joseph Kemp
        Hearts of Oak—Capt. Thomas Wayman
        Capt. Oakley Haddaway's Co.
        Capt. John Carroll's Co.
    Attached from 4th Maryland Militia Regiment
        Talbot Volunteer Artillery Co.—Capt. Clement Vickers
        Light Infantry Blues—Capt. George W. Smith
        Easton Fencibles—Capt. John L. Kerr

Capt. Jonathan Spencer's Co.
Attached from 9th Cavalry District
　　　Independant Light Dragoons—Capt. Robert H. Goldsborough
　　　Capt. Robert Banning's Troop
　　　Capt. Willam Dickinson's Troop

13 Aug British attack Queenstown—opposed by 38th Maryland Militia. (Queen Anne's County)
　　　Maj. William H. Nicholson, Commanding.
　　　　　Maj. Thomas Emory's Detachment, 9th Cavalry Distr.
　　　　　Capt. Gustavus Wright's Artillery Co.

1814

Patuxent Battles, June - July

First Battle of St. Leonard's Creek, 10 June 1814
U.S. Flotilla—Commodore Joshua Barney
31st Regiment, Maryland Militia—Col. Michael Taney (Calvert County)

Second Battle of St. Leonard's Creek, 26 June 1814
U.S. Flotilla—Commodore Joshua Barney
36th U.S. Infantry—Col. Henry Carberry (arr. 14 June)
2/38th U.S. Infantry—Maj. George Keyser
U.S. Artillery Det.—Col. Decius Wadsworth
U.S. Artillery Det.—Lt. Thomas L. Harrison
Capt. Samuel Miller's Co., USMC
31st Regiment Maryland Militia, (Calvert Co.) elements—Maj. Stephen Johns;
　　Col. Michael Taney

Other units in the Patuxent area:

Hq. 5th Brigade, Maryland Militia—Br. Gen. Philip Steuart

D.C. Militia—Maj. George Peter, Commanding (19-30 June)
　　Maj. George Peter's Georgetown Artillery
　　　　Capt. John J. Stull's Georgetown Riflemen
　　　　Capt. John C. William's Georgetown Hussars
　　　　Capt. William Thornton's Columbian Dragoons
　　　　Capt. Elias B. Caldwell's Washington Light Horse
　　Capt. John Davidson, Commanding (18 July-25 Aug)
　　　　Union Light Infantry—Capt. John Davidson

Washington Artillery—Capt. Benjamin Burch
Capt. John Doughty's Rifle Company

Battle of Bladensburg 24 August

U.S. 10th Military District—Br. William H. Winder, USA, Commanding

Detachments, 36th and 38th U.S. Infantry Regiments—Lt. Col. William Scott; Capt. Willoughby Morgan's Co., 12th U.S. Infantry, attached.

Squadron, 1st U.S. Dragoons—Lt. Col. Jacint Laval

11th Maryland Militia Brigade—Br. Gen. Tobias E. Stansbury (Baltimore City)
   1st Regiment—Lt. Col. John Ragan (Allegeny, Washington, Frederick Counties)
   2nd Regiment—Lt. Col. Jonathan Schutz
   5th Regiment—Lt. Col. Joseph Sterrett
      1st Rifle Battalion—Maj. William Pinkney
      Washington Battery—Capt. Joseph Myers
      American Artillery Co.—Capt. Richard B. Magruder
   17th Regiment—Col. William D. Beall (Prince George's County)
      Battalion, 32nd Regiment—Lt. Col. Thomas Hood (Anne Arundel
        County), attached
   34th Regiment, detachments (Prince George's County)
      Maj. Samuel Magruder's
      Maj. Henry Waring's

Maryland Militia Cavalry
   Det.—Lt. Col. Frisby Tilghman
   1st Cavalry District—Maj. Otho Williams
      American Blues—Capt. Jacob Barr
      Washington Hussars—Capt. Edward G. Williams
   2nd Cavalry District, Bladensburg Troop of Horse—Capt. John C. Herbert
   5th Cavalry District, Baltimore Light Dragoons—Lt. Jacob Hollingsworth
   5th Cavalry District, 1st Baltimore Hussars—Capt. James Sterrett

1st D.C. Brigade—Br. Gen. Walter Smith (1,070) arr. 20 August
   Capt. John Doughty's Rifle Co.
   Capt. John J. Stull's Rifle Co.
   1st Regiment—Col. George Magruder
   2nd Regiment—Col. William Brent
   Artillery Battalion—Maj. George Peter, 12 x 6 pdrs
      Georgetown Artillery—Maj. George Peter
      Washington Artillery—Capt. Benjamin Burch

Washington Light Horse—Capt. Elias B. Caldwell attached to Tilghman's Maryland command.

Georgetown Hussars—Capt. John C. Williams attached to Tilghman's Maryland command.

2nd D.C. Brigade (Alexandria)—Br. Gen. Robert Young (450) at Fort Washington
1st Regiment—Col. William A. Dangerfield
Columbian Dragoons—Capt. William Thornton attached to Tilghman's Maryland command.

Virginia Militia—60th Infantry Regiment—Col. George Minor (500) arr 23 August

Fairfax Light Dragoons—Capt. George Graham (100)

USN—Flotilla—Comm. Joshua Barney (500)

USMC—Capt. James Miller's Co. (103)

Caulk's Field 30 Aug

21st Regiment Maryland Militia—Lt. Col. Philip Reed (part of 6th Maryland Militia Brigade)
   Capt. Ezekial F. Chambers's Co.
   Lt. Henry Tilghman's Co. (vice Capt. Bedingfield Hand)
   Capt. Simon Wickes's Rifle Co.
   Capt. Samuel Griffiths's Co.
   Capt. Thomas Hynson's Co.
   Lt. Samuel Wickes's Co. (vice Capt. Henry Page)
   Lt. Aquila M. Usselton's Artillery Co. (vice Capt. James Morrison)

White House 1-5 Sept

Captain David Porter, USN
   Crew and marines from USS *Essex*

14th Virginia Brigade—Br. Gen. John P. Hungerford
   111th Infantry Regiment—Lt. Col. Richard Parker (Westmoreland County)
      Capt. Foushee G. Tebbs's Co., 41st Infantry (Westmoreland County) attached
      Capt. Joseph Janney's Co., 6th Infantry (Essex County) attched
      Capt. George Glassock's Cavalry Co., (Westmoreland County) (patrol from White House to Alexandria)
   36th Infantry Regiment—Lt. Col. Enoch Reno (Prince William County)

6th Infantry Regiment—Lt. Col. John Dangerfield (Essex County)
Lt. Col. John W. Green's Mounted Infantry Regiment
    Capt. George W. Ball's Co. (Loudoun County)
    Capt. Nicholas Osbourn's Co. (Loudoun County)
    Capt. Carver Willis's Dragoons (Jefferson County)
    Capt. George W. Humphrey's Rifles (Jefferson County)
Capt. David Griffith's Alexandria Artillery Co. (D.C. Militia)

Indian Head 6 Sept

Capt. Oliver H. Perry, USN
    Crew and marines from USS *Java*
    D.C. Militia
        Georgetown Artillery—Maj. George Peter
        Washington Artillery—Capt. Benjamin Burch
        Union Light Infantry—Capt. John Davivson
        D.C. Rifle Corps—Capt. John J. Stull
    Br. Gen. Philip Steuart, 5th Maryland Brigade
        Capt. John Barnes's Artillery Co. (Charles Co.) - Lt. William W. Lewis
        1st Infantry Regiment (elms) (Charles Co.) - Lt. Col. Samuel Hawkins

Defense of Baltimore Aug-Nov

1st Maryland Militia Brigade—Br. Gen. Thomas Foreman (Harford, Cecil, Ann Arundel Counties)
    30th, 40th, 42nd, 49th Infantry Regiments
    32nd Infantry Regiment—Col. Thomas Hood, 8th Brigade, (Ann Arundel County), attached

2d Maryland Militia Brigade—Lt. Col. John Ragan (Allegany, Washington Counties)
    8th, 10th, 24th, 50th Infantry, and 1st Cavalry Regiments

3d Maryland Militia Brigade—Br. Gen. John Stricker (Baltimore County)
(see North Point organization)

7th Brigade elements (Frederick County)
    Cos. from 3rd, 13th, 29th, 49th Infantry Regiments attached to 2d Brigade

8th Brigade
    32nd Infantry Regiment attached to 1st Brigade

9th Brigade elements (Frederick County)
    Cos. from 16th, 20th, 47th Infantry Regiments attached to 2nd Brigade

11th Brigade—Br. Gen. Tobias E. Stansbury (Baltimore County)
7th, 15th, 36th, 41st, 46th Infantry Regiments

1st Regiment Maryland Artillery—Lt. Col. David Harris
Franklin Artillery—Capt. Joseph Meyers
Columbia Artillery—Capt. Samuel Moale
Baltimore Union Artillery—Capt. John Montgomery (attched 5th Regiment)
Baltimore Fencibles—Capt. Joseph H. Nicholson
American Artillerists—Capt. John B. Magruder
Washington Artillery—Capt. John Berry
Baltimore Independent Artillerists—Capt. George J. Brown
1st Baltimore Volunteer Artillery—Capt. Abraham Pike
United Maryland Artillery—Capt. James Piper

Corps of Marine Artillery—Capt. George Stiles

Provisional Division, Pennsylvania Militia—Maj. Gen. Nathaniel Watson
1st Brigade—Br. Gen. John Foster
2nd Brigade—Br. Gen. John Addams
(Regiments and Companies from Berks, Bucks, Chester, Dauphin, Lancaster,
Lebanon, Schuylkill and York Counties)

Virginia Militia Division—Maj. Gen. John Pegram (see Virginia Militia section)
2nd Virginia Brigade—Br. Gen. Joel Leftwich
3rd Virginia Brigade—Br. Gen. John Breckenridge
6th Virginia Brigade—Br. Gen. Hugh Douglass

Detachments from 12th, 14th, 36th and 38th U.S. Infantry Regiments—Lt. Col.
William Steuart

Detachments from 1st U.S. Dragoons—Lt. Col. Jacint Laval

Detachments from 2nd U.S. Artillery—Capt. Frederick Evans

Lt. Joseph S. Kuhn's Co., USMC

Capt. M. Simmones Bunbury's Co., U.S. Fencibles

Capt. William H. Addison s Co., U.S. Fencibles

Detachments from U.S. ships *Guerriere, Erie, Java*

Detachments from U.S. Chesapeake Flotilla—Lt. Solomon Rutter

Western Maryland Units in Baltimore, July-Oct 1814

Washington County—raised 11 July.
Headquarters 1st Maryland Regiment—Lt. Col. John Ragan Jr.
Capt. George Shryrock's Co., Hagerstown
Homespun Volunteers, Hagerstown—Capt. Thomas Quantrill (at North Point)
Hagerstown Cavalry—Capt. Jacob Barr (attched to 5th Maryland Cavalry)
Capt. Gerard Stonebreaker's Co., Funkstown
Capt. Henry Lowry's Co.

Allegeny County—raised 11 Aug
Capt. William McLaughlin's Co.
Capt. Thomas Blair's Co.

Frederick County—raised 25 Aug
Frederick Artillery—Capt. Henry Steiner (assigned to 1st Maryland Regiment)
Frederick Minutemen—Capt. John Brengle
Capt. Nicholas Turnbull's Co.
Capt. George W. Ent's Co. (attched to 1st Maryland Regiment from 3rd Maryland Regiment)
Capt. John Galt's Co.

Battle of North Point, 12 Sept

3rd Brigade Maryland Militia—Br. Gen. John Stricker
5th Regiment Maryland Cavalry Militia—Lt. Col. James Biays (140)
Independent Light Dragoons—Capt. Jehu Bouldin
1st Baltimore Hussars—Capt. James Sterrett
Maryland Chasseurs—Capt. James Horton
Fell's Point Light Dragoons—Capt. John Hanna
1st Regiment of Artillery Maryland Militia—Lt. Col. David Harris (not present)
Baltimore Union Artillery—Capt. John Montgomery (75) (6 x 4 pdrs)
1st Rifle Battalion, Maryland Militia—Maj. William Pinkney (150)
Sharp Shooters—Capt. Edward Aisquith
Union Yagers—Capt. Dominic Bader
Fell's Point Riflemen—Capt. William B. Dyer
5th Regiment of Infantry, Maryland Militia—Lt. Col. Joseph Sterrett (550)
Baltimore Yeagers—Capt. Philip B. Sadtler
1st Baltimore Light Infantry—Capt. John Shrim
Mechanical Volunteers—Capt. Benjamin C. Howard
Washington Blues—Capt. George H. Steuart

Independant Co.—Capt. Samuel Sterrett
Baltimore United Volunteers—Capt. David Warfield
Union Volunteers—(Capt. Christian Adreon)/Ens. John Wilmot
  commanding.
Baltimore Patriots—Capt. Robert Lawson
Independant Blues—Capt. Aaron R. Levering
York (Pennsylvania) Volunteers—Capt. Michael H. Spangler
6th Regiment of Infantry Maryland Militia—Lt. Col. William McDonald (620)
  Capt. Thomas Sheppard's Co.
  Capt. Gerrard Wilson's Co.
  Capt. Peter Galt's Co.
  Capt. William Brown's Co.
  Capt. Thomas T. Lawrence's Co.
  Capt. Benjamin Ringgold's Co.
  Capt. Luke Kierstead's Co.
  Capt. Samuel McDonald's Co.
  Capt. Robert Conway's Co.
  Capt. Nicholas Burke's Co.
  Marietta (Pennsylvania) Volunteers—Capt. John G. Dixon
27th Regiment of Infantry, Maryland Militia—Lt. Col. Kennedy Long (500)
  Capt. James McConkey's Co.
  Capt. John Kennedy's Co.
  Capt. Benjamin Eades's Co.
  Capt. John McKane's Co.
  Capt. Peter Pinney's Co.
  Capt. George Steever's Co.
  Capt. Daniel Schwarzauer's Co.
  Capt. James Dillon's Co.
39th Regiment of Infantry, Maryland Militia —Lt. Col. Benjamin Fowler (450)
  Capt. Archibald Dobbin's Co.
  Capt. Thomas Warner's Co.
  Capt. Thomas Watson's Co.
  Capt. John D. Miller's Co.
  Capt. Andrew E. Warner's Co.
  Capt. Henry Myer's Co.
  Capt. Joseph K. Stapleton's Co.
  Capt. William Roney's Co.
  Hanover (Pennsylvania) Volunteers—Capt. Frederick Metzger
  Hagerstown (Maryland) Volunteers—Capt. Thomas Quantrill
51st Regiment of Infantry, Maryland Militia—Lt. Col. Henry Amey (700)
  Capt. Jacob Deems' Co.
  Capt. William Chalmer's Co.
  Capt. John H. Rogers's Co.

Capt. Michael Haubert's Co.
Capt. John Stewart's Co.
Capt. James Easter's Co.
Capt. Michael Peters' Co.
Capt. Andrew Smith's Co.

Virginia Militia in State and Federal Service

Norfolk 1812 Local militia from Norfolk, Pr. Anne, Nansemond, Warwick and
Elizabeth City Counties were called up immediately after the declaration of war.
They were reinforced by Lt. Col.Edmund Lucas's 500-man Greensville County
Regiment (50th Virginia Militia), called up for six months.

Background Gov. Barbour issued orders on 6 Feb 1813 to ensure continuous
manning of the Norfolk defenses. Three regiments were created to be filled by
companies rotating into them from throughout the state. Br. Gen. Robert B.
Taylor, 4th Virginia Cavalry, a Norfolk lawyer, was named first commander of
the entire force. When he received federal recognition on 9 Feb., he also
assumed command of the 5th Military District. Lt. Col. Constant Freeman,
USA, the senior regular in the district, reverted to command of Fort Nelson in
Norfolk.
Maj. Gawin Corbin's 1st Virginia Regiment was the first to be formed with a
battalion each in Hampton and Norfolk.
Lt. Col. William Sharp's 2nd Virginia Regiment garrisoned Norfolk in June and
Craney Island in August.
Lt. Col. Francis Boylan's 3rd Virginia Regiment occupied Portsmouth and had
other elements stationed at Fort Norfolk, Fort Nelson, and Craney Island.
Gen. Taylor mixed the county militias within each regiment to reduce nepotism
and to improve discipline.
British activity led Gov. Barbour to call up two more regiments: The 4th (Lt. Col.
Henry Beatty) and the 5th (Lt. Col. Armistead T. Mason) were activated on 24
March 1813 and served under various commanders with a mix of militia
companies until March 1815. The 4th Regiment occupied Fort Norfolk while
the 5th was stationed throughout the borough of Norfolk. Five additional
temporary regiments were raised in the summer of 1814 to reinforce the
Norfolk garrison, serving until disbanded in February 1815.

A Special command was formed in Sept-Nov 1814 with two brigades:
Maj. Gen. Thomas Parker, Commanding
1st Brigade—Br. Gen. Robert Taylor
8th Virginia, 9th Virginia, 1st/8th Brigade (Allen's) Regiments
2d Brigade—Col. Josiah Goodwyn, 35th U.S. Infantry
4th, 5th, 6th, 7th Virginia Regiments

Norfolk Command 1813-15

Commanding:Br. Gen. Robert Taylor (10 Jan 1813-7 April 1813)
  Br. Gen. Wade Hampton (7 April-2 June 1813)
  Br. Gen. Robert Taylor (2 June 1813-5 Feb 1814)
  Br. Gen. Thomas Parker (5 Feb 1814- 1 Nov 1814)
  Br. Gen. Moses Porter (1 Nov 1814- March 1815)

1 Aug 1812-31 Jan 1813 4th Virginia Militia (Bedford, Southampton, Brunswick, Isle of Wight, Greensville, Pr. George)—Lt. Col. Edmund Lucas (d. 5 Dec 1812); Lt. Col. Langley C. Wells

6 Feb 1813-14 Aug 1813 1st Virginia Regiment (Powhatan, York, Essex, Dinwiddie)—Lt. Col. James Clarke
  Detachment at Hampton—Maj. Gawin L. Corbin

9 Feb 1813-14 Aug 1813 2nd Virginia Regiment (Nansemond, King and Queen, King William, New Kent, Charles City, Dinwiddie, Pr. Anne, Norfolk, Isle of Wight, Petersburg, Richmond)—Lt. Col. William Sharp

6 Feb 1813-14 Aug 1813 3rd Virginia Regiment (Dinwiddie, Southampton, Nansemond, Norfolk, Pr. Anne, Isle of Wight)—Lt. Col. Francis M. Boykin

1 April 1813-22 Feb 1815 4th Virginia Regiment (Frederick, Rockbridge, Fauquier, Jefferson, Sussex, Orange, Chesterfield, Loudoun, Albemarle, Louisa)—Lt. Col. Henry Beatty at muster; Lt. Col. Thomas H. Wooding at discharge

5 May 1813-March 1815 5th Virginia Regiment (72 Piedmont and Valley Companies)—Lt. Col. Armistead Mason at muster; Lt. Col. Isaac Booth at discharge

26 Aug 1813-Feb 1815 6th Virginia Regiment (Mecklenburg, Lunenburg, Chesterfield, Amelia, plus later companies from throughout the state)—Lt. Col. Grief Green at muster; Lt. Col. Isaac Booth at discharge

Aug 1814-10 Feb 1815 7th Virginia Regiment (Southside and Mountain)—Lt. Col. David Saunders

19 Aug 1814-Oct 1814 8th Virginia Regiment (Norfolk, Southampton, Isle of Wight, Surrey, Pr. Anne, Hanover, Nansemond)—Lt. Col. Bernard Magnien

Aug 1814-Oct 1814 9th Virginia Regiment (Norfolk, Nansemond, Pr. Anne, Hanover, Sussex, King and Queen)—Lt. Col. William Sharp

2 April 1813 1st Virginia Regiment Det. at Hampton redesignated Crutchfield's
Battalion—Maj. Stapleton Crutchfield
    Capt. Nimrod Ashby's Co. (Fauquier)
    Capt. Reuben Herndon's Co. (Albemarle)
    Capt. Thomas O. Jenning's Co. (Fauquier)
    Capt. Thomas Miller's Co. (Orange)
    Capt. Brazure W. Pryor's Artillery Det. (Elizabeth City) eff. Aug 1813

Militia Artillery Organized April 1813 into 1st Virginia Artillery Regiment (eight
companies)—Lt. Col. Thomas Reade Jr.; redesignated Oct 1813, Battalion of
Artillery (sixteen companies) and mustered into federal service—Col. Constant
Freeman

Militia Cavalry Eight Tidewater companies under Capt. Samuel Carr served various
periods between March 1813 and Feb 1814.
    Maj. William Sale's Battalion (Amherst, Greenville, Pittsylvania) served between
March 1814 and July 1814.
    Maj. Thomas Hunter's Command (Mecklenburg, Loudoun, Sussex, Fauquier)
served from Dec 1813-April 1814.

On Craney Island 20-22 June 1813

Lt. Col. Henry Beatty, Commanding post

Maj. Andrew Waggoner, Commanding infantry

Maj. James Faulkner, Commanding artillery (2 x 24 pdr, 1 x 18 pdr)
    Battalion, 4th Virginia Regiment—Maj. Andrew Waggoner (416)
    Capt. Thomas Robert's Co. of Riflemen (Frederick County) (50)
    Portsmouth Light Artillery—Capt. Arthur Emmerson (38) (4 x 6 pdr)
    Capt. John D. Richardson's Co. of Light Artillery (Charlotte County) (53) (served
as infantry)

Reinforcements 21 June
    Capt. Richard Pollard's Co., 20th U.S. Infantry (30)
    Det., Capt. Jesse Naile's Co., 5th Virginia Regiment—Lt. Johnson (Culpeper) (15)
    Det., Riflemen—Capt. Hamilton Shields Co., 3rd Virginia Regiment—Ens.
Archibald Atkinson (Isle of Wight) (15)
    Det., USS *Constellation* Crew—Lt. B. J. Neale, Lt. W. Brandford Shubrick, Lt.
James Saunders (100)
    Det., USS *Constellation* Marines—Lt. Henry B. Breckenridge, USMC (50)

Hampton 25 June 1813

Maj. Stapleton Crutchfield's Battalion (also post commander)
    Capt. Nimrod Ashby's Co. (Fauquier)
    Capt. Reuben Herndon's Co. (Albemarle)
    Capt. Thomas O. Jennings' Co. (Fauquier)
    Capt. Thomas O. Miller's Co. (Orange)

Maj. Gawin L. Corbin's Battalion, 1st Virginia Regiment
    (Capt. John Goodall, 2rd U.S. Artillery, vol. deputy cdr.)
    Capt. Richard B. Servant's Rifles (Hampton)
    Capt. Samuel Shield's Co. (Elizabeth City, Warwick, York)
    Capt. John E. Browne's Light Infantry (York)
    Capt. Brazure W. Pryor's Artillery Co. (Elizabeth City, York)
    Capt. John B. Cooper's Cavalry Co. (Elizabeth City, Warwick, York)

(349 Infantry, 62 Artillery, 25 Cavalry = 439 men)

Virginia Militia Deployment during crisis of Aug-Sep 1814

2nd Virginia Brigade—Br. Gen. Joel Leftwich, 1 Sep 1814-1 Dec 1814
    3rd Virginia Regiment—Lt. Col. William Dickinson (Bedford, Campbell,
        Pittsylvania, Halifax)
    4th Virginia Regiment—Lt. Col. William Greenhill (Pittsylvania, Halifax,
        Charlotte) (stationed in Baltimore area 27 Oct-9 Nov 1814)

3rd Virginia Brigade—Br. Gen John Breckenridge, Aug-Nov 1814
    Nine miscellaneous Valley Companies (including two Cavalry troops)
    6th Virginia Regiment—Lt. Col. Daniel Coleman
    (stationed in Baltimore area 5 Oct-Nov 1814)

6th Virginia Brigade—Br. Gen. Hugh Douglass, Aug-Nov 1814
    1st Virginia Regiment, 16th Virginia Brigade—Lt. Col. Griffin Taylor (Frederick,
        Berkeley, Jefferson)
    56th Virginia Regiment—Lt. Col. Timothy Taylor (Loudoun)*
    57th Virginia Regiment—Lt. Col. Armstead Mason (Loudoun)
    60th Virginia Regiment—Lt. Col. George Minor (Fairfax)*
    Capt. Eben Taylor's Cavalry Co. (Frederick)
    (stationed at Baltimore Aug-Nov 1814, participated in defense of city)

* consolidated 19 Sept under Lt. Col. Minor

Alexandria Sept-Oct 1814

Maj. John Kemper's Command
　　Capt. John Ashby's Co. (Fauquier)
　　Capt. Edward Digges's Co. (Fauquier)

Along Potomac

1st Virginia Regiment, Madison's Brigade (Aug-Dec 1814)—Lt. Col. Stapleton Crutchfield
　　12 Piedmont companies based at Fredericksburg and along Potomac River

Mounted Infantry Regiment (Aug-Sep 1814)—Lt. Col. John W. Green
　　Capt. George W. Ball's Co. (Loudoun)
　　Capt. Nicholas Osburn's Co. (Loudoun)
　　Capt. Carver Willis's Dragoons (Jefferson)
　　(stationed at Dumfries)

(Sources: Butler, S., Va. Militia; Hogue, Northern Neck; Huntsberry, Militia; Marine, Invasion; Niles, Register; Scharf, Western Maryland; Baltimore; Tilghman, Talbot County; Todd, D.C. Militia; USNARA, RG94.)

Regular Army units associated with Chesapeake region sites:

UNIT	RECRUITING DISTRICT	ASSIGNMENT IN JULY 1814
12th Infantry Regiment	Staunton, VA	Right Div., 9th Dist. (NY)
14th Infantry Regiment	Baltimore, MD	Right Div., 9th Dist. (NY)
20th Infantry Regiment	Fredericksburg, VA	Norfolk, VA
35th Infantry Regiment	Petersburg, VA	Norfolk, VA
36th Infantry Regiment	Georgetown, D.C. Richmond, VA	St. Mary's Co., MD
38th Infantry Regiment	Norfolk, VA Baltimore, MD	1st Bn., Norfolk, VA 2nd Bn., Baltimore, MD
Rifles	Shenandoah Valley Cumberland Valley	Left Div., 9th Dist. (NY)

(Source: American State Papers: Military Affairs, Vol.1; Army Register, 1813.)

Distribution of Regular Forces in the Fifth and Tenth Military District

			1 July 1814	30 Sept 1814
Norfolk	Artillery		224	
	Infantry	20th US		153
		35th US	873	362
		1/38th US		103
Baltimore	Artillery			65
	Infantry	2/38th	300	103
	Sea Fencibles		167	
Annapolis	Artillery		40	
Southern Maryland	Infantry	36th US	320	136
Fort Washington	Artillery		79	

Appendix C

ॐ

ORDER OF BATTLE
CHESAPEAKE OPERATIONS, 1812-15
BRITISH ORGANIZATIONS

April and May 1813

Royal Marine shipboard companies.

Lt. Frederick Robertson's Det. from Capt. George Crawford's Company, Royal Artillery.

June - August 1813

Land Force commander—Col. Sir Sydney Beckwith
    102nd Regiment—Lt. Col. Charles Napier
    1st Battalion Royal Marines—Lt. Col. Richard Williams
    2nd Battalion Royal Marines—Maj. James Malcolm

1st Independent Co. of Foreigners—Capt. Sylvester Smith
2nd Independent Co. of Foreigners—Capt. Monduet

Shipboard Marine Companies
    1st Co. Royal Marine Artillery—Capt. John Montgomerie
    2nd Co. Royal Marine Artillery—Capt. Thomas Parke
    Rocket Co. Royal Marine Artillery—Lt. George Bulchild

For the attack on Craney Island Lt. Col. Napier led a brigade composed of the 102d Regiment, 2nd Battalion RM, 1st Co. of Foreigners and 2nd Co. RMA; Lt. Col. Williams' brigade consisted of the 1st Battalion RM, 2nd Co. of Foreigners and 1st Co. RMA. At the attack on Hampton, Napier's brigade consisted of the 102nd Regiment, both companies of foreigners and three companies of shipboard marines. Lt. Col. Williams' brigade had both marine battalions and all the artillery.

21-30 August 1814 Operations Against Washington

Naval Commander— Rear Adm. George Cockburn
                Lt. James Scott, RN, ADC

Army Commander— Maj. Gen. Robert Ross
                Capt. Thomas Falls, ADC
                Capt. Harry Smith, Asst. Adj. Gen.
                Lt. George De Lacy Evans, Acting Dep. QMG

1st (Light) Brigade—Lt. Col. William Thornton, Jr.
    85th (Light Infantry) Regiment—Lt. Col. William Wood
    Light Companies, 4th, 21st, 44th Regiments—Maj. Timothy Jones
    Co., 2nd Battalion, Royal Marines—Lt. Stephens
    Co., Colonial Marines—Capt. James Reed

2nd Brigade—Col. Arthur Brooke
    4th Regiment—Maj. Alured D. Faunce
    44th Regiment—Maj. Thomas Mullins

3rd Brigade—Lt. Col. William Patterson
    21st Regiment—Maj. John A. Whitaker
    2nd Battalion, Royal Marines—Maj. George Lewis

Royal Navy Landing Party
    Provisional Battalion, Royal Marines—Capt. John Robyns
    Division of Armed Seamen—Capt. Palmer, RN

Detachment, Royal Artillery—Capt. Lewis Carmichael

2nd Co. Royal Marine Artillery—Capt. James Harrison

Rocket Section, Royal Marine Artillery—Lt. John Lawrence

Royal Artillery Drivers—Capt. William Lempière

2nd Co., 4th Battalion Royal Sappers and Miners—Capt. Thomas Blanchard

11-15 September Operations Against Baltimore

Naval Commander— Rear Adm. George Cockburn
             Lt. James Scott, RN, ADC

Army Commander— Maj. Gen. Robert Ross (to 12 Sept)
             Col. Arthur Brooke (from 12 Sept)
             Maj. Henry Debbeig, Asst. Adj. Gen.
             Lt. George De Lacy Evans, Actg. Dep. QMQ
             Lt. Frederick Williams, Asst. QM

1st (Light) Brigade— Col. Arthur Brooke (to 12 Sept)
             Maj. Timothy Jones (from 12 Sept)
   85th (Light Infantry) Regiment—Maj. Richard Gubbins
   Light Companies 4th, 21st, 44th Regiment—Maj. Norman Pringle, later Maj.
      Robert Renny

2nd Brigade—Lt. Col. Thomas Mullins
   4th Regiment—Maj. A.D. Faunce
   44th Regiment—Maj. John Johnson
   Provisional Battalion, shipboard Marines—Capt. John Robyns
   Naval Landing Party—Capt. Edward Crofton, RN

3rd Brigade—Lt. Col. William Patterson
   21st Regiment—Maj. John H. Whitaker
   2nd Battalion, Royal Marines—Maj. George Lewis

Capt. Lewis Carmichaels' Co., Royal Artillery

Capt. John Mitchell's Co., Royal Artillery

2nd Co., Royal Marine Artillery—Capt. James Harrison

Rocket Section, Royal Marine Artillery—Lt. John Lawrence

Det., Royal Artillery Drivers—Capt. William Lempière

2nd Co., 4th Battalion Royal Sappers and Miners—Capt. Thomas Blanchard

(Sources: Army List, 1814; Brooke, Report; Cockburn, Report; Field; Fortescue; Fraser; Gleig; James; Pack.)

Bibliography

Archives:

American Antiquarian Society
185 Salisbury St.
Worcester, MA 01609
  Orderly books of Gen. Robert B. Taylor *in re* Norfolk, Virginia defenses

Calvert Museum
Solomons, MD 20688
  Clem Hollyday letter *in re* war on Patuxent
  Joshua Barney *in re* Leonard's Creek Skirmish, 1814

Crawford County History Society
848 N. Main St.
Meadville, PA 16355
  Henry Shippon on the capture of Washington

Detroit Public Library
Burton History Collection
5201 Woodward Ave.
Detroit, MI 48202
  Cutts family papers *in re* fall of Washington

Duke University
Perkins Library
Durham, NC 27706
  Samuel B. Clark papers
  William B. Chamberlayne papers
  Samuel Kello papers
  William Kemp papers

Fort McHenry National Monument
Baltimore, MD 21230
  Letters to and from Capt. George Armistead

Glassboro State College Library
Glassboro, NJ 08028
  Benjamin Howell Fort McHenry account

Illinois State Library
Old State Capitol
Springfield, IL 62706
  Duncan family papers *in re* Chesapeake
  Journal of the privateer *Rossie* out of Baltimore

Maryland Hall of Records
Annapolis, MD 21402
  C.N. Causins and James Forrest to Maj. James Thomas
  9 Apr. 1813—Gift Collection, Box G-176/260

Maryland Historical Society
201 W. Monument St.
Baltimore, MD 21201
  Archives of Maryland Vols. 22 and 26
  Contractor Robert C. Jennings *in re* supplies for Virginia and North Carolina
  troops
  Gen. Samuel Smith papers
  War of 1812 in Maryland and Baltimore papers
  Zach Spratt coll. *in re* Star Spangled Banner
  James Jarboe papers, incl. 12th Maryland Regiment Accounts
  Samuel A. Harrison papers *in re* war in Talbot County
  Wm. H. Winder and John Stricker papers *in re* Baltimore Battle
  Thomas Beall *in re* Burning of Washington
  Militia unit items

Naval Historic Foundation
Washington Navy Yard
Washington, DC 20390
　Adm. Alexander Cochrane *in re* the burning of Washington

National Archives of Canada
Ottowa, KIA OK2, Canada
　RG8, I C Series
　MGII, CO42, Q Series

North Carolina Division of Archives and History
109 E. Jones Street
Raleigh, NC 27611
　Mordecai family papers *in re* life in Washington

New York Historical Society
170 Central Park West
New York, NY 10024
　Descriptions of the capture of Washington by Mary Hunt and Allen McLane

Peabody Institute Library
Danvers, MA 09123
　Moses Porter papers

Pennsylvania Historical and Museum Commission
Box 126
Harrisburg, PA 17120
　Gen. Gabriel Hiester, reflections on the Balto.-Wash. campaigns

Pennsylvania Historical Society
1300 Locust Street
Philadelphia, PA 19107
　Vincent Gray in Shaler family papers *in re* capture of Washington and Battle of New
　Orleans
　Barney papers in Dreer Collection

Public Record Office
66 Balmoral Avenue
Belfast, BT96NY, N. Ireland, U.K.
　Sir Arthur Brooke, Diary/Autobiography, (Ref. D 3004/D/2; Microfilm 840)

University of Michigan
Clements Library
Ann Arbor, MI 48104
 John Wilson Croker Coll., Adm. George Cockburn papers

University of North Carolina
Wilson Library
Chapel Hill, NC 27514
 Records of Maryland Militia in papers of Gen. Joel Leftwich (Southern Historical
 Collections)

University of Virginia
Alderman Library
Charlottesville, VA 22901
 Papers by Joel Leftwich *in re* the Northwest and the Virginia Militia

United States Library of Congress
Washington, DC 20540
 Adm. George Cockburn papers
 Sir Charles Napier, Campaigning in the Chesapeake
 James James, Attack on Craney Island
 Joshua Barney, Defense of the Chesapeake
 Clement Hollyday to Urban Hollyday, 12 Jul 1814
 John Rodgers papers
 Charles Simms papers (Mayor of Alexandria, 1814)
 Constant Freeman papers
 Fort Nelson Orderly Book

United States National Archives and Records Administration
Record Group 15: Records of the Veterans Administration
 Selected Pension Applications, War of 1812 series (M313)
 Selected Bounty-Land Warrant Application Files, 1800-1815 (M804)
Record Group 45: Records of the Secretary of the Navy
 Letters Received, Miscellaneous (M124, R.64)
Record Group 94: Records of the Office of the Adjutant General
 Letters Sent, 1812-1815 (M565)
 Letters Received, 1812-1815 (M566)
 Muster Rolls of Volunteer Organizations of the War of 1812: Virginia
 Returns of Army Commands: War of 1812
 Carded Records, Volunteer Organizations, War of 1812: Virginia
 Manuscript File for the War of 1812
 Returns of Killed and Wounded in Battles and
 Engagements with Indians, British, and Mexican Troops, 1790-1848 (Eaton's

Compendium)
Record Group 107: Records of the Office of the Secretary of War
    Letters Sent, 1812-1815 (M420)
    Letters Received, 1812-1815 (M221, R.67)

United States Naval Academy Library
Annapolis, MD 21402
    Joshua Barney letter *in re* a naval battle
    British officer's journal *in re* Chesapeake campaigns

Virginia State Library & Archives
Richmond, VA 22320
    Governor James Barbour Executive papers, 1812-14
    Militia Commissions, 1812-15
    Hailey Cole papers
    Andrew Stevenson papers
    Aylette Waller papers
    David Watson papers
    6th Virginia Regiment papers
    93d Virginia Regiment papers

Virginia Historical Society
Richmond, VA 23221-0311
    James Barbour papers
    William Butt Order Book, 1813
    Brigade and Regimental Order Book, Norfolk, 1813
    Richard Corbin Order Book, 1813
    Stapleton Crutchfield militia papers
    Benjamin Graves Order Book, 1813-14
    Henderson family papers, 1778-1830
    George Hannah Order Book, 1813-14
    Charles Porterfield Order Book, 1814
    Thomas Reeke Order Book, 1813-14
    Vincent Shackleford Order Book, 1813
    Andrew Waggoner Order Book, 1814
    Claiborne Watts Gooch papers, 1812
    Fifth Virginia Order Book, 1814-15
    Joseph Kent papers, 1813
    Christopher Tompkins papers, 1813

Western Michigan Univ. Library
Kalamazoo, MI 49001
    Sgt. Greenburg Keene 1812-13 Journal, Pennsylvania Militia

Books:

Adams, Henry. *The War of 1812.* Washington: Infantry Journal, 1944. (Repr. 1891 ed.)

"An Officer" (Gleig). *A Narrative of the Campaigns of the British Army...* London: John Murray, 1821.

The Annual Register, or a View of the History, Politics, and Literature for the year 1813. London: Baldwin, Cradock & Jay, 1823.

Anon. *Historical Record of the Fourth, or the King's Own Regiment of Foot.* London: Longman, Orme & Co., 1839.

Armstrong, John. *Notices of the War of 1812.* Vol. I, New York: George Dearborn Publ, 1836; Vol. II, New York: Wiley and Putnam, 1840.

Auchinleck, G. *A History of the War Between Great Britain and the United States of America.* Toronto: Maclear & Co., 1855.

Ball, Charles. *Slavery in the United States, A Narrative of the Life and Adventures of Charles Ball, A Black Man.* New York: Negro Universities Press, 1969. (reprint of 1837 ed.)

Barlett, C. J. *Castlereigh.* New York: Charles Scribner's Sons, 1966.

Barney, Mary, ed. *A Biographical Memoir of the Late Commodore Joshua Barney: From Autobiographical Notes and Journals in Possession of His Family, and Other Authentic Sources.* Boston: Gray & Bowen, 1832.

Barrett, C. R. B., ed. *The 85th King's Light Infantry.* London: Spotteswoode & Co. Ltd., 1913.

Beirne, Francis F. *The War of 1812.* New York: E. P. Dutton and Co. Inc., 1949.

Bourchier, Lady. *Memoir of the Life of Admiral Sir Edward Codrington.* London: Longmans, Green & Co., 1873.

Brackenridge, Henry M. *History of the Late War Between the United States and Great Britain.* Philadelphia: James Kay Jr. & Bro., 1839.

Brannan, John, ed. *Official Letters of the Military and Naval Officers of the U.S. During the War of 1812.* Washington: Way & Gideon, 1823.

Brant, Irving. *James Madison: President.* Vol.6, *James Madison: Commander-in-Chief 1812-1836.* New York & Indianapolis: Bobbs-Merrill, 1961.

Brenton, Edward P. *The Naval History of Great Britain From the Year 1783 to 1836.* London: Henry Colburn, Publ., 1837.

Brugger, Robert J. *Maryland, A Middle Temperament, 1634-1980.* Baltimore: Johns Hopkins Univ. Press in assoc. with Maryland Historical Society, 1988.

Buchan, John. *The History of the Royal Scots Fusiliers (1678-1918).* London: Thomas Nelson and Sons, Ltd., 1926.

Buel, Richard, Jr. *Securing the Nation: Ideology in American Politics, 1789-1815.* Ithaca: Cornell Univ. Press, 1972.

Burns, James M. *The Vineyard of Liberty.* New York: Alfred A. Knopf, 1982.

Bushong, Millard. *A History of Jefferson County, West Virginia.* Charles Town, West Virginia: Jefferson Publ. Co., 1941.

Butler, Stuart L. *A Guide to Virginia Militia Units in the War of 1812.* Athens, Ga.: Therian Publ. Co., 1988.

Butler, William F. *Sir Charles James Napier.* London: MacMillan, 1890.

Byron, Gilbert. *The War of 1812 on the Chesapeake Bay.* Baltimore: Maryland Historical Soc., 1964.

Caffrey, Kate. *The Twilight's Last Gleaming: Britain vs. America 1812-1815.* New York: Stein & Day Publs., 1977.

Callcott, Margaret L. ed. *Mistress of Riversdale: The Plantation Letters of Rosalie Stier Calvert, 1795-1821.* Baltimore: Johns Hopkins Univ. Press, 1991.

Calloway, Colin G. Crown and Calument: *Crown and Calument: British-Indian Relations, 1783-1815.* Norman: Univ. of Oklahoma Press, 1987.

Cannon, Richard. *Historical Records of the British Army.* London: Parker, Furnival & Parker, 1849.

Cassell, Frank A. *Merchant Congressman in the Young Republic, Samuel Smith of Maryland, 1752-1839.* Madison: Univ. of Wisc. Press, 1971.

Chamier, Frederic. *The Life of a Sailor.* 2 Vols., London: Richard Bentley, 1855.(New Edition) (First Edition 1833)

Chapelle, Howard I. *The History of the American Sailing Navy: The Ships and Their Development.* New York: W. W. Norton & Co., 1949.

Chesterton, George L. *Peace, War, and Adventure: An Autobiography of George Laval Chesterton.* 2 Vols., London: Longman, Brown & Green, 1853.

Chichester, Henry M., and George Burges-Short. *The Records and Badges of Every Regiment and Corps in the British Army.* London: Gale & Polden Ltd., 1900.

Clarke, William P. *Official History of the Militia and the National Guard of the State of Pennsylvania.* N.P.: Capt. Charles J. Hendler, 1909.

Cole, John W. *Memoirs of British Generals Distinguished During the Peninsula War.* 2 Vols., London: Richard Bentley, 1856.

Coles, Harry L. *The War of 1812.* Chicago & London: Univ. of Chicago Press, 1965.

Connolly, T. W. J. *The History of the Corps of Royal Sappers and Miners.* 2 Vols., London: Longman, Brown, Green, and Longmans, 1855.

Cowper, L.I. *The King's Own, The Story of a Royal Regiment.* 2 Vols., Oxford: Univ. Press for the Regiment, 1939.

Cress, Lawrence D. *Citizens in Arms: The Army and Militia in American Society to the War of 1812.* Chapel Hill: Univ. of North Carolina Press, 1982.

Dangerfield, George. *The Era of Good Feelings.* New York and Burlingame: Harcourt, Brace and World, Inc., 1963.

Dagg, John L. *Autobiography.* Harrisonburg, Va: Gan Books, 1982 (reprint 1878 ed.)

Davis, Paris M. *An Authentic History of the Late War Between the United States and Great Britain.* Ithaca: Mack and Andrus, 1829.

Davis, Paris M. *The Four Principal Battles of the Late War.* Harrisburg: Jacob Baab, 1832. (reprint Tarrytown, NY, 1917)

Dobyns, Kenneth W. *The Patent Office Pony: A History of the Early Patent Office.* Fredericksburg, Va.: Kirkland s Museum And History Society, 1994.

Dudley, William S. *The Naval War of 1812, A Documentary History.* 2 Vols., Washington, D.C.: Naval Historical Center, 1985.

Duncan, Francis. *History of the Royal Regiment of Artillery.* 2 Vols., London: John Murray, 1873.

Egle, William H. *History of the Counties of Dauphin and Lebanon in the Commonwealth of Pennsylvania.* Philadelphia: Everts and Peck, 1883.

Elting, John R. *Amateurs to Arms: A Military History of the War of 1812.* Chapel Hill, N.C.: Algonquin Books, 1991.

Ellis, Franklin and Samuel Evans. *History of Lancaster County Pennsylvania with Biographical Sketches.* Philadelphia: Everts and Peck, 1883.

Emmons, George F. *The Navy of the United States from the Commencement 1775 to 1853.* Washington, D.C.: Gideon & Co., 1853.

Emory, Frederic. *Queen Anne's County, Maryland, Its Early History and Development.* Baltimore: Maryland Historical Society, 1950.

Evans, George D. *Facts Relating to the Capture of Washington.* London: Henry Colburn, 1829.

Farmer, John S. *The Regimental Records of the British Army.* London: Grant Richards, 1901.

Fauquier County Bicentennial Committee. *Fauquier County, Virginia 1759-1959.* Warrenton, Va.: The Committee, 1959.

Fay, Herman A. *Collection of the Official Accounts, in detail, of all the Battles Fought by Sea and Land Between the Navy and Army of the United States and the Navy and Army of Great Britain.* New York: E. Conrad, 1817.

Field, Cyril. *Britain's Sea Soldiers: A History of the Royal Marines.* 2 Vols., Liverpool: Lyceum Press, 1924.

Footner, Hulburt. *Rivers of the Eastern Shore.* New York: Farrar & Rinehart, 1944.

Footner, Hulburt. *Sailor of Fortune: The Life and Adventures of Commodore Barney USN.* New York & London: Harper & Bros., 1940.

Forbes-Lindsay, C. H. *Washington, the City and the Seat of Government.* Philadelphia: John C. Winston Co., 1908.

Forester, C. S. *The Age of Fighting Sail: The Story of the Naval War of 1812.* Garden City, New York: Doubleday & Co., 1956.

Fortescue, J. W. *A History of the British Army.* 13 Vols., London: Macmillan & Co., Ltd., 1899-1930.

Fraser, Edward and L. G. Carr-Laughton. *The Royal Marine Artillery 1904-1923.* 2 Vols., London: Royal United Services Inst., 1930.

Gibson, John. (ed.) *History of York County, Pennsylvania.* Chicago: F.A. Battey Publ. Co., 1886.

Gleig, G. R. *The Campaigns of the British Army at Washington and New Orleans.* E. Ardsley, Eng.: E.P. Publ. Ltd., 1972. (reprint 1847 ed.)

Godcharles, Frederic A. *Pennsylvania Political, Governmental, Military, and Civil.* New York: The American Historical Society, N.D.

Hallahan, John M. *The Battle of Craney Island: A Matter of Credit.* Portsmouth, Va.: N.P., 1986.

Hammet, Regina C. *History St. Mary's County, Maryland 1634-1990.* Ridge, Md.: The Author, 1991.

Hanna, John S. *A History of the Life of Samuel DeWee.* Baltimore: Robert Neilson, 1844.

Harland, John. *Seamanship in the Age of Sail.* Annapolis: Naval Institute Press, 1984.

Harrison, Eliza C. (ed.) *Philadelphia Merchant: The Diary of Thomas Cope, 1800-1851.* South Bend, In.: Gateway Editions, 1978.

Hassler, Warren W. Jr. *The President as Commander in Chief.* Menlo Park, Ca.: Addison-Wesley Publs. Co., 1971.

Heitman, Francis. (ed.) *Historical Register and Dictionary of the U.S. Army, 1789-1903.* Washington: GPO, 1903.

Hickey, Donald R. *The War of 1812.* Urbana & Chicago: Univ. of Ill. Press, 1989.

Hickman, Nathaniel. (ed.) *The Citizen Soldiers at North Point and Fort McHenry...* Baltimore: Hickman, 1858. (reprint with additions 1889 by Charles C. Saffell)

Hopkins, Fred W. Jr., Donald G. Shomette. *War on the Patuxent: A Catalog of Artifacts.* Solomons, Md.: Nautical Archaeological Assocs. Inc. & the Calvert Marine Museum Press, 1981.

Horn, R. Lee Van. *Out of the Past: Prince Georgians and Their Land.* Riverdale, Md.: Prince George's County Historical Society, 1976.

Horsman, Reginald. *The War of 1812.* New York: Alfred A. Knopf, 1969.

Huntsberry, Thomas V. *Western Maryland, Pennsylvania, and Virginia Militia in Defense of Maryland.* N.P.: 1983.

Huntsberry, Thomas V. and Joanne M. *Maryland War of 1812 Privateers.* Baltimore: J. Mart, 1983.

Ingraham, Edward D. *A Sketch of the Events Which Preceded the Capture of Washington.* Philadelphia: Cary and Hart, 1849.

Jacobs, James R. and Glenn Tucker. *The War of 1812: A Compact History.* New York: Hawthorn Books Publs., 1969.

James, William. *The Naval History of Great Britain from the Declaration of War by France in 1793 to the Accession of George IV.* London: MacMillan & Co. Ltd., 1902.

Jones, Elias. *New Revised History of Dorchester County, Maryland.* Cambridge, Md.: Tidewater Publishers, 1966. (reprint of 1925 ed.)

Kennedy, John P. *Memoirs of the Life of William Wirt.* 2 Vols., Philadelphia: W. J. Neal, 1834. (reprint 1872)

Klapthor, Margaret B. *The History of Charles County, Maryland.* La Plata, Md.: Charles County Tercentenary, 1948.

Kreidberg, Marvin A. and Merton G. Henry. *History of Military Mobilization in the United States Army, 1775-1945.* Washington: USGPO, 1955. (DA PAM 20-212)

Lavery, Brian. *Nelson's Navy: The Ships, Men, and Organisation, 1793-1815.* Annapolis: Naval Institute Press, 1994.

Laws, M. E. S. *Battery Records of the Royal Artillery, 1716-1859.* Woolwich: Royal Artillery Inst., 1952.

Lee, Sidney. (ed.) *Dictionary of National Biography.* 22 Vols., London: Smith, Elder & Co., Inc. 1899.

Lehmann, Joseph H. *Remember You Are An Englishman: A Biography of Sir Harry Smith 1787-1860.* London: Jonathan Cape, 1977.

Lemmon, Sarah M. *Frustrated Patriots: North Carolina and the War of 1812.* Chapel Hill: Univ. of North Carolina Press, 1973.

Lessem, Harold I. and George C. Mackenzie. *Fort McHenry National Monument and Historic Shrine.* Washington, D.C.: National Park Service Historical Handbook Series No. 5, 1954. (reprint 1961)

Lewis, Michael. *A Social History of the Navy, 1793-1815.* London: George Allen & Unwin Ltd., 1960.

Linn, John B. *Annals of Buffalo Valley Pennsylvania, 1775-1855.* Harrisburg: Lane S. Hart, 1877.

Linthicum, John C. *The Part Played by Fort McHenry and the "Star Spangled Banner" in our Second War with Great Britain.* Washington D.C.: GPO, 1912.

Lloyd, Alan. *The Scorching of Washington: The War of 1812.* Washington, D.C.: Luce, 1974.

Long, David F. *Nothing Too Daring: A Biography of Commodore David Porter, 1780-1843.* Annapolis: U.S. Naval Institute, 1970.

Lord, Walter. *The Dawn's Early Light.* New York: W. W. Norton & Co., Inc., 1972.

Lossing, Benson J. *The Pictorial Field Book of the War of 1812.* Glendale, Ny: Benchmark Publ. Corp., 1970. (reprint 1868 ed.)

Lovell, William S. *Personal Narrative of Events From 1799 to 1815.* London: William Allen & Co., 1879.

Mahon, John K. *The War of 1812.* Gainesville: Univ. of Florida Press, 1972.

Manarin, Louis H. and Clifford Dowdey. *The History of Henrico County.* Charlottesville: Univ. Press of Virginia, 1984.

Marine, William M. *The British Invasion of Maryland, 1812-1815.* Hatboro, Pa.: Tradition Press, 1965. (reprint 1913 ed.)

Meade, William. *Old Churches, Ministers, and Families of Virginia.* 2 Vols., Philadelphia: J.B. Lippincott Co., 1900. (reprint of 1857 ed.)

Moody, Robert E. ed. *The Saltonstall Papers, 1607-1815.* 2 Vols., Boston: Massachusetts Historical Society, 1974.

Muller, Charles G. *The Darkest Day: 1814, the Washington-Baltimore Campaign.* Philadelphia & New York: J. B. Lippincott Co., 1963.

Napier, Elers. *The Life and Correspondence of Admiral Sir Charles Napier.* London: Hurst and Blackett Publs., 1862.

Napier, William. *The Life and Opinions of General Sir Charles Napier.* London: John Murray, 1857.

The Naval Chronicle for 1813. London: Joyce Gold, N.D.

Netherton, Nan et al. *Fairfax County, Virginia: A History.* Fairfax, Va.: Fairfax Co. Board of Supervisors, 1978.

Nicolas, Paul H. *Historical Record of the Royal Marine Forces.* 2 Vols., London: Thomas & William Boone, 1845.

Niles, Hezekiah. *Weekly Register.* Vol. 1 (Sep 1811) to Vol. 7 (Feb 1815) facsimile reprint by *Microbook of English Literature.* Chicago: Library Resources, 1972.

Norris, Walter B. (ed.) *Westmoreland County, Virginia, 1653-1983.* Montross, Va.: Westmoreland Co. Board of Supervisors, 1983.

O'Brian, Patrick. *Men-of-War.* Ny: W. W. Norton and Co., 1995.

O'Byrne, William R. *A Naval Biographical Dictionary.* London: John Murray, 1849.

Owens, Hamilton. *Baltimore on the Chesapeake.* New York: Doubleday, Doran & Co. Inc., 1941.

Pack, James. *The Man Who Burned the White House: Admiral Sir George Cockburn, 1772-1853.* Annapolis: Naval Inst. Press, 1987.

Paine, Ralph D. *The Fight for a Free Sea: A Chronicle of the War of 1812.* New Haven: Yale Univ. Press, 1920.

Pancake, John. *Samuel Smith and the Politics of Business, 1752-1839.* University, Alabama: Univ. of Alabama Press, 1972.

Paullin, Charles O. *Commodore John Rodgers.* New York: Arno Press Inc., 1980. (reprint 1910 ed.)

Pellew, George. (ed.) *The Life and Correspondence of the Right Honorable Henry Addington, First Viscount Sidmouth.* 3 Vols., London: J. Murray, 1847.

Perkins, Bradford. *Castlereigh and Adams: England and the United States, 1812-1823.* Berkeley & Los Angles: Univ. of California Press, 1964.

Perkins, Bradford. *Prologue to War, 1805-1812: England and the United States.* Berkeley: Univ. of California Press, 1961.

Porter, David D. *Memoir of Commodore David Porter of the United States Navy.* Albany, Ny.: J. Munsell, Publishers, 1875.

Preston, Dickson J. *Talbot County, A History.* Centreville, Md.: Tidewater Publs., 1983.

Preston, Walter W. *History of Harford County, Maryland.* Regional Publ. Co., 1972. (reprint of 1901 ed.)

Pringle, Norman. *Letters by Major Norman Pringle, Late of the 21st Royal Scots Fusiliers.* Edinburgh: S.N., 1834?

Publications of the Champlain Society. *Select British Documents of the Canadian War of 1812.* Toronto: Champlain Soc., N.D.

Ralfe, J. *The Naval Biography of Great Britain.* 4 Vols., London: Whitmore & Fenn, 1828.

Reilly, Robin. *The British at the Gates: The New Orleans Campaign in the War of 1812.* New York: G. P. Putnam's Sons, 1974.

Riley, Elihu S. *The Ancient City, A History of Annapolis in Maryland. 1649-1887.* Annapolis: Records Printing Co., 1887.

Roosevelt, Theodore. *The Naval War of 1812.* Annapolis, Md.: Naval Inst. Press, 1987. (reprint 1882 ed.)

Rutland, Robert A. (ed.) *James Madison and the American Nation, 1751-1836: An Encyclopedia.* New York: Simon and Schuster, 1994.

Rutland, Robert A. *James Madison, The Founding Father.* New York: Macmillan Publ. Co., 1987.

Rutland, Robert A. *The Presidency of James Madison.* Lawrence: Univ. of Kansas Press, 1990.

Saffell, Charles C. *The Citizen Soldiers at North Point and Fort McHenry, September 12 and 13.* Baltimore: Charles C. Saffell, N.D. (1889?)

Sapio, Victor. *Pennsylvania and the War of 1812.* Lexington: Univ. of Kansas Press, 1970

Scharf, J. Thomas. *The Chronicles of Baltimore: Being a Complete History...* Baltimore: Turnbull Bros., 1874.

Scharf, J. Thomas. *History of Baltimore City and County.* 2 Vols., Baltimore: Regional Publ. Co., 1971. (reprint of 1881 ed.)

Scharf, J. Thomas. *History of Western Maryland.* 2 Vols., Baltimore: Regional Publ. Co., 1968. (reprint of 1882 ed.)

Scott, James. *Recollections of a Naval Life.* 3 Vols., London: Richard Bentley, 1834.

Scott, Winfield. *Memoirs of Lieutenant General Scott, LL.D.* 2 Vols., New York: Sheldon and Co. Pubs., 1864.

Sheads, Scott S. *Fort McHenry.* Baltimore, Md.: Nautical and Aviation Publ., 1995.

Sheads, Scott S. *The Rocket's Red Glare: The Maritime Defense of Baltimore in 1814* Centreville, Md.: Tidewater Publs., 1986.

Shomette, Donald. *Flotilla: Battle for the Patuxent.* Solomons, Md.: Calvert Marine Museum Press, 1981.

Shomette, Donald G. *Tidewater Time Capsule: History Beneath the Patuxent.* Centreville, Md.: Tidewater Publs., 1995.

Skeen, C. Edward. *John Armstrong, Jr., 1758-1843, A Biography.* Syracuse: Syracuse Univ. Press, 1981.

Smith, G. C. Moore, ed. *The Autobiography of Lieutenant General Sir Henry Smith.* 2 Vols., London: John Murray, 1901.

Smith, Margaret B. (Gaillard Hunt ed.). *The First Forty Years of Washington Society.* New York: Charles Scribner's Sons, 1906.

Stagg, J. C. A. *Mr. Madison's War: Politics, Diplomacy, and Warfare in the Early American Republic 1783-1830.* Princeton: Princeton Univ. Press, 1983.

Stahl, John M. *The Invasion of the City of Washington: A Disagreeable Study in and of the Military Unpreparedness.* Argos,Indiana: Van Trump Co., 1918.

Stein, Charles G. *A History of Calvert County, Maryland.* 3d ed., Baltimore: Schnerdereith & Sons, 1977.

Stevens, Sylvester K. *Pennsylvania, Birthplace of a Nation.* New York: Random House, 1964.

Stuart, Reginald C. *War and American Thought: From the Revolution to the Monroe Doctrine.* Kent, Oh: Kent State Univ. Press, 1982.

Swanson, Neil H. *The Perilous Fight.* New York & Toronto: Farrar and Reinhart, 1945.

Taylor, Blaine. *Battle of North Point, 1814, Defenders' Day 1990.* Towson, Md: Baltimore County Government, 1990.

Thomson, W. W. *Chester County and Its People.* Chicago and New York: Union History Co., 1898.

Tilghman, Oswald. *History of Talbot County, Maryland.* 2 Vols., Baltimore: Regional Publ. Co., 1967. (reprint of 1915 ed.)

Travers, Paul J. *The Patapsco, Baltimore's River of History.* Centreville, Md.: Tidewater Publishers, 1990.

Tucker, Glen. *Poltroons & Patriots: A Popular Account of the War of 1812.* 2 Vols., Indianapolis and New York: Bobbs-Merrill Co. Inc., 1954.

Tuckerman, Henry T. *The Life of John Pendleton Kennedy.* New York: G.P. Putnam and Sons, 1871.

U.S. Army, Adjutant and Inspector General's Office. *Military Laws and Regulations for the Armies of the United States.* Washington: 1813.

U.S. Army, Infantry School. *Battle of Bladensburg.* Camp Benning, Ga.: Inf. School Press, 1921.

U.S. Congress. *American State Papers: Military Affairs.* Vol. I, Washington: Gale & Seaton, 1832.

U.S. Congress, House Committee on the Invasion of Washington. *Report of the committee appointed on the 23rd of September last to inquire into the causes and particulars of the invasion of the city of Washington by British forces in the month of August, 1814.* Washington: A. G. Way, 1814.

Usilton, Frederick G. *History of Kent County, Maryland 1630-1916.* Chesterton: Perry Publs., 1916 (1980 reprint with additions).

Walton, William. *The Army and the Navy of the United States From the Revolution to the Present Day.* 11 Vols., Boston: George Barrie Publs, 1889-1896.

Watts, Steven. *The Republic Reborn: War and the Making of Liberal America, 1790-1820.* Baltimore and London: Johns Hopkins Univ. Press, 1987.

Wertenbaker, Thomas J. *Norfolk, Historic Southern Port.* 2d ed. edited by Marvin W. Schlegel, Durham, N.C.: Duke University Press, 1962.

Wharton, Anne H. *Social Life in the Early Republic.* Williamstown, Ma.: Corner House Publs., 1970. (reprint 1902 ed.)

White, Leonard D. *The Jeffersonians: A Study in Administrative History 1801-1829.* New York: Macmillan Co., 1956.

Whitelaw, Ralph W. *Virginia's Eastern Shore, A History of Northampton and Accomack Counties.* 2 Vols., Gloucester, Ma.: Peter Smith, 1968.

Williams, John S. *History of the Invasion and Capture of Washington, and of the Events Which Preceded and Followed.* New York: Harper, 1857.

Williams, Noel H. *The Life and Letters of Admiral Sir Charles Napier.* London: Hutchinson & Co., 1917.

Williams, T. J. C. and Folger McKinsey. *History of Frederick County, Maryland.* Baltimore: Regional Publishing. Co., 1967.

Wilstack, Paul. *Potomac Landings.* New York: Tudor Publishing Co., 1937.

Winter, Frank H. *The First Golden Age of Rocketry.* Washington & London: Smithsonian Institute Press, 1990.

Wright, F. Edward. *Maryland Militia, War of 1812.* 7 Vols., Silver Spring, Md.: Family Line, 1979-1986.

Writers Program, W.P.A. *Maryland, A Guide to the Old Line State.* New York: Oxford University Press, 1940.

Young, James S. *The Washington Community, 1800-1828.* New York: Columbia University Press, 1966.

Articles:

Anderson, Robert. "Operations at and near Hampton During War of 1812." *Virginia Magazine of History and Biography* Vol. 36 (Jan. 1929): 1-11.

Andrews, Matthew P. "Maryland in the War of 1812." *Tercentenary of Maryland* 4 Vols., Chicago: S. J. Clarke, 1925.

Anon. "Narrative of the Naval Operations in the Potomac." *Coulburn's United Services Magazine* No. 53 (1833): 469-481.

Anon. (Old Sub.) "Recollections of the Expedition to the Chesapeake and Against New Orleans, in the Years 1814-15." *Coulburn's United Services Magazine* (April 1840): 443-456; (May 1840): 25-36; (June 1840): 192-195; (July 1840): 337-352.

Anon. "The Vigilance Committee: Richmond During the War of 1812." *Virginia Magazine of History and Biography* Vol. 7 (Jan. 1900): 225-241.

Anon. "The Robbery of St. Inigo's House." *American Historical Record.* Vol. 2 (Nov. 1873): 553-557.

Anon. "The War of 1812 Battle of the Patuxent (Two sides of the same war)." *Calvert Historian* Vol. 9 (Spring 1994): 7-20.

Anon. "War's Wild Alarm, Richmond 1813, Baltimore 1814." *Virginia Magazine of History and Biography* Vol. 49 (July 1941): 217-233.

Balch, Lewis P. "Reminiscences of the War of 1812." *Historical Magazine* Vol. 7 (Sept. 1863): 383-384.

Barrett, Richard J. "Naval Recollections of the Late American War." *Coulburn's United Services Magazine* (April 1841): 455-467; (May 1841): 13-23.

Barrett, Robert. "A White Squall off the Chesapeake." *United Service Magazine* Pt. 1 (Jan 1831): 57-59.

Baylor, Anne L. "Jefferson County War of 1812 Soldiers..." *Magazine of Jefferson County Historical Society* Vol. 7 (1941): 35-37.

Beitzell, Edwin W. "The Raid on St. Inigoes, Oct 30, 1814." Typescript, St. Mary's County Historical Society, Leonardstown, Md.

Beitzell, Edwin W. "A Short History of St. Clements Island." *Chronicles of St. Mary's* Vol. 6, No. 11 (Nov. 1958): 245-253.

Booker, James M. "Battle of Munday Point." *Bulletin of the Northumberland County Historical Society* Vol. I, No. I (1964): 1-19.

Bradford, J. Stricker. "Battle of Bladensburg." *Maryland Historical Magazine* Vol. 5 (1910): 341-349.

Bradford, S. Sidney. "Ft. McHenry, 1814." *Maryland Historical Magazine* Vol. 54 (1959): 188-209.

Brant, Irving. "Madison and the War of 1812." *Virginia Magazine of History and Biography* Vol. 74 (1966): 51-67.

Brant, Irving. "Timid President? Futile War?" *American Heritage* Vol. X (Oct 1959): 46-47, 85-89.

Brown, Roger H. "A Vermont Republican Urges War. Royall Tyler, 1812, and the Safety of Republican Government." *Vermont History* Vol. 36 (Winter 1968): 13-18.

Brynn, Edward. "Patterns of Dissent: Vermont's Opposition to the War of 1812." *Vermont History* Vol. 40 (Winter 1972): 10-27.

Bushong, Millard K. "Jefferson County in the War of 1812." *Magazine of Jefferson County Historical Society* Vol. 6 (1940): 4-14.

Calderhead, William L. "Naval Innovation in Crisis: War in the Chesapeake." *American Neptune* Vol. 36 (1976): 206-220.

Carroll, Charles. "Charles Carroll of Carrollton's letter describing the battle of Baltimore." *Maryland Historical Society* Vol. 39 (1939): 244-245.

Cassell, Frank A. "Baltimore in 1813: A Study of Urban Defense in the War of 1812." *Military Affairs* Vol. 33 (Dec. 1969): 349-361.

Cassell, Frank A. "The Great Baltimore Riot of 1812." *Maryland Historical Magazine* Vol. 70 (1975): 241-259.

Cassell, Frank A. "Response to Crisis: Baltimore in 1814." *Maryland Historical Magazine* Vol. 66 (1971): 261-287.

Cassell, Frank A. "Slaves of the Chesapeake Bay Area and the War of 1812." *Journal of Negro History* Vol. 57 (April 1972): 144-155.

Chartrand, René. "An Account of the Capture of Washington, 1814." *Military Collector and Historian* Vol. 37 (Winter 1985): 182.

Clinton, Amy C. "Historic Fort Washington." *Maryland Historical Magazine* Vol. 32 (Sept. 1937): 228-247.

Cockburn, George. "Admiral Cockburn's plan." *Maryland Historical Society* Vol. 6 (1911): 16-19.

Coles, Harry L. "1814: A Dark Hour Before the Dawn." *Maryland Historical Magazine* Vol. 66 (1971): 219-21.

Colston, Frederick M. "The Battle of North Point." *Maryland Historical Magazine* Vol. 2 (1907): 111-125.

Commager, Henry S. "The Second War of American Independence." *New York Times Magazine* (17 June 1962): 15-16.

(Crain, R. M.). "Orderly Book of Harrisburg Volunteer Company of Artillery, Captain Richard M. Crain, 1814." *The Pennsylvania Magazine of History and Biography* Vol. 37 (1913): 129-151.

Cress, Lawrence D. "'Cool and Serious Reflection': Federalist Attitudes Toward War in 1812." *Journal of the Early Republic* Vol. 7 (Summer 1987): 123-145.

Dangerfield, George. "If Only Mr. Madison had Waited." *American Heritage* Vol. VII (April 1956): 8-10, 92-94.

Davis, Milton S. "The Capture of Washington." *U.S. Naval Institute Proceedings* Vol. 63 (June 1937): 839-851.

Dickson, Alexander. "Artillery Services in North America in 1814 and 1815." *Journal of the Society for Army Historical Research* Vol. 7, (April 1929): 79-85.

Eaton, H. B. "Bladensburg." *Journal of the Society for Army Historical Research* Vol. 55 (Spring 1977): 8-14.

Elting, John R. "Those Independent Companies of Foreigners." *Military Collector and Historian* Vol. 40 (Fall 1988): 124-125.

Emmerson, John C. "War in the Lower Chesapeake and Hampton Roads Areas— 1812-1815—As Reported in the *Norfolk Gazette and Public Ledger* and the *Norfolk and Portsmouth Herald*." Typescript, 1946.

"Enemy in the Chesapeake." *Chronicles of St. Mary's* Vol. I, No. 4 (Sept. 1953): 13-16.

Engelman, Fred L. "The Peace of Christmas Eve." *American Heritage* Vol. XII, No. 1 (Dec. 1960): 28-31, 82-88.

"Excerpts from *Nile's Weekly Register*, Part I." *Chronicles of St. Mary's* Vol. 8, No. 7 (July 1960): 70-76; "Part II." Vol. 8, No. 9 (Sept. 1960): 90-97.

Fabel, Robin. "The Laws of War in the 1812 Conflict." *Journal of American Studies* 14 (1980): 199-218.

Flournoy, Fitzgerald. "Hugh Blair Grigsby: A Virginia Boy during the War of 1812." *Virginia Magazine of History and Biography* Vol. 66 (1958): 423-431.

Forester, C. S. "Bloodshed at Dawn." *American Heritage* Vol. XV (Oct 1964): 40-45; 73-76.

Gaines, Edwin M. "George Cranfield Berkeley and the *Chesapeake-Leopard* affair of 1807." in John B. Boles. (ed.) *America the Middle Period, Essays in Honor of Bernard Mays.* Charlottesville: Univ. of Virginia Press, 1973.

Gaines, William H. "Craney Island or Norfolk Delivered." *Virginia Cavalcade* Vol. 1 (1951): 32-35.

Garred, Martin. "Amphibious Warfare: Why?" *Journal of the Royal United Services Institute* (Winter 1988): 25-30.

George, Christopher T. "The Family Papers of Major General Robert Ross, The Diary of Col. Arthur Brooke, and the British Attacks on Washington and Baltimore of 1814." *Maryland Historical Magazine* Vol. 88 (Fall 1993): 300-316.

Gilje, Paul A. "Le Menu People in America: Identifying the Mob in the Baltimore Riots of 1812." *Maryland Historical Magazine* Vol. 81 (1986): 50-66.

Graves, Donald E. "The Royal Navy and Amphibious Operations in the 18th Century—an Aspect of the 'Military Revolution'?" unpublished paper read before the Conference on Naval History, Annapolis, Md., September 1991.

Groene, Bertram H. "A Trap for the British: Thomas Brown and the Battle of the 'White House'." *Virginia Cavalcade* Vol. 18 (1968): 13-19.

Guy, John. "Action at Hampton, 1813." *Virginia Magazine of History and Biography* Vol. 31 (Oct. 1923): 351-353.

Guy, John. "Operations at and near Hampton During the War of 1812." *Virginia Magazine of History and Biography* Vol. 37 (Jan. 1929): 1-11.

Haarman, Albert W. "The Independant Companies of Foreigners at Hampton, Virginia, June 1813." *Military Collector and Historian* Vol. 38 (Winter 1986): 178-179.

Hadel, Albert K. "The Battle of Bladensburg." *Maryland Historical Magazine* Vol. 1 (1906): 155-167; 197-210.

Harpster, John W. (ed.). "Maj. William Darlington's Diary." *Western Pennsylvania Magazine of History* Vol. 20 (1937): 197-220.

Hatzenbuehler, Ronald L. "Party Unity and the Decision for War in the House of Representatives, 1812." *William and Mary Quarterly* Vol. XXIX (1972): 367-390.

Hecht, Arthur. "The Post Office Department in St. Mary's County in the War of 1812." *Maryland Historical Magazine* Vol. 52 (June 1957): 142-152.

Hendry, Douglas L. "British Casualties Suffered at Several Actions During the War of 1812." unpublished report, Directorate of History, Canadian Forces, March 1994.

Hill, Maurice. "A Short History of the New South Wales Corps, 1789-1818." *Journal of the Society for Army Historical Research* Vol. XIII: 135-140.

Hickey, Donald R. "The darker side of democracy: The Baltimore riots of 1812." *Maryland Historian* Vol. 7 (1976): 1-14.

Hitsman, J. Mackay, and Alice Sorby. "Independent Foreigners or Canadian Chasseurs." *Military Affairs* Vol. 25 (Spring 1961): 11-17.

Hoge, William A. "The British Are Coming Up the Potomac." *Northern Neck of Virginia Historical Magazine* Vol. 14 (Dec 1964) 1265-1279.

Hoyt, William D. "Civilian Defense in Baltimore, 1814-1815." *Maryland Historical Magazine* Vol. 39 (1944): 199-224, 293-309; Vol. 40 (1945): 7-23, 137-232.

Hunter, Wilbur H. "Baltimore's War." *American Heritage* Vol. 3 (1952): 30-33.

Irwin, Ray W. (ed.) "The Capture of Washington in 1814." *Americana* (Jan. 1934): 7-26.

Jarvis, James. "A Narrative of the Attack on Craney Island." *Virginia Historical Register* Vol. 1 (July 1848): 137-141.

Jenkins, B. Wheeler. "The Shots that Saved Baltimore." *Maryland Historical Magazine* Vol. 77 (1982): 362-364.

Jones, J. Webster. "The British in the Patuxent." *Chronicles of St. Mary's* Vol. 8, No. 1 (January 1960): 1-10.

Jones, Virgil C. "The Sack of Hampton." *American History Illustrated* Vol. 9 (1974): 32-44.

Jones, Wilbur D. "A British View of the War of 1812 and the Peace Negotiations." *Mississippi Valley Historical Review* Vol. 45 (1958-1959): 481-487.

Judge, C. B. "Navy Powder Goes on a Journey: An Episode of the War of 1812." *U.S. Naval Institute Proceedings* Vol. 69 (Sept. 1943) 1223-1228.

Kerby, Robert L. "The Militia System and the State Militias in the War of 1812." *Indiana Magazine of History* Vol. 73 (June 1977): 102-124.

Kochan, James L. "Virginia Cavalry in the War of 1812." *Military Collector and Historian* Vol. 38 (Fall 1986): 110-113.

Lingel, Robert. "The Manuscript Autobiography of Gordon Gallie Macdonald." *Bulletin of the New York Public Library* Vol. 34 (1930): 139-147.

"Log of HMS *Dragon*." *Chronicles of St. Mary's* Vol. 13, No. 8 (August 1965): 177-180.

"Log of HMS *Hebrus*." *Chronicles of St. Mary's* Vol. 15, No. 10 (October 1967): 112-117.

"Log of HMS *Jaseur*." *Chronicles of St. Mary's* Vol. 8, No. 12 (December 1960): 127-128; Vol. 9, No. 1 (January 1961): 136; Vol. 10, No. 2 (February 1962): 244-246; Vol. 11, No. 12 (December 1963): 107.

"Log of HMS *Loire*." *Chronicles of St. Mary's* Vol. 8, No. 10 (October 1960): 102-107; Vol. 8, No. 12 (December 1960): 126-127.

"Log of HMS *Royal Oak*." *Chronicles of St. Mary's* Vol. 15, No. 2 (February 1967): 9-16.

"Log of HMS *St. Lawrence*." *Chronicles of St. Mary's* Vol. 11, No. 12 (December 1963): 107-108; Vol. 13, No. 4 (April 1965): 161-167.

"Log of HMS *Severn*." *Chronicles of St. Mary's* Vol. 14, No. 8 (August 1966): 292-294.

"Log of HMS *Tonnant*." *Chronicles of St. Mary's* Vol. 14, No. 8 (August 1966): 294-296.

Lohnes, Barry J. "British Naval Problems at Halifax During the War of 1812." *The Mariner's Mirror* Vol. 59, No. 3 (August 1973): 317-333.

London Gazette Extraordinary (27 Sep 1914), Reprint of dispatch by Major General Ross of 30 Aug 1814.

Lord, Walter. "Humiliation and Triumph." *American Heritage* Vol. 23, No. 5 (Aug. 1972): 50-72; 91-93.

Maguire, W. A. "Major General Ross and the Burning of Washington." *The Irish Sword* XIV (No. 55): 1-12.

Mahon, John K. "British Command Decisions in the Northern Campaigns of the War of 1812." *The Canadian Historical Review* Vol. 46 (1965): 219-237.

Marrien, R. J. "85th (Bucks Volunteers) Light Infantry, 1812-14 War With America." *Tradition* Vol. 4, No. 24, 24-27.

Martell, J. S. "A Side Light on Federalist Strategy during the War of 1812." *American Historical Review* XLIII (1938): 553-566.

Morgan, James D. "Historic Fort Washington on the Potomac." *Records of the Columbia Historical Society* Vol. 7 (1904): 1-19.

Morgan, Michael. "The Flag Was Still There." *Maryland Magazine* Vol. 22 (1989): 6-13.

Mullaly, Franklin E. "The Battle of Baltimore." *Maryland Historical Magazine* Vol. 54 (1959): 61-103.

Muller, Charles G. "Fabulous Potomac Passage." *U.S. Naval Institute Proceedings* Vol. 90 (May 1964): 84-91.

Pancake, John S. "The 'Invisibles': A Chapter in the Opposition to President Madison." *The Journal of Southern History* Vol. 21 (1955): 17-37.

Parker, Thomas. "A Narrative of the Battle of Bladensburg in a Letter to Henry Banning, Esq." Typescript, Military History Institute, Carlisle, Pa.: N.D.

Piper, James. "Defense of Baltimore, 1814." *Maryland Historical Magazine* Vol. 7, No. 4 (1912): 375-384.

Pomeroy, Earl S. "The Lebanon Blues in the Baltimore Campaign, 1814: Extracts From a Company Orderly Book." *Military Affairs* Vol. 12 (Fall 1948): 168-174.

Quebec Gazette, 25 August 1814.

Robinson, Ralph. "Controversy over the Command at Baltimore During the War of 1812." *Maryland Historical Magazine* Vol. 39 (1944): 177-198.

Robinson, Ralph. "New Light on Three Episodes of the British Invasion of Maryland in 1814." *Maryland Historical Magazine* Vol. 37 (1942): 273-290.

Robinson, Ralph. "Retaliation for the Treatment of Prisoners in the War of 1812." *American Historical Review* Vol. 38 (Oct. 1943): 65-70.

Robinson, Ralph. "The Use of Rockets by the British in the War of 1812." *Maryland Historical Magazine* Vol. 40, No. 1 (1945): 1-6.

Rouse, Parke. "The British Invasion of Hampton in 1813: Reminiscences of James Jarvis." *Virginia Magazine of History and Biography* Vol. 76 (1968): 318-336.

Rouse, Parke. "Low Tide at Hampton Roads." *U.S. Naval Institute Proceedings* Vol. 95 (1969): 79-86.

Rowland, Kate M. "Armistead Thomas Mason Letters, 1813-1818." *William and Mary Quarterly* Vol. 23 (April 1915): 228-239.

Rowley, Peter. "Captain Rowley Visits Maryland; Part II of a Series." *Maryland Historical Magazine* Vol. 83 (1988): 247-253.

Sanford, John L. "The Battle of North Point." *Maryland Historical Magazine* Vol. 24, No. 4 (1929): 356-364.

Sapio, Victor. "Maryland's Federalist Revival, 1808-1812." *Maryland Historical Magazine* Vol. 64 (Spring 1969): 1

Sellers, Nicholas. "Lt. Col. Samuel Smith: Defender of Fort Mifflin, 1777." *Cincinnati Fourteen* Vol. XXXI, No. 1 (Oct. 1994): 17-24.

Sharrer, G. Terry. "The Patuxent, Maryland's Heartland River." *Maryland Magazine* Vol. 21 (1989): 6-22.

Sheads, Scott S. "A Black Soldier Defends Fort McHenry, 1814." *Military Collector and Historian* Vol. 41 (Spring 1989): 20-21.

Sheads, Scott S. "And the Carcasses Red Glare, 'The Bomb Bursting in Air,' 13 September 1814." *Military Collector and Historian* Vol. 40 (Winter 1988): 172-173.

Sheads, Scott S. "U.S. Sa Fencibles at Fort McHenry." *Military Collector and Historian* Vol. 34 (Winter 1982): 159-163.

Skinner, J. S. "Incidents of the War of 1812." *Maryland Historical Magazine* Vol. 32 (1937): 340-347.

Skirven, Percy C. "The Battle of Caulk's Field." *Patriotic Marylander* Vol. 2 (1916): 20-38.

Smith, Eric M. "Leaders Who Lost: Case Studies of Command Under Stress." *Military Review* Vol. 61 (April 1981): 41-45.

Smith, Theodore C. "War Guilt in 1812." *Proceedings* Massachusetts Historical Society, Vol. LXIV (1932): 319-345.

Sparks, Jared. (ed.) "Conflagration of Havre de Grace." *North American Review and Miscellaneous Journal* No. XIV (July 1817): 157-163.

Spaulding, Thomas M. "The Battle of North Point." *The Sewanee Review* (1 Sept. 1914): 319-329.

Stacey, C. P. "An American Plan For a Canadian Campaign." *American Historical Review* XLVI (1941): 348-358.

Stewart, Robert G. "The Battle of the Ice Mound, February 7, 1815." *Maryland Historical Magazine* Vol. 70 (1975): 373-78.

Sweeney, Mrs. William M. "Orderly Book, Virginia Militia, War of 1812." *Virginia Magazine of History and Biography* Vol. 46 (July 1938): 246-253; (Oct. 1938): 329-338.

Syrett, David. "The Methodology of British Amphibious Operations During the Seven Years and American Wars." *The Mariner's Mirror* Vol. 58, No. 3 (August 1972): 269-280.

Talmadge, John E. "Georgia's Federalist Press and the War of 1812." *Journal of Southern History* Vol. 19 (1953): 488-500.

Tarlton, Moses. "The Robbery of St. Inigoes House." *American Historical Record* Vol. 2 (Nov. 1873): 553-557.

Thornton, Willis. "The Day They Burned the Capitol." *American Heritage* Vol. 6, No. 1 (1954): 48-53.

Todd, Frederic P. "The Militia and Volunteers of the District of Columbia, 1783-1820." *Records of the Columbia Historical Society* Vol 50 (1952): 379-439.

Tucker, Lillian H. "Sir Peter Parker, Commander of HMS *Menelaus*." *Bermuda Historical Quarterly* Vol. 1 (1944): 189-195.

Van Why, Joseph S. "Martin Gillette's Letters About the War of 1812." *Connecticut Historical Society Bulletin* Vol. 23 (July 1958): 81-84.

Wallace, Lee A., Jr. "The Petersburg Volunteers, 1812-1813." *Virginia Magazine of History and Biography* Vol. 82 (Oct. 1974): 458-485.

Wallace, S. A. (ed.) "Georgetown is saved from the British! From the Diary of Wilham B. Thornton, 1814." *The Social Studies* (October 1952): 233-237.

Walsh, Richard. "The Star Fort: 1814." *Maryland Historical Magazine* Vol. 54
(1959): 296-309.

Wehjte, Myron F. "Opposition in Virginia to the War of 1812." *Virginia Magazine
of History and Biography* Vol. 78 (1970): 65-86.

Woehrmann, Paul. "National Response to the Sack of Washington." *Maryland
Historical Magazine* Vol. 66 (1971): 222-260.

Index

࿊